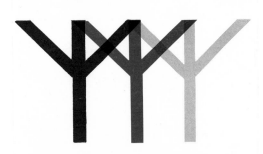

**Civic Garden Centre
Library**

FINE HERBS
Ornamental Plants
for the Garden

Peony (Paeonia officinalis)

To Judith and Simon Hopkinson,
with whom I shared several happy years of herb growing.

(opposite) The golden, cut-leaved form of red elder: an aristocrat among foliage plants.

FINE HERBS
Ornamental Plants for the Garden

DENI BOWN

UNWIN

HYMAN

LONDON SYDNEY WELLINGTON

First published in Great Britain by the Trade Division
of Unwin Hyman Limited, 1988.

Unwin Hyman Limited
15/17 Broadwick Street
London W1V 1FP
and
Allen & Unwin Australia Pty Ltd
8 Napier Street, North Sydney, NSW 2060, Australia

Allen & Unwin New Zealand Pty Ltd with the Port Nicholson Press
60 Cambridge Terrace, Wellington, New Zealand

Bown, Deni
Fine herbs: ornamental plants for the garden.
I. Gardens. Herbs. Cultivation
I. Title
635′7

ISBN 0–04–440133–7

Designed by Elizabeth Palmer
Typeset by Nene Phototypesetters Ltd, Northampton
Printed in Italy by New Interlitho S.P.A.

All black and white illustrations are from
The Herball or Generall Historie of Plants
by John Gerard (1597)
with kind permission of the Lindley Library.

Photograph of author by Robin Bown

CONTENTS

INTRODUCTION

Although the appreciation of fragrance surfaces now and again, most garden plants are enjoyed solely on a visual level. They tend to be purchased on impulse when at their showiest, and the main pleasure derived from this is that of the display – be it of new leaves, flowers, autumn colour or fruits. As a result, many gardens are like cocktail parties – eyecatching, but offering limited satisfaction. As with people, though first impressions count, many plants have much more to them than appearance and merit closer acquaintance.

In particular, most herbs – plants used for culinary, medicinal or aromatic purposes – have fascinating histories, memorable aromas and an impressive diversity of uses. The most outstanding characteristic of plants, beyond their beauty, is the astonishing range of chemicals they produce. As plants are rooted to the spot and cannot wrestle with attackers or run away, these compounds are often their main defence against the hordes of ever-hungry insects and animals. In sufficient quantity, such toxins kill, but one of the greatest discoveries made by human beings is that in very small and carefully calculated amounts, those same poisons become medicines which can cure. It is estimated that one in seven plant species has curative properties – a figure which may well be higher in tropical rain forests. Regardless of this, I have encountered many people, including experienced gardeners and professional horticulturists, who have a sceptical, even disparaging, attitude to herbal medicine and are most reluctant to use the word 'herb' for anything but those most popular for flavouring food. Sadly, there is a whole side to plants that they have been missing.

Admittedly, few gardeners aspire to becoming biochemists or herbalists but a great deal can be discovered about plants with nothing more technical than curiosity and the senses, applied with the necessary common sense and sensitivity. But first we must rid ourselves of preconceptions. Herbs are not just those in the spice rack and we must be prepared for some surprises when it is revealed how many common garden plants – and weeds – are used for medicinal purposes and have potent chemical compounds. Once we can accept that plants as different as pasque flowers (*Pulsatilla vulgaris*), ornamental conifers such as *Thuja occidentalis*, and the pernicious weed ground elder (*Aegopodium podagraria*) are important herbs, then we may be interested in learning why and how they are used and even inspired to investigate them in more depth.

However, it is my experience that getting people to do anything more than look at plants is no easy task! For all their beauty, the distrust of them at closer quarters is on a par with that felt towards animals with which we are not familiar. Our approach to any but the domesticated and well known, presumes that the encounter will probably result in attack, in the case of animals, or poisoning where plants are concerned. Any naturalist will tell you that such fears are usually exaggerated and may be dispelled by a little understanding of the subject. I am not suggesting that one goes round blithely sampling all manner of vegetation, but it is rewarding to experience, for example, the astringency of leaves containing tannin or the typically unpleasant smell of those that are rich in alkaloids. I have watched the look of enlightenment spread across many a student's face as the word 'mucilage' becomes real: the cut surface of a root such as comfrey (*Symphytum officinale*) exudes a slimy substance which forms a protective coating on the fingertips and once this has been felt, it is easy to appreciate how such compounds work as buffering agents, externally or internally, to prevent irritation of damaged tissues and im-

prove healing. Experiencing textures, smells and tastes is an integral part of our relationship with plants: one that is often neglected in our preoccupation with the visual and something that no amount of looking at plants or reading about them can give.

It could be argued that such suspicion is a good thing and is an instinct which may save us from being poisoned. Equally well, it can be seen as ignorance which cuts us off from any real awareness of plants and their healing powers. Suspicion and ignorance about the vegetation surrounding us does not bode well for our future. At one time human beings must have exercised all their faculties with regard to plants and thus discovered that a great many were not only decorative, but edible and possibly curative as well. In some parts of the world where traditional medicine survives intact, such skills are still to be found. But for the most part this depth of knowledge – and

Pelargonium crispum 'Variegatum' has lemon-scented leaves and is perfect for pots.

the respect for plants that it inspires – has disappeared and plants have become mere commodities to be cultivated if useful or ornamental, valued if profitable, but otherwise ignored or destroyed. It is this lack of relationship and understanding that permits the senseless extermination of plant communities, whether it be a hedgerow or a rain forest, for short-term economic gain. And it is noticeable that where there are last minute pleas for conservation, they largely rely for their success on visual appeal – our strongest and often last remaining link with the natural world.

So what went wrong? Why do we find ourselves alienated from our heritage: tourists in our own landscape? It is a long and complex story, as is the break-up of any deep relationship, but at the end of the nineteenth

7

century (in the western world at least), the gathering of wild plants for food, medicine and other uses, and the cultivation of a wide range of herbs in the garden entered a period of decline from which it is only just beginning to emerge. It was occasioned by the Industrial Revolution: an era of scientific discoveries which affected every aspect of life, including medicine, and heralded a drastic change in attitude towards all that was traditional and natural in origin. Until then, home-made herbal remedies eased most afflictions. Many were based on herbs either grown in cottage gardens or collected from the surrounding countryside and prepared in the kitchen – often by experienced women ('old wives') in the community. In the rush for material prosperity which followed on the heels of technological innovation, such domestic skills became outmoded and herbalism was viewed as a thing of the past. (This is not to say that herbs themselves became entirely redundant – even today about a quarter of all pharmacy prescriptions contain active ingredients ex-tracted from plants – but the processing of herb-based preparations passed into the hands of commercial concerns.) And so began the dark age for herbal plants, in which all but the culinary elite – sage, parsley, thyme, mint, marjoram, rosemary and bay – together with a few that were both pretty and scented (such as lavender) were ousted from our gardens.

The tide began to turn in the sixties. In many respects, the recent upsurge of interest in herbs can be seen as an offshoot of the environmental movement which was ushered in by hippies and flower-power. The naïvety of those early days has fallen on stony ground in the hardened hearts of the eighties, but con-cern for the fate of the natural world – and our own – is, if anything, more urgent. The future may be less rosy but it is also less bleak! In the last twenty years, there have been many changes in the right direction. We use far more herbs in cooking; herb-based cosmetics and toiletries are commonplace; supermarkets stock health foods, herbal and vegetarian products; and every chemist and drug store keeps a range of herbal and homoeopathic medicines. There is still, however, a great deal to be done. We are, for example, a long way from achieving the integration of western and traditional medicine, as China has done so successfully. There is also the problem that plants remain the poor relations in terms of conservation and respect, with the lion's share of resources and sympathy going to – if not lions, then to other creatures first and plant life second. The unique fascination of herbs could do a great deal to change this and is already playing an important role in the campaign to save tropical rain forests.

The renaissance of herbs is also leading to changes in the garden. A decade ago, when I first worked as a herb grower with Hollington Nurseries, few gardeners were familiar with any but the common culinary herbs. Since then, herbs have begun to make the transition from a corner of the vegetable garden to the flower border and are being grown as much for the pleasure of their company as for strictly utilitarian purposes. More and more gardeners are beginning to buy and enjoy plants for their interesting uses and associations – magical, romantic or historical – as well as for their more obvious attractions. Like all new de-velopments, it does, however, mean some adjusting of perspective. An example of this occurred in 1983 when Hollington Nurseries (which specializes in herbal and romatic plants) was awarded its first Gold Medal at the Chelsea Flower Show. Judith and Simon Hopkinson's display incorporated a range of herbs far exceeding the culinary, but the judges nevertheless had to make the award in the vegetable section, where herbs were then considered to belong! Undaunted, they went on to exhibit further successful displays which served to elevate herbs from vegetable to foliage and floral (and much more) in the eyes of both the judges and the gardening public. These designs, and the accompanying in-formation and publicity, have been influential in re-introducing aromatic and medicinal plants, along with colourful forms of common herbs to our gardens. Imagine the delight when visitors to the Nurseries found multi-coloured thymes and sages side-by-side with mighty angelica, ancient woad, mysterious henbane and Mediterranean oleanders! Herbs were not boring little green plants after all!

In the renaissance of herbs as garden plants, the visual is bound to play an important part, even though other dimensions – fragrance, history, uses, and even the wider aspects of medicine and plant life – emerge in the process. The herb gardener of today wants the best of both worlds – beauty and interest – and it is this combination which has inspired the plant profiles of *Fine Herbs*. The purpose has therefore been twofold: firstly, to describe some of the loveliest forms of commonly grown herbs, in the hope of encouraging a wider appreciation of them as garden plants. And secondly, to draw attention to a number of outstanding varieties of popular garden plants which also happen to be herbs, in order to add interest to their appeal. Unfortunately, for reasons of space and availability of material, some of my favourites have had to be left out. I especially regret that there wasn't room for white-flowered foxgloves (*Digitalis purpurea* 'Alba'), yellow-berried guelder rose (*Viburnum opulus* 'Xanthocarpum'), the purple-leaved grape vine (*Vitis vinifera* 'Purpurea') and ornamental forms of arbor vitae (*Thuja occidentalis*), such as 'Ellwangeriana Aurea' and 'Hetz Midget'; that I was never in the right place at the right time to get good photographs of either the pink-flowered or the variegated lily-of-the-valley (*Convallaria majalis* 'Rosea' and 'Variegata'); and that I failed to find the gorgeous variegated coltsfoot (*Tussilago farfara* 'Variegata') described by Frances Perry in her book *Beautiful Leaved Plants*, which, as far as I can determine, is not currently listed by any nursery in the British Isles.

The horticultural varieties of culinary and medicinal herbs include those with variegated leaves, double flowers, or with differently coloured foliage or flowers from the common species. Contrary to expectations perhaps, these variations do not affect their usefulness as herbs. Indeed, in the case of some (purple sage and double-flowered chamomile, for example) it appears to be an asset and the variety is preferred by many herbalists. When it comes to garden design, these varieties give infinitely greater scope. In the case of double flowers, they last longer and are often more fragrant than their single counterparts, and may flower earlier or later. The great thing about variegation (or coloured foliage such as golden or bronze) is that it gives interest to a plant that would otherwise be of little or no merit in the garden. Variegated ground elder and red rat's tail plantain are choice foliage plants, whereas no one willingly cultivates the plain green ground elder or rat's tail plantain! In addition, variegation often produces weaker plants, rendering rampant nuisances such as ground elder tame enough (just!) for inclusion in the flower bed or shrubbery. Even well-loved garden plants can be enhanced immeasurably by variegation. Orris and jasmine have lovely, if short-lived, flowers: growing their variegated forms turns them into foliage plants with a much longer period of interest.

After the thrill of first impressions – from virginal white double primroses and 'Brazen Hussy' celandines with pale orange flowers and brown leaves, to mounds of lime-green marjoram and smartly striped green and white swords of sweet flag – comes the practical information. This explains how the plant grows, which are its closest relatives, what makes it important as a herb and the stories – some true and some to be taken with a pinch of salt – which are told about it. And that, unfortunately, is about all that can be conveyed in a book, leaving you to explore the more intimate details for yourself. The hostess can only invite the most interesting guests and make the introductions! Some you may not take to, but I am sure many will become close friends and serve as ambassadors to other forgotten allies of the plant world.

Deni Bown, November 1987.

FINE HERBS

PINK AND YELLOW YARROWS
Achillea millefolium 'Cerise Queen' and
'Flowers of Sulphur'

About ten years ago an article in the
journal *Science* described a prehistoric
find in northern Iraq. It was the grave of a
Neanderthal man who, 60,000 years ago, had
been buried surrounded by flowers in the
depths of a cave. Analysis of the plant frag-
ments identified them as belonging to eight
different genera. Even more remarkable,
further investigation showed that nearly all of
them are still used medicinally by local people.
One of them was yarrow.

The use of herbs to cure illness may be even
older than this extremely ancient find and
could be described as pre-human. Animals are
known to seek out certain plants when ailing,
in the same way that they have an instinct to
vary their diet according to nutritional requirements. Of all the thousands of known
medicinal plants, few have such a well-
documented use throughout human history as
yarrow (*Achillea millefolium*). One factor is its
abundance. It is a very common weed of the
immensely prolific daisy family (Compositae)
which accounts for a tenth of all species of
flowering plants. Yarrow is found wild all over
Europe, North America, Asia and Australasia.
Its close relatives (200 or so species of *Achillea*), many of which are similar in appearance,
extend the range of habitats colonized by the
genus to almost every temperate region.

*Pink-flowered forms of yarrow are common in the
wild but none are more vivid than 'Cerise
Queen'.*

Another factor in its widespread use is its effectiveness as a herb. Its chemistry is complex and its applications many, from healing wounds and lowering fevers to relieving high blood pressure and controlling diarrhoea and urinary tract infections. Much of its reputation in traditional medicine rests on its wound-healing powers. The genus name *Achillea* was given because Achilles was supposed to have treated his soldiers' wounds with it during the Trojan War. The Greek physician Dioscorides, an exceedingly observant doctor and botanist who travelled widely with the Roman army, used it as a haemostatic (a herb which stops bleeding, either internal or external) and found it invaluable for wounds caused by metal. It was believed that you had to have scrapings of the actual weapon to ensure the healing of such wounds, and one account of the origin of yarrow was that it grew from the scrapings of Achilles' spear. Several of yarrow's names reflect its use on the battlefield – herbe militaris, soldier's woundwort, knight's milfoil – and in the workshop, another place renowned for injuries, where it was known as carpenter's weed. So respected is yarrow for healing that the present-day herbalist Maurice Mességué called it 'the iodine of the meadows and fields'. Though lotions and ointments can be made from yarrow, it is worth remembering that the traditional way of applying the herb for emergencies 'in the field' is to chew a mouthful of the plant into a wad and apply it to the wound there and then.

Yarrow's reputation as a fever herb is so high that at times it has been used as a substitute for quinine (the classic treatment for malaria). The feverish stages of common illnesses such as measles, 'flu and colds respond well to piping hot infusions of yarrow heads, the top few inches of flowers and leaves being gathered in summer for this purpose. Any herbalist will tell you that as a household remedy for colds and 'flu, there is nothing to beat yarrow, elderflower and peppermint tea – made even more potent with a dash of cayenne pepper. It will bring you out in a cleansing sweat, lower your temperature and clear congestion.

Though beyond the scope of household remedies, the circulatory effects of yarrow are of particular interest. Medical herbalists use it in conjunction with herbs, such as limeflowers (*Tilia* spp), nettle (*Urtica dioica*) and melilot (*Melilotus officinalis*), to treat high blood pressure and thrombosis. Drinking yarrow tea occasionally might help safeguard against such conditions. It is a pleasant-tasting, aromatic drink which improves digestion and has a tonic effect on the whole metabolism.

Extending the list of yarrow's benefits further, strong infusions mixed with Fuller's earth are good for greasy skins and acne; the fresh juice was a traditional treatment for aching ears; and the leaves may be chewed for toothache. In the Orkneys, off the north coast of Scotland, yarrow tea is considered an anti-depressant and in China, Siberian yarrow (*A. sibirica*) – known inscrutably as skyflying centipede grass – is used for almost all the aforementioned traumas, as well as snakebite.

Should you still be short of uses for yarrow, there are yet more possibilities: the Scandinavians, who call it the field hop, traditionally used it for brewing and reckon the beer is more potent as a result, and in the German wine trade yarrow seeds were once added to the wine barrels as a preservative. Another of its common names – old man's pepper – describes its use as snuff and tobacco. If you enjoy experimenting with unusual herbs in cooking, try small amounts of finely chopped yarrow leaves (omitting the tough midrib) in sauces, salads and soups. Tom Stobart, in his book *Herbs, Spices and Flavourings*, recommends it as an acceptable substitute for chervil (*Anthriscus cerefolium*), a herb which does not dry well, is difficult to buy fresh and which, if you grow it yourself, has an awful tendency to bolt just when you need it most.

One of yarrow's other names, milfoil, like the specific name *millefolium*, means 'a thousand leaves', referring to the appearance of the dark green leaves which are finely cut into numerous feathery leaflets. Plants may be anything from 10–60 cm (4–24 in) or more, depending on conditions, branching out at the top into flat clusters of greyish-white to pale pink flowers which open in midsummer right through to late autumn. All parts are tough and wiry, including the creeping rhizome which enables it to spread over a wide area. It is not fussy about soils but prefers sunny grassy places and can be found in fields, hedgerows, wasteland and the verges of roads at altitudes of up to 2,000 m (5,500 ft).

Yarrow has always been popular in cultivation. Apart from its medicinal uses, it makes a good border plant with long-lasting flowers which cut and dry well. Occasionally in the wild, you can find a plant which has much pinker flowers than its neighbours. Such variants have caught the eye of plant breeders and their selections have resulted in some outstanding colour forms. Seeds of pink-flowered yarrow, A. millefolium 'Rosea', are sometimes offered but even better are 'Cerise Queen' whose flowers are vivid carmine, and 'Flowers of Sulphur' which, as the name suggests, bears flowers exactly the same colour as sulphur – an entrancing clear pale yellow a shade or two darker than primrose. 'Cerise Queen' retains the vigorous growth of the species, but 'Flowers of Sulphur' is not nearly as rampant.

Over the centuries the abundance, usefulness and popularity of yarrow have led to rampant growth in other directions too: namely in myths and legends concerning it. In Britain there are a host of verses about yarrow, mostly for recital by young women to find out about the trueness of their loves. Some involve accompanying actions, such as 'Yarroway, yarroway, bear a white blow, if my lover loves me, my nose will bleed now', which was said (probably with some difficulty) while tickling the inside of the nostrils with yarrow leaves. The irritation could well cause a nosebleed and, interestingly, this was also a technique for using yarrow to relieve migraine in humans and fevers in domestic animals. The nosebleed

Yarrow (Achillea millefolium)

was, of course, nothing to worry about, as you had on hand the very herb to cure it: the crushed leaves having long been employed as a plug for bleeding nostrils.

A more sophisticated kind of divination, known as the *I Ching* or *Book of Changes*, also calls for yarrow. For consulting this oracle you need 50 yarrow stalks (though only 49 are used) but, even with the instructions given in the book, it is a complicated business which explains why the alternative of tossing three coins is usually chosen instead. The stalks must be carefully prepared, cutting them exactly the same length but otherwise preserving their individuality as 'the symbols of heaven and the spirit'. The ritual of casting the yarrow stalks is carried out in solitude and in a meditative frame of mind. It is regarded not as magic (though yarrow's association with certain magical practices is reflected in names such as devil's plaything), but as a means of revealing the pattern of forces prevalent at that moment. The *I Ching*, whose origin may be traced to the second millenium BC, is one of the earliest attempts by human beings to account for their place in the universe – the start of the wisdom and morality which later produced Confucian and Taoist philosophy.

One of our commonest weeds is therefore rather remarkable in its close association with the evolution of *Homo sapiens*. Unless we are gardeners or herbalists, yarrow may no longer play much part in our daily lives, but if nothing else its history as a medicinal and divinatory plant provides food for thought.

VARIEGATED SWEET FLAG
Acorus calamus 'Variegatus'

Most people's idea of a herb garden is a neat bed of mainly Mediterranean plants – thyme, sage, rosemary, lavender – bathed in sunshine and buzzing with bees. But there are other possibilities. Many beautiful, interesting and useful herbs will grow in damp shady spots, even in unpromising quagmires and wet ditches, as well as on the margins of pools and the banks of streams, if your water-logged areas include such assets.

Personally, I have always had a soft spot for mud and one of my dreams is to plant a wetland herb garden. Needless to say, I have a well-drained sunny garden where wild roses, marjoram and pinks run riot and thus my beloved bog plants are confined ignominiously to a couple of old baths. If ever I do lay claim to an area of mud, glorious mud, it will soon be transformed into a lush and mysterious jungle of marshmallow (*Althaea officinalis*), angelica (*Angelica archangelica*), meadowsweet (*Filipendula ulmaria*), comfrey (*Symphytum officinalis*), bogbean (*Menyanthes trifoliata*), skunk cabbage (*Symplocarpus foetidus*), all kinds of mints (*Mentha* spp) and last, but not least – sweet flag.

Of them all, sweet flag is possibly the least well known and probably the least showy – that is, unless you plant the variegated form. Characteristic of wetland vegetation are plants with rush-like foliage. Though plain in themselves, their simple linear leaves punctuate more complex shapes and are invaluable in landscaping such areas. Variegation gives additional emphasis to such focal points. *Acorus calamus* 'Variegatus' is one such plant. Its sword-shaped leaves rise to 1 m (3 ft) or more and are cream-striped with rose pink bases that are particularly noticeable when the new foliage emerges from the mud (or shallow water) in early spring.

Cultivating sweet flag should present no problems if a suitably wet site is available, whether marshy ground, or still or flowing water. Plants of the variegated form are obtainable from specialist herb nurseries and from aquatic centres. If planting in water, it is best to place the root ball, along with some extra soil and a few large stones, in a piece of sacking, to weigh it down until it becomes established. Alternatively, use one of the basket-type pots sold in aquatic centres. The plant should be potted more firmly than usual and topped with a thick layer of stones to prevent both soil and plant floating away when submerged. Sweet flag dies down in the winter but is extremely hardy. It is also virtually pest- and disease-free.

Acorus calamus is an aroid, a member of the arum family (Araceae), though you would be hard pressed to see much resemblance between it and the familiar European lords-and-ladies (*Arum maculatum*) and North American Jack-in-the-pulpit (*Arisaema triphyllum*). In fact, it looks far more like a reed or bulrush as regards foliage, and grows in the same kinds of places: marshes, river banks and lake margins. You can, however, tell it apart from reeds and

13

The bright new leaves of variegated sweet flag emerge from the pond each spring.

reedmaces by the prominent midrib which can be felt as a ridge down the centre of the leaf. Furthermore, the blade tends to be slightly crimped or wavy in places and both it and the 2–3 cm (1 in) thick horizontal rhizome are fragrant when bruised. Flowering (in the summer) also helps in distinguishing sweet flag from rushes (and irises, which it resembles too). The flowers are well camouflaged, borne on a greenish cylindrical spoke (technically a spadix) some 9 cm (3½ in) long, which juts out at an angle from the ridged flower stalk. Below it emerges a bract-like spathe, up to 80 cm (32 in) in length, which is little different from a leaf. In some regions (Europe, for example), wild sweet flag virtually never sets seed as the entire population is composed of sterile triploid plants. It therefore relies for propagation upon pieces of rhizome breaking off during floods and floating away to begin new growth wherever they lodge: a surprisingly effective technique which has enabled it to spread almost worldwide, from close on the Arctic Circle to south of the equator in New Guinea.

Compared with its showy relatives, such as the glossy scarlet anthuriums and snow-white arum lilies, the sweet flag inflorescence is unexciting. Upon closer inspection, one might, however, be tempted to agree with Roy Genders, who, in his encyclopedic work *Scented Flora of the World*, describes the spike as having 'a sombre beauty in appearance resembling the spire of a church, being greenish-brown in colour with the surface

14

In summer, the sword-shaped leaves of variegated sweet flag arch gracefully over the water.

covered in a gold mosaic' – the minute tightly packed flowers forming this intricate pattern. Neither would one imagine that the general appearance of the plant, for all its landscape potential, is anything to wax lyrical about in comparison with its famous houseplant relatives, the monsteras (Swiss cheese plants) and philodendrons (elephant ears) which have some of the most dramatic leaf shapes in creation. Yet Walt Whitman, no less, found it intensely inspiring and wrote a long poem entitled *Calamus* in which he sings its praises at length and refers to it as 'scented herbage of my breast'.

Sweet flag is an important herb historically and has some interesting medicinal applica-

tions that are still in use today. It was one of the earliest herbs in cultivation and as a result its place of origin is uncertain. Most likely it was first found in central Asia, but there is evidence that it may also be native to North America. It was introduced to Europe from Mongolia and Siberia in the sixteenth century, and long before this westward expansion it was used in Chinese and North American Indian medicine, found in ancient Egyptian tombs and mentioned several times in the Bible.

In England its cultivation once centred on the Norfolk Broads, a low-lying wetland area. Here it was known as gladdon and gathered by boat at the annual gladdon harvest. The leaves were mostly used for strewing floors in the days before carpets. Originally rushes and fragrant herbs such as meadowsweet were used for this purpose, but when sweet flag was introduced, its aromatic resilient leaves were found superior. So popular did it become that when Cardinal Wolsey fell from favour with Henry VIII, one of the charges laid against him was of his extravagance in having large quantitites of sweet flag brought from Norfolk for the floors of his London residence.

All parts of sweet flag are fragrant. The rhizome is the part used medicinally. It contains a volatile oil which has tranquillizing and antibiotic effects and was once listed in the pharmacopoeias of 24 countries. William Salmon, in his herbal of 1710, listed numerous different ways of preparing the rhizome, from a powder and a decoction in wine to the more obscure 'collegium' and 'cataplasm'. He claimed that the juice would 'prevail against the bitings of mad dogs and other venomous creatures. It is a peculiar thing against poison, the plague and all contagious diseases.'

Anyone reading old herbals is bound to form the impression that our ancestors had more than their share of mad dogs, poisonous beasts and plagues. It is easy to dismiss the constant references to these as lurid turns of phrase, and their antidotes as more wishful thinking than pharmacology. The truth is that they did have to contend with horrors such as rabies and infectious diseases, such as the rat-flea-borne Black Death which decimated the population of Europe in the fourteenth century. The Great Plague of London killed more than, 68,000 people in one year (1664–65), more than one-sixth of the city's inhabitants. Needless to say, contact with the dead and dying was greatly feared. Crosses were put on doors and bells rang before hearses as a warning. Yet, during this time, a gang of thieves managed to rob corpses with the most astonishing impunity and immunity. Eventually they were caught and tried, but promised pardon if they would divulge the secret of their resistance to this virulent infection. It turned out to be a herbal potion which they drank and liberally doused themselves with before going about their gruesome business. It became known as the 'Four Thieves' Vinegar' and one of its ingredients was sweet flag.

In many countries sweet flag is used in traditional remedies for gastric disturbances. A recent (1986) Soviet study concluded that it is indeed effective against organisms which cause such serious complaints as septicaemia and dysentery. It is also helpful for toothache: chewing the raw root is a North American Indian cure. It probably works, as the volatile oil contains eugenol which is the active ingredient in oil of cloves, a proven household remedy for dental pain.

The spicy fragrance of sweet flag makes it useful in other ways too. We may not strew our floors but we are still avid users of food flavourings and perfumes. In many countries the essential oil is distilled commercially. It has a long-lasting fragrance and is used in the making of liqueurs and in toiletries and perfumes, especially those with woody or leathery notes. The ground root can be used like cinnamon or nutmeg and is not unlike lemon grass in aroma. At one time, pieces of the rhizome were crystallized and sucked as a lozenge to ward off infections and relieve coughs and indigestion. The foliage is less often used, but Nicholas Culpeper, whose enduringly popular work *The Complete Herbal* was completed in 1653, reported that 'The leaves, having a very grateful flavour, are by some nice cooks put into a sauce for fish.'

Sweet flag is not a showy plant but its interesting history, easy disposition (given a wet spot), effective simplicity amongst more ornate aquatic and marginal plants, and tangerine-like scent make it one that grows in our admiration and affection.

VARIEGATED GOUTWEED
Aegopodium podagraria 'Variegata'

Trying to persuade gardeners to grow a form of goutweed, or ground elder as it is perhaps better known, is no easy task. One of the first things we learn as gardeners is to recognize and wage constant war on weeds, the great enemies of cultivation, and the ruthless dislike of years is difficult to overcome. Many common weeds are valuable medicinal herbs – nettles (*Urtica dioica*), dandelion (*Taraxacum officinale*) and couch grass or twitch (*Agropyron repens*), to mention a few. However, among the most pestiferous, only ground elder has a form which is sufficiently attractive and well behaved to elevate it from weed to ornamental, giving us a desirable garden plant which also has, as a bonus, a long history of use as an edible and medicinal plant.

One problem with variegated plants is that they are often weaker than their plain equivalents. In the case of variegated goutweed, this turns out to be a saving grace, tempering its invasive weediness just enough to merit consideration as a ground cover plant. Like the species, it will grow almost anywhere but on acid soils, and seems to thrive in any situation from full sun to heavy shade. It is most useful as deciduous ground cover under trees and between shrubs, in shade or dappled woodland conditions where the white-splashed leaves show to best effect. If the flowering shoots are removed, its height remains at 10–20 cm (4–8 in) throughout the growing season. Winter-flowering bulbs such as snowdrops (*Galanthus* spp) and aconites (*Eranthis hyemalis*) should prove good companions, coming into growth when its foliage has died down, and fading as its fresh new leaves unfold in spring.

. Goutweed is a member of the Umbel-liferae, a family with characteristic flat-topped umbels of tiny flowers and a distinctive, though variable smell. Closely related to gout-weed are such well-known edible plants as carrots (*Daucus carota*) and parsnips (*Pastinaca sativa*), and the popular herbs, fennel (*Foeniculum vulgare*), dill (*Anethum graveolens*) and coriander (*Coriandrum sativum*). It is found throughout Europe in woodland and hedgerows and on roadsides, waste ground and cultivated land, and has been introduced by European immigrants to many areas of North America where it is just as much a nuisance as in its original homelands. Like many umbellifers, goutweed has white flowers and matt mid-green divided leaves. The segments are in three groups of three, ovate and toothed at the margins – 'snipped about', according to Culpeper's description. Each leaf measures 10–20 cm (4–8 in) in length and the whole plant at flowering time is some 60–80 cm (24–32 in) tall.

Goutweed and ground elder are only two of the common names that *Aegopodium podagraria* has acquired over the ages. Several refer to the likeness of its leaves to those of the ash (*Fraxinus excelsior*): ground ash, white ash and ashweed. They are also similar to elder (*Sambucus nigra*) leaves, hence ground elder. Less obvious is goatweed. My goats would rarely eat it, so I can hardly believe it got this name because it is supposed to be one of their favourite foods. On the other hand, it goes under the name of pigweed as pigs enjoy it greatly. (In Anglo-Saxon England, it also had the reputation of protecting pigs from sudden death if hung in the pigsty.) Perhaps the association with goats came as a result of the

Goutweed or ground elder
(Aegopodium podagraria)

generic name; *Aegopodium* being derived from the Greek words *aix, aigos*, meaning a goat, and *pous, podos*, foot or feet, though, again, in the case of my goats, the shape of their feet was nothing like that of goutweed leaves. More realistic is the species name, *podagraria*, which is from the Latin for gout (an inflammation of the joints, especially of the big toe and foot, caused by deposits of sodium urate), for which it is used medicinally. The common names goutweed and goutwort also refer to its effectiveness for this complaint. As the herbalist Nicholas Culpeper said: 'It is not to be supposed goutwort hath its name for nothing'.

Perhaps bishops were particularly afflicted by this painful condition, as it is also called bishopswort and bishopsweed. A more likely explanation, however, is that, in the British Isles at least, it used to be found mostly near ecclesiastical ruins because herb gardens were

17

(above and opposite) The fresh green and white leaves of variegated goutweed make eyecatching deciduous ground cover under shrubs or over winter- and spring-flowering bulbs.

originally the province of monks. There is, in fact, a story and a name which combine both possibilities. Once upon a time, certain monks were sorely afflicted with gout and prayed to St Gerard for help. They started using goutweed and, lo and behold, their gout was cured, so they named it herb Gerard. Less esoteric are names such as Jack-jump-about, referring to the seeds which are ejected from the plant when shaken by the wind; and the prosaic, utterly self-explanatory Irish name – farmer's plague.

As a medicinal herb, goutweed is a mild diuretic and sedative, and whether taken internally or used externally, is a good anti-inflammatory. In the form of a tea or infusion it not only helps to relieve gout, but sciatica and all aches and pains in the joints. It is a useful, if at times all too plentiful remedy. Externally, a poultice of the leaves, or a pad of cotton wool soaked in a strong infusion, makes a soothing compress for inflamed joints, haemorrhoids, burns, wounds and insect bites. In homoeopathy it is regarded as beneficial for arthritis and rheumatism.

Anyone who has pulled goutweed out of their garden in the hope of restricting its progress will have noticed its strong, fairly unpleasant smell. I once read that this diminishes when it is cooked, but my culinary endeavours resulted in a vegetable which tasted exactly as it smelled and one which I hesitate to recommend. No doubt it would be more palatable in soup. However, in Scandinavia and eastern Europe it has long been enjoyed as a spring vegetable, both raw in salads or cooked. Its high vitamin content and medicinal properties should be sufficient in themselves to encourage us to try it, spurred on

18

by the knowledge that the more we eat (of the plain green species, that is), the less there is to take over the rest of the garden. Its tough creeping rhizomes may be unstoppable, but they are certainly weakened by constant defoliation.

The herbalist John Gerard (who did not give his name to the plant) wrote at the end of the sixteenth century that 'Herbe Gerard groweth of itself in gardens without setting or sowing and is so fruitful in its increase that when it hath once taken roote, it will hardly be gotten out againe, spoiling and getting every year more ground.' Gardeners today find exactly the same problem and it is therefore with a sense of guilt – or at least of incongruity – that after years of struggling against the all-pervasive spaghetti-like roots of goutweed in my garden, I am now nurturing the variegated form, welcoming each new leaf and every increase in its spread – though I do so with every confidence that it will never achieve the wall-to-wall carpeting of its predecessor. Such are the powers of attraction that colour variation and pattern have over the plant enthusiast!

COLOURED BUGLES
Ajuga reptans 'Atropurpurea', 'Burgundy Glow', 'Rainbow' (syn. 'Multicolor') and 'Variegata'

Plants, like clothes and decor, go in and out of fashion. As a medicinal herb, bugle is definitely 'out' at the moment. On the other hand, its current vogue as a garden plant goes from strength to strength. Over the years it has proved to be one of the best carpeters for moisture-retentive soil, providing neat colourful foliage all year round and a display of attractive flowers in spring. It now comes in such a range of colours that there is a variety for almost any planting scheme – indeed, the only problem it is likely to cause the gardener is that he or she is spoilt for choice!

Bugle is a perennial creeping plant found all over Europe in damp woods and grassland. It is similar in appearance and closely related to self-heal (*Prunella vulgaris*). Both are members of the Labiate family (Labiatae) which has yielded so many important culinary and medicinal herbs. Plants tend to form dense colonies as each rosette of shiny green obovate leaves sends out runners some 30 cm (1 ft) long during the growing season. At first the runners bear pairs of leaves along their length and, as these develop, roots are sent down from the nodes. The sections of runner between the plantlets decay in the winter and the following spring the juvenile plant enlarges and, in its turn, sprouts runners. Mature rosettes flower in the spring. The flower stalks are leafy and 15–30 cm (6–12 in) tall, square in cross-section and hairy on two sides (distinguishing it from *A. genevensis* and *A. pyramidalis* whose stems are hairy all round). They bear whorls of (usually) deep blue flowers, though pink-flowered forms are not uncommon in the wild. Even plants with white flowers may be found occasionally. Bees are attracted to the small, lipped tubular flowers and seed is sometimes set, but there is no doubt that bugle's main method of reproduction is vegetative.

Bugles are remarkably undemanding. They thrive in sun or shade and, though happiest in moisture-retentive soil, will tolerate a range of conditions, from heavy wet soils to soils that dry out in summer. They are seldom invasive enough to be a problem and all in all are indispensable evergreens for filling gaps, covering banks and planting at the front of borders. They also associate well with many kinds of bulbs and grasses which come up happily through the rosettes during the spring and summer. Propagation is child's play, for bugle is similar in habit to the ubiquitous spider plant (*Chlorophytum*) in obligingly producing an endless supply of ready-made plantlets which only need separating from the parent to start a whole new dynasty.

The palest, smallest and most delicate bugle is 'Variegata'. Its leaves are a haphazard mixture of light green, grey-green and ivory and the flowers are porcelain blue. In habit, this variety is ground-hugging and restrained, taking much longer to cover an area than its more robust relatives. It is best kept in the shade to protect the variegation from scorching, and is perhaps the only bugle to be trusted on the rock garden near alpines and other choice small-growing plants which do not tolerate invasion. Elsewhere it is very pretty as ground cover around plants with predominantly grey or blue-green coloration – the most restful of planting schemes and the basis of 'silver gardens'. (Purists might exclude *A. reptans* 'Variegata' from a silver border because of its blue flowers, in which case 'Alba' might be used instead. It has pure white flowers, but lacks the pretty variegation, being basically green with a bronze tinge.)

Where something much more vigorous and dramatic is welcome, 'Atropurpurea' is the obvious choice. It bounds along with the greatest of ease, depositing big bold rosettes of dark purplish-brown at regular intervals and soon forming an impenetrable mass of glossy leaves which, in the spring, are punctuated with stocky spires of intense blue flowers. For dazzling contrast I once planted it with pineapple mint (*Mentha suaveolens* 'Variegata'), but more subtle effects can be obtained by using the bronze bugle to complement other plants with purple, brown, pink or reddish-coloured flowers or foliage. Imagine it beneath a chocolate-brown hazel (*Corylus maxima* 'Purpurea') or bronze elder (*Sambucus nigra* 'Purpurea'), along with pink cow parsley (*Chaerophyllum hirsutum* 'Roseum') and bright pink forms of yarrow (*Achillea millefolium*).

The most vivid of all bugles is 'Burgundy Glow', whose leaves are a delightful blend of bright pink, unripe plum and pinkish-cream. Sunlight intensifies the colours: shade mutes them, introducing more grey and green; either way the overall effect is pink throughout summer and winter. This should be sufficient recommendation in itself, but in spring the deep blue flowers make this an astonishingly colourful plant – the more so because the leaflets on the flower stems and the bracts extend the foliage colour up into the flowers. Like 'Variegata', it looks most effective near blue-green and silver plants – but should be kept well away from anything yellow!

Whereas 'Burgundy Glow' would tarnish any gold, a variety of bugle known as 'Multicolor' or 'Rainbow' is the perfect choice for enhancing yellow shades. It has shiny bronze leaves that are more brown than purple and they are dappled with salmon pink, cream and pale yellow. The colours are retained in shade so it may be used as ground cover between shrubs.

I have always wondered how bugle got its name when nothing about the plant resembles a bugle. There is no easy explanation. Some sources blind us with science and claim that *Ajuga* is from Greek words meaning 'without a yoke' – apparently referring to the calyx having just one lip (not two as is the case with most Labiates). Or, possibly, it may be from *abigo*, from the Latin for 'to drive away', in the sense of getting rid of sickness and ill health. Others admit defeat and propose that both *Ajuga* and bugle are the results of inevitable changes in such early words for the plant as *abija*, *abuga* and *bugula* – whose origins are lost in obscurity. Another explanation links the word 'bugle' with tubular glass beads known as bugles which are used in embroidery and look vaguely like the corolla tube of the bugle flower. We shall probably never know which, if any, of these is correct. Some of its other names are more straightforward: *reptans* means 'creeping' and its other common names, herb carpenter and middle comfrey, refer to its healing properties.

In spite of the fact that one of its names likens it to comfrey (*Symphytum officinale*), there is little evidence that it is anywhere nearly such an effective herb for healing wounds. Traditionally it was used mainly for internal injuries and slow-healing wounds and

sores, though it was also prescribed (mixed with peppermint) for gall bladder problems. In homoeopathy it has been used quite differently – for mouth ulcers and throat infections.

For hundreds of years bugle was undoubtedly an important herb. In the seventeenth century the herbalist Nicholas Culpeper swore by it, advising that 'if the virtues of it make you fall in love with it (as they will if you be wise) keep a syrup of it to take inwardly, and an ointment and plaster of it to use outwardly, always by you. . . . It is so efficacious for all sorts of hurts in the body that none shall be without it.' Apart from curing 'inward wounds, thrusts or stabs in the body or bowles', it was apparently just the thing for a hangover too. In Culpeper's words: 'Many times such as give themselves to drinking are troubled by strange fancies, strange sights in the night time and some with voices . . . Those I have known cured by taking only two spoonfuls of the syrup of this herb after supper two hours, when you go to bed.'

Though largely rejected by modern herbal medicine, there may well be uses for the plant that have not yet been fully investigated. It is known, for example, to have an action on the heart which is comparable to that of digitalis, though what is responsible for this has not been determined. Its relative, the African bugle (A. remota) is used in native medicine to treat high blood pressure and has recently been found by scientists to contain compounds which interfere with moulting in insect larvae – a discovery which could prove valuable in crop protection. In some ways, then, bugle is a bit of a mystery. It is blessed with odd names and its usefulness as a medicinal herb may be an old wives' tale, but as a garden plant its reputation is unsullied. Perhaps in deference to its undoubted value in horticulture, it should be renamed herb carpeter?

Bugle 'Burgundy Glow': one of the most colourful of all evergreen foliage plants.

SILVER WORMWOODS
Artemisia absinthium 'Lambrook Silver' and 'Powis Castle'

There are over 200 species of *Artemisia* and they include some of the bitterest herbs known. Wormwoods of various kinds have been used medicinally since earliest times: in ancient Egypt, Rome and Greece; in Middle Eastern countries where some of the first advances in medicine and chemistry took place; by the Celts; by North American Indian tribes; and in traditional Chinese medicine, in which the smouldering of compacted *Artemisia* leaves on the skin of a patient is an important branch of therapy known as moxibustion and is used in conjunction with acupuncture.

Wormwood was evidently a household word in biblical times and often used as an analogy for the consequences of sin: 'For the lips of a strange woman drop as an honeycomb, And her mouth is smoother than oil: But her end is bitter as wormwood.' (Proverbs 5: 3–4.) A dire warning is given in the Book of Revelation too: 'And the third angel sounded, and there fell a great star from heaven, burning as it were a lamp, and it fell upon the third part of the rivers, and upon the fountains of waters; And the name of the star is called Wormwood: and the third part of the waters became wormwood; and many men died of the waters, because they were made bitter.' (Revelation 8: 10–11.) Most chilling of all, Chernobyl is the Ukrainian word for wormwood.

The chemistry behind the bitterness is complex and has a great many medicinal applications. It consists of potent substances which promote glandular and gastric secretions, relieve spasms and fevers, cause abortion, kill insects and expel 'worms' – intestinal parasites. Its species name, *absinthium*, means 'without sweetness': an understatement for its intense, nauseating bitterness. The complaints that have been treated with wormwood are numerous and diverse, but in modern herbal medicine it is prescribed mainly with butternut bark (*Juglans cinerea*) for worms in children; for anorexia, debility and lassitude with poor appetite and digestion; and for hepatitis. It has also been found effective in cases of lead poisoning.

Wormwood is strongly aromatic and contains a dark green volatile oil. Herein lies a tale. The German word for wormwood is *Wermut*, meaning 'preserver of the mind', as wormwood was held to be a great restorer of the nerves and mental functions. Perhaps as an extension of this, it was also thought to prevent intoxication and hangovers, and sprigs of the herb were steeped in wine for this purpose. In small carefully controlled doses, wormwood may well achieve these and other improvements to health and well-being, but unfortunately it does not necessarily follow that larger amounts will do even more good. The sad truth of this was demonstrated in the nineteenth century when addiction to absinthe – a wormwood-based spirit – became a social problem in many countries. It all started in 1797 when Henri Louis Pernod bought a recipe from a doctor in Switzerland. It was for the herb-flavoured alcoholic drink which became known as absinthe after its main ingredient, absinthol, the oil of *A. absinthium*. The yellowish-green spirit also contained extracts from sweet flag, fennel, liquorice, aniseed and star anise, angelica and dittany. Like many alcoholic herbal drinks, it was probably intended as a tonic. In any case, it proved enormously popular and, far from preventing hangovers and improving mental acuity, wormwood in this form caused the worst alcoholism ever seen. It was certainly strong stuff – 68 per cent alcohol by volume – and soon absinthe drinking became a serious problem in the United States and in several European countries, especially France. Several artists, including Manet, painted the miserable absinthe drinker whose death would be preceded by vertigo, numbness, stupefaction, hallucinations, convulsions and irreversible brain damage. Consumption of absinthe rose in France from 6,713 hectolitres (147,686 gal)

in 1873 to 360,000 hectolitres (7,920,000 gal) in 1911 (a hectolitre is 100 litres). Switzerland took the lead and banned it in 1908; France in 1915, and other countries, including the United States, soon after. Absinthe is now a forgotten drink, but we are familiar with its less potent successors: the aniseed-based Pernod and the herb-flavoured wine vermouth (vermouth being the French version of the German word for wormwood, *Wermut*).

All this is a far cry from wormwood as a garden plant, which is sheer – and harmless – delight. Wild plants are found on roadsides and wasteland in many areas of Europe, North America, Siberia and western Asia. Occasionally they cover large areas of poor stony soil where nothing else will grow and, protected by their intense bitterness, are touched by neither man nor beast. They are perennials of the daisy family (Compositae) with stems 60–100 cm (24–40 in) tall which are almost woody at the base. The leaves are 7–8 cm (3 in) long, divided and subdivided into narrow segments and covered in the finest silky hairs which give them a silvery appearance. Small drooping yellow flowers, like closely cropped tassels, are borne in leafy racemes during the summer.

The horticultural varieties of wormwood have distinctly silver foliage, making filigree mounds which complement more colourful herbaceous plants and shrubs. 'Lambrook Silver' has a neat, non-invasive habit and reaches about 50 cm (20 in). Its delicate spires of flowers are lovely in flower arrangements. However, should the flowers be of no interest, the non-flowering 'Powis Castle' may be an even better choice. Its foliage resembles that of the doubtfully hardy *A. arborescens*, but at 60 cm (24 in) it is a much smaller plant than this southern European species which can reach 1.8 m (6 ft) tall. The origin of 'Powis Castle' is uncertain but it may be a hybrid between *A. arborescens* and *A. absinthium*. Both 'Lambrook Silver' and 'Powis Castle' provide a note of sophistication with bronze foliage, or with flowers in shades of blue, purple or pink – and

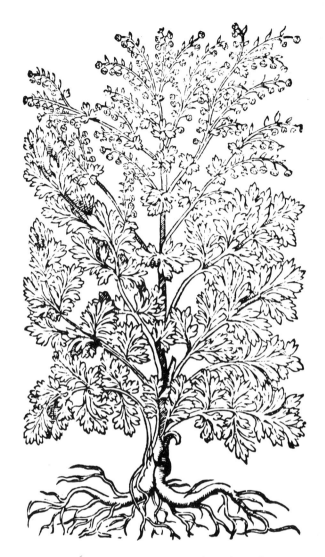

Wormwood (Artemisia absinthium)

are quite ethereal with white flowers. They ask nothing more than sunshine and good drainage and, if anything, look and smell better on a spartan diet. If necessary, they can be divided during the winter and cut back in spring to keep them tidy.

Wormwood was once an important strewing herb. William Tusser, whose *Five Hundred Pointes of Good Husbandrie* was published in 1573, advised that:

> While wormwood hath seed get a handful or twain,
> To save against March, to make flea refraine,
> Where the chamber is swept and the wormwood is strowne,
> No flea for his life dare abide to be knowne.

Updated advice would be to sprinkle crushed dried wormwood in amongst the bedding of cat and dog baskets (though I hesitate to compose a poem on the subject). Its insect-repellent properties can also be utilized in sachets for

(above) Sprigs of flowering wormwood 'Lambrook Silver' surround black basil.
(opposite) An ethereal combination: wormwood 'Powis Castle' and white mallow flowers.

GOLD AND SILVER BOX

Buxus sempervirens 'Elegantissima' (syn. 'Elegans' and 'Variegata') and 'Latifolia Maculata' (syn. 'Aurea' and 'Japonica Aurea')

linen. Culpeper was at his most discursive on the subject of wormwood and was of the opinion that the herb 'being laid among cloathes will make a moth scorn to meddle with cloathes as much as a lion scorns to meddle with a mouse or an eagle with a fly.'

Wormwood is a plant of contrasts, with a reputation both protective and destructive. Folklore tells us that wormwood should be planted along the boundaries of the garden to keep adders away. Another myth describes how wormwood grew from the track of the serpent as it slithered out of the Garden of Eden. Like the proverbial wolf in sheep's clothing, beneath its silver fleece is hidden a dangerous nature.

There is nothing to compare with box (*Buxus sempervirens*) for dense neat hedges of whatever shape and size. Those at Powis Castle in Powys, Wales, are giants at over 4.5 m (15 ft) but many are miniatures scarcely 20 cm (8 in) high. The slender twigs and tiny close-set leaves makes box a favourite with topiarists, being ideal for cutting into mathematically accurate lines. On the one hand box is slow-growing and therefore does not need cutting often, and on the other hand it can take drastic pruning if necessary. And whatever attention is lavished on it is worthwhile, for this is not the kind of hedge that defines boundaries and covers eyesores in a

26

season, but a slow-growing, immensely long-lived feature that gives dignity to a garden.

Topiary is an ancient art. There are many records of this skill from Roman times, notably in the letters of Pliny the Younger who, in the first century AD, had various shapes of box in his garden. The word topiary is from the Latin *topia*, meaning decorative garden work, and it is probably no coincidence that most wild box in Great Britain is found near Roman sites. Though the popularity of topiary has waxed and waned according to garden fashion (reaching its height in England in the late seventeenth century during the reign of William and Mary), there will always be a certain fascination in bushes which are painstakingly cut into shapes. From the basic wall-shape of the hedge and simple pillars and domes – which are little more than tidy versions of the shrub's natural habit – human imagination, spurred on no doubt by the love of a challenge, has produced the most extraordinary three-dimensional objects out of bushes: centaurs, whales, hounds chasing deer, carts, chessmen and the ever-popular peacock, to mention just a few. Hedges in themselves have also taken many elaborate turns in gardening history, becoming more decorative than functional in labyrinths, mazes and intricate geometric knot gardens. A fine example of box used in such delights is at Ludstone Hall, Shropshire, which has miniature box hedges enclosing box topiary of clubs, hearts, diamonds and spades, with a centrepiece of box cut like a corkscrew.

The family Buxaceae has only six genera and about 100 species, some 70 of which belong to the genus *Buxus*. Most important is the common box, *B. sempervirens*, an evergreen shrub or small tree which seldom reaches more than 6 m (20 ft) but can live over 600 years: hence the name *sempervirens*, meaning 'living for ever'. On average the trunk of a box tree adds a mere 3–5 cm (1–2 in) to its diameter in twenty years. It is found wild in central and more southerly parts of Europe and in northern Africa through to the foothills of the western Himalayas. The bark on branches is yellowish but that on the trunk is grey-brown and patterned like crocodile skin. The dark green leaves are smooth, leathery and oval, and are set in pairs at close intervals on the four-angled twigs. Clusters of greenish flowers, with one female and several males, are borne in the axils during the spring, followed by fruits which are basically egg-shaped but triangular at the top.

Box is a poisonous plant and is not suitable for hedging near livestock. However, its toxins have curative properties which have long been used in medicine. It contains a volatile oil, which is extracted for use in dentistry, and several alkaloids (mostly buxine which is a bitter steroidal compound). Its most outstanding effect is in lowering fevers, for which it is comparable with quinine. Among its other uses are homoeopathic preparations for rheumatism and a traditional cure for baldness. The latter is made by soaking chopped box leaves in alcohol and its effectiveness is legendary – at least if you believe the tale told of a peasant woman who was an enthusiastic user of the lotion. She applied it not only to her scalp but to her face and neck as well, with the result that she grew more hair than even she had hoped for and ended up, so the story goes, looking more simian than human.

It is surprising to learn that such a toxic plant had a place in the kitchen, but it did, though only for decoration. It was part of the ornamentation for gilt gingerbread which was a traditional English confection often given as a celebratory gift. A firm dough was made from flour, honey, butter, ground ginger and other spices, then baked in a cool oven. While still lukewarm it would be painted with egg white, overlaid with gold leaf (tissue-thin and quite edible) and finally decorated with groups of green or gilt box leaves arranged in a fleur-de-lis, interspersed with box seeds or stuck with cloves that again were gilded.

The yellowy-orange wood from box was once commonly used for making boxes and that is how containers of this sort got their name. It sinks in water and is certainly the toughest, heaviest wood of any European tree. Unsurpassed for density and fine grain, it is extremely hard wearing and at one time was widely used in mathematical, nautical and musical instruments. Thomas Bewick (1753–1828), the artist and wood engraver who invented block printing, recounted how one of his boxwood blocks was still serviceable after being used 900,000 times – which probably puts it on a par with brass for durability. The root is supposed to be even harder and was once used for the handles of teapots and knives (the latter being known as dudgeon-hafted daggers – dudgeon being another name for box). Pill boxes, chess pieces and mallets are other items that were often made from box.

Cultivating box needs one thing above all else: patience! If you prefer plain dark green, the best forms of *B. sempervirens* are 'Suffruticosa', a dwarf variety that is excellent for small hedges, and 'Handsworthensis' where something taller is needed. Should you aspire to something more colourful – even perhaps to an unshorn specimen – then there are several delightful varieties available. *B. sempervirens* 'Latifolia Maculata' (also called 'Aurea' and 'Japonica Aurea') has relatively large oval leaves which are a soft green handsomely marked with yellow in spring. It colours best in a sunny position, forming a mound about 1.8 m (6 ft) high and as much across if left to its own devices. Making a compact dome-shaped bush with smaller, narrower foliage is the silver-variegated box. Known as 'Elegantissima' (or 'Elegans' or 'Variegata'), it has leaves irregularly bordered with creamy-white. This is a particularly fine form for a specimen shrub and has little tendency to revert. All varieties of common box are reasonably hardy, though the variegated forms are generally less vigorous. For cold northern regions, it might be better to plant *B. microphylla*, the Korean box, or its dwarf form 'Compacta', which are very hardy with equally dense, but more slender leaves than common box. Its neat, slow-growing habit and resistance to freezing and dryness makes 'Compacta' a good choice for containers.

Box will grow in sun or partial shade and likes well-drained neutral to alkaline soil. For hedges, plants should be set 20 cm (8 in) apart and have leading shoots shortened by 7 cm (3 in). Trimming is best done in late summer. At this time cuttings may also be taken, put round the sides of a pot containing sandy compost and kept in a cool shady place. It will be two years before young plants from cuttings can be planted out. Some bushes are amenable to division in their early years if further stocks are needed.

The Victorians were keen on the symbolism of plants and found meaning in their characteristics. Today we are familiar only with roses for love and white lilies for purity, but their vocabulary was much more extensive. They evolved a kind of horticultural morse code known as florigraphy (literally, writing with flowers) so that one could send a posy or bouquet whose message was contained solely in the meaning of the flowers or foliage chosen. Box signified stoicism – no doubt in recognition of the way this long-suffering plant continues to thrive, apparently undeterred by efforts to control and direct its growth in the interests of aesthetics.

DOUBLE-FLOWERED CHAMOMILE
Chamaemelum nobile (syn. *Anthemis nobilis*) 'Flore Pleno'

Chamomile has been a major herb in the traditional medicine of many countries for over two thousand years. In earliest times it was a sacred herb because it relieved 'ague'; later a cure-all which eased 'all colds, aches, and pains whatsoever'; and now a wonder drug for its role as a safe relaxant and anti-allergenic agent. Apart from these shifts of emphasis, the verdict on chamomile's usefulness and effec-

(opposite) A fine specimen of silver box in Esther Merton's garden at The Old Rectory, Burghfield, Berkshire.
(above) The shaggy pompom daisies and feathery aromatic leaves of double chamomile.

tiveness has always been unanimous. In contrast, certain other aspects of this interesting herb are quite confusing and have been the subject of a great deal of disagreement: namely, which species is the genuine chamomile, what is the correct name for it, and last but not least, how on earth do you spell it?

To take the last point first, it matters not a jot whether you spell it chamomile or camomile. Both are acceptable. The English word is derived from the Old French camomille which, in turn, came from medieval Latin chamomilla and ultimately from the Greek khamaimelon, meaning 'earth-apple' (referring to its ground-hugging habit and apple-like scent).

The next point is much more problematic. Chamomile is the general name given to two different species belonging to the daisy family (Compositae): the perennial Chamaemelum nobile and the annual Chamomilla recutita. The interesting thing is that they belong to different genera. This is an unusual situation in herbal medicine, as rarely is the chemistry sufficiently similar in two closely related species – never mind species in different genera – for them to be used interchangeably. However, the former was at one time classified as Chamomilla nobilis, so perhaps they are not very far apart after all. Botanists have obviously had a number of rethinks on this group of species – the chamomiles, mayweeds and feverfews – as there has been a good deal of chopping and changing. Chamaemelum nobile has also gone under the name Anthemis nobilis and the annual Chamomilla recutita was once known as Matricaria recutita. Common names are scarcely more helpful: the former being referred to variously as Roman, lawn or true chamomile, and the latter as scented mayweed, German, Belgian, Hungarian, or sweet false chamomile.

Which brings us to the herbalist's dilemma of which of the two is the true chamomile? Most likely both species have been in regular use since earliest times, the determining factor being availability. German chamomile has a wider and more northerly distribution and in early times was presumably the only species to be found in much of northern Europe. Roman chamomile favours western and southern regions, and was probably the species used by the ancient Egyptians (and the Romans, as the name Roman chamomile suggests). The distinction became blurred in the sixteenth century when the double-flowered form ('Flore Pleno') of Roman chamomile was introduced from Spain to Germany. Its cultivation and use spread rapidly and it soon became favoured by herbalists throughout Europe.

In spite of their similarity, there are slight differences between the two chamomiles. Botanically one can tell them apart by splitting

Double-flowered chamomile
(Chamaemelum nobile *'Flore Pleno'*)

the yellow dome-shaped centre of the flower. If it is solid in the middle, it is Roman chamomile; if hollow, it is German. As far as taste goes, the German is less bitter and is best for herb teas. It does, however, tend to be more of an irritant as a result of substances contained in the yellow centres which make up most of the dried herb. Herbalists generally prefer the more aromatic, but bitter Roman chamomile for the preparation of medicinal tisanes, tinctures and liquid extracts.

Both chamomiles have the effect of reducing tension, soothing and healing irritations and soreness. Herbalists prescribe chamomile as part of herbal mixtures for digestive problems, especially those caused by tension and exhaustion. It is also particularly good for women, helping many cases of morning sickness, premenstrual headaches and menstrual cramps. Strong infusions may be used to bathe wounds, eczema and ulcers, and have been known to cure conjunctivitis. Extracts of chamomile are used commercially in preparations for nappy rash and in cosmetics to reduce allergic reactions. They are also added to shampoos and rinses, having a conditioning, lightening effect on fair hair. The essential oil of chamomile is pale blue when fresh. A few drops can be added to vegetable oil for massage purposes or the flowers themselves can be left to steep in oil for several days and then strained before use. Whichever way it is used, chamomile is a comforting herb.

From the gardener's point of view, there is no doubt which chamomile is best. The German chamomile or scented mayweed, an erect annual with daisy-like flowers, is undistinguished, but the Roman chamomile is quite delightful with its heady scent and thick mats of finely cut ferny foliage. Again it has daisy flowers, pendent in bud, with conical yellow centres and white rays which droop like skirts toward the end of flowering. Even better though is the double-flowered form, 'Flore Pleno', whose shaggy pompon flowers have a dishevelled look which is quite unlike the innocent neatness of daisies. The plants themselves are creeping evergreen perennials and each produces at least a dozen offsets in a season. These are the usual method of propagation, as seed produces a high proportion of single-flowered plants.

The best place for chamomile is at the side of paths or between paving stones where it will be trodden on to release its intoxicating fragrance. There is a saying that 'Like a chamomile bed – the more it is trodden the more it will spread', and though not exactly tough enough for a football pitch, it can be planted as a lawn. Chamomile lawns originated in Tudor times and although they were then planted on quite a large scale, they are admirably suited to small gardens – even to miniature lawns made by taking up just a paving slab or two. For a lawn you will need to plant rooted offsets at 10–15 cm (4–6 in) apart – in other words, about 100 will cover 2.5 sq m (3 sq yd). The soil must be well drained but can be slightly acid to alkaline. Its surface should be free from stones and ideally have some sand and fertilizer raked into it. The site chosen should be reasonably sunny. Newly planted lawns need regular weeding but once established should need no more than a trim with shears (or on a high blade setting with a mower if the area warrants it). The best variety for lawns is undoubtedly the non-flowering form known as 'Treneague' as its foliage stays neatly prostrate all year round, instead of elongating in an effort to flower.

Chamomile is not only good for ailing people (and animals). It is said to cure sick plants and has been called 'the plant's physician'. An infusion of chamomile – some left-over tea perhaps – added to a vase of water is said to revive drooping cut flowers and make them last longer. Sickly garden plants are also supposed to perk up if chamomile is planted near them, so a healthy garden is presumably guaranteed if you grow lots of chamomile.

These and the more orthodox medicinal uses of chamomile were probably what inspired Victorian compilers of florigraphy to consider chamomile as a symbol of energy in adversity. It is certainly a great restorer of equilibrium and, if for no other reason, a chamomile lawn should be planted for therapeutic purposes. To appreciate the experience fully, you should walk barefoot. It is softer and more springy than grass and the scent that envelops you instantly is of surprising intensity. Culpeper was right when he said chamomile 'takes away weariness'. The scent alone does this. Another herbalist recommended that, 'To comfort the brain, smell camomile, eat sage . . . wash measurably, sleep reasonably, delight to hear melody and singing', which is a simple and pleasurable recipe for health and happiness.

DOUBLE WHITE MEADOW SAFFRON
Colchicum autumnale 'Alboplenum'

Colchicum autumnale has a number of common names which describe its habit and appearance well: meadow saffron, autumn crocus, upstart, pale maidens, naked ladies and other variations on the same theme – such as the rather naughty naked nannies and naked boys, which describe the pink- and white-flowered forms growing together. It does indeed grow in meadows and is fairly common throughout Europe in damp grassland on calcareous soil. And it looks similar to the saffron crocus, *Crocus sativus*, from which the stigmas are gathered for flavouring and colouring food. Most noticeably, the pale flowers appear suddenly in early autumn, bare of leaves and vulnerable on their fragile and even paler 'stalks' (which are actually an elongation of the flower). Superficially they resemble crocuses, though a closer look reveals that they have six stamens and three styles whereas a crocus has but one style and only three stamens. (Also, colchicums are in the lily family, Liliaceae, and crocuses are related to irises, Iridaceae.) Likewise, the genus name, *Colchicum*, describes the centre of distribution for the genus – Colchis, an ancient country south of the Caucasus in what is now the Georgian Soviet Socialist Republic – and the species name *autumnale* records the time of flowering. The strange thing is that there appears to be no name which indicates its toxicity and yet this plant is so poisonous that it has been referred to as 'vegetable arsenic'.

Four thousand years ago the ancient Egyptians probably knew about the poisonous properties of the colchicum, and the ancient Greeks were certainly well versed in its use. They took it in minute, carefully measured doses to cure asthma, dropsy, kidney complaints and gout, and, with perhaps less precision, used it as a poison to dispense of rivals and enemies. Even slaves dosed themselves with just the right amount to make themselves ill enough to get back at their masters without putting themselves in danger. Obviously the quantity that could be taken safely was well known. Somewhere along the line, this knowledge seems to have been lost and later European herbalists write about the uses of meadow saffron with a degree of uncertainty.

Its toxicity was never in doubt, however. In 1563, William Turner affirmed that 'much of it is stercke poyson, and will strongell a man and kill him in the space of one day'. John Gerard, writing at the end of the sixteenth century, repeated the warning that, if eaten, colchicums 'are very hurtfull to the stomacke' and 'kill by choaking as Mushromes do, according unto Dioscorides; whereupon some have called it *Colchicum strangulatorium*'. Very sensibly, he advises 'those which have eaten of the common Medow Saffron must drinke the milke of a cow, or else death presently ensueth'. Nevertheless, some herbalists had the courage to use it: Sir Theode Mayerne, seventeenth-century physician to James VI and I of England prescribed it ground with a 'powder of unburied skulls' for the King's gout.

The scientific use of colchicum in medicine is ascribed to Anton Stoerck who, in 1763, evaluated several poisonous plants, including the equally deadly aconites (*Aconitum* spp), and came up with therapeutic doses. Since then, although herbalists have very rarely used it (preferring gentler remedies, such as celery seed), it has been invaluable in allopathic medicine as the standard treatment for gout, relieving pain and inflammation in acute attacks and warding off further attacks by improving the excretion of urates (salts of uric acid which cause the unpleasant symptoms as they lodge in the joints and kidneys). It works almost instantly, but is not usually given to elderly patients or those with heart, liver, kidney or digestive problems. In spite of its disappearance from the herbal pharmacopoeia, homoeopaths use it not only for gout and other joint complaints, but also for abdominal colic and – please note, dear reader – dimness of vision caused by too much reading.

Unfortunately, its reinstatement as an important medicinal plant did nothing to halt the tide of destruction which began when farming became more intensive. In many areas of Europe, including most of the British Isles, meadow saffron is now an uncommon sight in the wild, having been exterminated in pastures because of its danger to cattle. I once went to Dorset at the behest of a friend to see 'fat and fertile medowes' – as Gerard described the habitat – where meadow saffron was flowering. I can confirm William Cobbett's remarks made in one of his *Rural Rides* that it was 'one of the prettiest sights in the flowering that ever I saw in my life'. Sadly, it is a sight few people will ever see and for the most part we must be content to grow our own.

As gardeners we have particular cause to be grateful to the meadow saffron. Not because we are more prone to gout or eyestrain than anyone else, nor even because it is a most beautiful flower. The fact is that many 'improved' varieties of garden plants owe their existence to the poisonous alkaloid colchicine which is extracted from the seeds and corms. If plant cells are subjected to colchicine while dividing, the normal course of events is disrupted and there is a doubling or trebling (or even greater increase) in the chromosome number. The next generation will therefore differ significantly, showing increased size and vigour, or perhaps, in the case of fruits, seedlessness, greater palatability and better keeping qualities. Doubling the chromosome number can also render sterile hybrids fertile, so that the 'dead ends' of plant breeding are brought back into circulation.

For most of us, the seeds and corms of colchicums are not for extracting, but for growing, and will involve nothing more complex than working out where to put them for greatest enjoyment. Seed should be sown in summer when ripe and the tiny plants should be watered but otherwise left undisturbed for two years before moving to a permanent site during dormancy. They take three to five years to reach flowering size. Corms and cormlets –

which have brown tunics and resemble tulip bulbs – need planting at least 10 cm (4 in) deep. They are happy in sun or light shade but need moisture-retentive soil (even clay) which does not dry out when they are dormant in summer. The warning must be given, however, that the voluminous shiny leaves, which reach up to 30 cm (1 ft) long and last through much of the growing season, are far from lovely and for this reason as much consideration

The rare double white form of meadow saffron, whose fragile autumn blooms arise like the ghosts of summer flowers.

should be given to where the leaves will be least obtrusive as to where the flowers will be best displayed. (The foliage cannot be cut off or the corms will fail to develop.) Once this problem is sorted out, there is nothing to do but enjoy the flowering – which always takes

35

me by surprise – year after year.

The life cycle of the meadow saffron greatly puzzled our ancestors. It was once called *filius ante patrem* – son before father – because of its peculiar habit of producing seed in the spring before flowering at the end of summer. Gerard complained that 'it bringeth forth leaves in Februarie, seed in May, and flowers in September; which is a thing clean contrarie to all other plants whatsoever.' The truth is that when it flowers, the plant is rootless and leafless, and the ovary is below ground. After flowering, growth gets under way and by early spring the leaves emerge and the subterranean flower stalk elongates to push the developing seed pod above the surface where it ripens in early summer. Then the leaves die down and the plant becomes completely dormant once again.

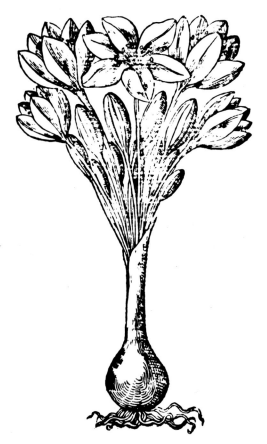

Meadow saffron (Colchicum autumnale)

Colchicums pose more problems for botanists than for gardeners. The genus is full of look-alike species which, in turn, are very variable. As always, the botanist's nightmare is the gardener's delight, and there is a tremendous variety of forms, both in the wild and in cultivation. As far as the meadow saffron is concerned, the flowers are most commonly a pinkish-lilac but may be striped, chequered (tessellated) or white. The rarest perhaps are double forms, which flower later and last longer. 'Pleniflorum', the mauve double, is delightful, but loveliest of all is 'Alboplenum' whose double white blooms rise from the newly fallen leaves of autumn like the ghosts of summer flowers. Victorian florigraphers took meadow saffron to symbolize 'my best days are past' – presumably meaning the end of summer – but for colchicum lovers, the best has only just begun.

VARIEGATED AND GOLDEN MEADOWSWEETS
Filipendula ulmaria 'Aurea' and 'Variegata'

Meadowsweet has been described as the herbalist's aspirin, and with good reason. The plant contains methyl salicylate, a substance which is also found in wintergreen (*Gaultheria procumbens*) and accounts for the characteristic smell of its foliage. When dried the methyl salicylate changes to salicylic acid: the basis of aspirin. Though now one of the most widely used medications in the world, aspirin has only been with us since 1899, following discoveries in chemistry which began in 1838 with the synthesis of salicylic acid. Before then, people had to depend on plants such as meadowsweet for this valuable chemical which, among other things, lowers fever and relieves pain.

Fortunately, salicylic acid is not uncom-

36

mon in the plant world, occurring in the roots, foliage, flowers and fruits of many different plants, and particularly in the essential oils of various species of *Spiraea* – a genus in the rose family (Rosaceae) – from which the word aspirin was derived. Meadowsweet was once known as *Spiraea ulmaria*, but it and its closest relatives are now split off into a separate genus, *Filipendula*.

However useful aspirin may be, it remains purely and simply an isolated synthetic chemical, whereas the chemistry of a plant such as meadowsweet is much more complex. Meadowsweet is therefore not merely the herbal equivalent of aspirin. Admittedly, it has some similar effects but, in addition, has far more curative – rather than just palliative – properties. Neither does it cause the same unpleasant side effects (namely, erosion of the stomach wall). Among its other constituents, meadowsweet contains healing tannins and soothing mucilage which act as buffers to the corrosive salicylates. It is even prescribed by herbalists for peptic ulcers, hiatus hernia, acid indigestion and heartburn – the very complaints which are made worse by aspirin – as it actually reduces stomach acidity and heals inflammation in the digestive tract. In addition, it controls diarrhoea and is particularly good for digestive upsets in children.

Like aspirin, meadowsweet is also used to relieve the pains of rheumatism, arthritis and gout. However, unlike aspirin, which only relieves pain and does nothing to influence the progression of these conditions, meadowsweet may bring about improvements. It is a good diuretic and antiseptic, and has a tonic effect on the whole metabolism – thus neutralizing and aiding excretion of inflammatory toxins such as uric acid (which causes gout), and increasing general vitality. These applications are also put to good use in urinary tract infections, such as cystitis, and in reducing cellulite (a puffiness of the tissues, especially on the thighs and upper arms in women, caused by fluid retention and a hardening of the connective fibres).

As a household remedy, meadowsweet makes a pleasant tea for the feverish stages of colds, 'flu and mild attacks of common infectious diseases such as measles. The herb should be gathered when flowering in the summer: the top 15 cm (6 in) or so of both flowers and leaves being picked and dried carefully at no more than 35°C (95°F). Infusions of 1–2 teaspoonfuls per cup are then made using water which has gone off the boil, so that the salicylic acid does not evaporate.

When you are gathering meadowsweet, you are sure to notice that the leaves smell quite different from the flowers. The cool medicinal tang of the foliage is in sharp contrast to the drowsy almond-and-honey fragrance of the cream-coloured flowers: the former like wintergreen, the latter closer to hawthorn (*Crataegus monogynus*). The divided leaves have two to five pairs of pointed ovate leaflets, each 2 cm (1 in) or more in length and interspersed with much smaller ones. They are dark green on the upper surface and corrugated by deep-set veins, giving them a resemblance to those of elm (*Ulmus* spp) – hence the species name, *ulmaria*. The undersurfaces are covered in greyish-white down which releases the odour of the essential oil if pressed. The individual five-petalled, many stamened flowers are tiny but are borne in such large terminal clusters that from a distance they look like foam. The seedheads are interesting if examined closely, consisting of spiral-shaped fruits twisted together. All in all, with its frothy cream flowers, deep green leaves and red stems, it is a beautiful plant, as acknowledged by its common name: queen (or pride or lady) of the meadow. In rich soil it reaches 120 cm (4 ft) and large stands of it in flower are one of the great joys of wetlands in summer.

Even lovelier are two varieties which are occasionally seen in gardens: the golden form, *F. ulmaria* 'Aurea' and the variegated, *F. ulmaria* 'Variegata'. The only problem with the golden one is that it is less vigorous and scorches badly in sun, so it must be grown in shade. It really is worth accommodating though, with light yellow foliage so glorious in spring that it is tempting to remove the flowers (which anyway do not show up very well against it) to encourage fresh new leaves later on in the season. The variegated form is more striking still, its bottle-green leaflets unfolding to reveal butter-yellow slashes, with here and there both the large and the mini-leaflets wholly yellow – a marvellous combination with the red stalks. It appears to tolerate higher light levels than the golden form, though its colour fades as summer advances and the stems lengthen for flowering.

All forms of meadowsweet need ample moisture and have a tendency to develop powdery mildew in dry conditions. Even wet ground, provided that it is not too acid, suits them, in either full sun or partial shade (with the exception of the golden form which is better in a shady spot). The fact that it is found wild throughout Europe from near the Arctic Circle to southern regions and is naturalized almost the length and breadth of eastern North America, indicates that meadowsweet is both hardy and adaptable. Given constant moisture, it is usually very easy to grow. Propagation is by seed sown in spring at 10–13°C (50–55°F), or from divisions taken after the plant dies down for winter dormancy.

For reasons best known to themselves, the Victorian florigraphers decided that meadowsweet symbolized uselessness. Its medicinal uses alone are sufficient to contradict this, but there are other practical applications. Centuries ago it held pride of place as a strewing herb, for in the days before damp-proof courses and carpets, stone or earthen floors were covered with rushes and fragrant plants. In 1636, John Gerard wrote in his *Herball* that 'The leaves and floures farre excell all other strowing herbes, for to decke up houses, to straw chambers, halls, and banqueting houses in the Summer time; for the smell thereof makes the heart merrie, delighteth the senses: neither doth it cause head-ache . . .' From the same period, John Parkinson (1597–1650), the royal apothecary and herbalist, told how

'Queen Elizabeth of famous memory did more desire it than any other herbe to strewe her chambers withall.'

Few of us would want to return to strewing our floors, but one of life's pleasanter tasks is gathering (or buying) and using herbs to flavour food and drink. One of its other common names – meadwort – describes yet another of its uses: as an ingredient in beers and wines (mead being a wine made from honey and spices). If you enjoy making country wines, it is well worth trying meadowsweet blossoms in winemaking, perhaps as a substitute for elderflowers. The fresh flowers also make an interesting addition to summer drinks of white wine and fruit juice ('wine coolers') and to stewed fruit such as apples, gooseberries and rhubarb.

Far from being useless, the queen of the meadows is, therefore, a very useful plant, with the bonus that the golden and variegated forms are most attractive hardy perennials for the damp garden.

BRONZE FENNEL
Foeniculum vulgare 'Purpureum'

Over the thousands of years that fennel has been in cultivation, several varieties have been developed. The finest in appearance is bronze fennel (*Foeniculum vulgare* 'Purpureum'). The new leaves emerge as a tight tan-coloured brush, becoming a rich dark brown when expanded. It is a magnificent foliage plant which can be used to great effect near fiery colours such as those of *Rudbeckia* daisies, *Canna* hybrids or Chinese lanterns (*Physalis* spp), or the soft salmon tints of the plume poppy (*Macleaya microcarpa*). It comes true from seed and, if anything, is hardier than the plain green species.

Though none can compare with the bronze form, common fennel and its varieties are all

handsome plants. The so-called Florence fennel (*F. vulgare* var. *azoricum*) is grown as an annual for its swollen bulbous stalk bases which are a sweet-tasting vegetable. In contrast, *F. vulgare* var. *piperitum* is known as bitter fennel because of its high content of essential oil. It is grown for its seeds which are used in the pharmaceutical, food and distilling industries. Deceptively similar to *F. vulgare* in appearance is giant fennel (*Ferula communis*). This is indeed a plant to behold! At over 3 m (10 ft) tall and with huge umbels of yellow flowers, it is an inspiring sight against the blue skies and tawny hillsides of Greek islands. The only disappointment is that it is completely scentless and no use at all in cooking or medicine.

There is an old saying that if you sow fennel, you sow trouble, but as far as the gardener is concerned, nothing could be further from the truth. Fennel is refined yet robust, both in habit and flavour, and as decorative as it is useful. Imbued with the warm bittersweet

(above left) The variegated form of meadowsweet: a colourful plant for damp places.
(above) Bronze fennel and marigolds.

aroma of aniseed, it produces a haze of the most finely cut foliage and at the same time forms substantial clumps which are a striking feature in the herbaceous border. It sows itself with moderation, is reliably hardy in sunny well-drained soils, does not become woody and sparse with age like sage and thyme, or need regular replacing like parsley, and all in all, is practically trouble-free – a bounteous beautiful plant which is indispensable to the cook, herbalist and gardener alike.

Though generally regarded as Mediterranean, fennel has been in cultivation so long that its origin is by no means certain. It may equally well have first been found in North Africa, for its use in Middle Eastern countries has as long a history as in southern Europe. But whether it comes from Syria or the Azores – which have both been proposed as likely sources – it can now be found wild in many parts of the world and is as much at home in California as Casablanca. Records show that it was established as far north as Great Britain before the Norman Conquest (1066), where it is fairly common along the south coast on dry sunny hillsides, cliffs and wasteland.

Fennel belongs to the very large family Umbelliferae, which has around 300 genera and 3,000 species and is characterized by umbels of tiny five-petalled flowers and a distinctive chemistry. Among the best-known umbellifers are celery (*Apium graveolens*) and parsley (*Petroselinum crispum*), together with the deadly hemlock (*Conium maculatum*) and the spectacular giant hogweed (*Heracleum mantegazzianum*). Many umbellifers have divided leaves and white flowers and are difficult to tell apart – a matter of concern when some are so poisonous. Fortunately, fennel is more distinctive and should not pose problems in identification, even if gathered from the wild.

When at its height in summer, fennel can reach 2 m (6½ ft). It dies down completely in winter, but its skeleton remains for months to mark its position. The compound leaves are divided into glossy, almost thread-like lobes and their stalks clasp the stem with broad fleshy sheaths. In summer the yellow flowers are produced. Each umbel has from fifteen to twenty rays and these later bear clusters of ribbed seeds which are grey-brown when ripe. In the herb garden, seedlings of fennel and dill (*Anethum graveolens*) can look confusingly alike, but if they are closely compared, it can be seen that fennel has a shine to it and dill is slightly glaucous and a greyer green. (There is, however, no possibility of confusing bronze fennel with dill, as even the first leaves of bronze fennel seedlings are brown.) Fennel and dill may also be told apart by their smell and taste: fennel being sweeter and rather like liquorice, whereas dill is closer to caraway. The seeds are quite different, those of dill being perfectly flat and oval. Lastly, dill is an annual and never attains the height or bulk of fennel.

Fennel is reputedly the best of all herbs with fish, especially those which are oily or rich. The traditional way of imparting the flavour of fennel to the fish is to make a bed of stalks – fresh or dried, but with the leaves still attached – and lay the fish on top before baking. It may also be used in a stuffing for the fish, or in a sauce to be served with it – added to either a hot white sauce, or cold whipped cream seasoned with freshly ground black pepper, sea salt and lemon juice. However you use it, it will help the digestion of oils and fats, as well as providing a most appetizing aroma. In Italy, where fennel is a great favourite, it is considered excellent with pork, and the seeds are used as a flavouring and preservative in a salami called *finocchiona*. The ancient Romans baked bread over fennel leaves. Adding a small amount of seeds directly to the dough imparts a still stronger flavour. Fennel bread is good with both sweet or savoury spreads and sandwich fillings, and is especially nice with honey. Fennel is also used in distilling. The liqueur *fenouillette* is based on it, and the root was one of the flavourings in the popular Elizabethan mead known as sack.

The medicinal uses are largely based on the properties of its complex volatile oil and another bitter substance which have a pronounced effect on the digestive system. Fennel seeds are an almost instant cure for flatulent indigestion, especially the kind caused by swallowing too much air through talking or nervousness while eating. Commercially fennel is added to babies' gripe water – the effectiveness of which is in no doubt – and to purgatives to prevent griping pains. The seeds are pleasant-tasting and may simply be chewed to bring relief, or, if preferred, a teaspoonful may be infused in a cup of boiling water and drunk as a tea. This remedy is so safe that it is suitable for children and babies if made at half-strength and given lukewarm.

Chewing the seeds is also a time-honoured way of allaying the pangs of hunger. This, along with another traditional use – that of reducing weight – suggests that fennel may have a role to play in slimming regimes. The seventeenth-century herbalists Nicholas Culpeper and William Coles both recommended it for this purpose. As Coles put it (none too delicately): 'both the seeds, leaves and root of our garden fennel are much used in drinks and broths for those that are grown fat, to abate their unwieldiness and make them more gaunt and lank.' And long before their time, Olympic athletes were taking it to increase strength and stamina while preventing excessive weight gain. It is easy to dismiss such claims, but present-day herbalists find that fennel does balance glandular functions and water levels, and stimulates the lymphatic system – all of which could result in weight loss if the excess was due to such causes. In short, fennel is an anti-sluggish herb and one that merits regular consumption as a delightful herb tea, and both raw or cooked in a variety of foods.

Fennel is also supposed to be good for the eyes, but its prowess in treating failing eyesight and eye infections has some rather odd credentials. The Roman encyclopaedist Pliny the Elder recorded that 'snakes eat it when they cast their old skins, and they sharpen their sight with the juice by rubbing against the plant.' This strange observation led William Coles to warn that fennel must be washed very carefully before use in case any snakes are still lurking in the foliage!

Cultivating fennel should present few problems if full sun and good drainage are ensured. Where the soil is heavy, it may succumb in a cold wet winter, in which case it is worth nurturing a few of the self-sown seedlings in a protected place. Even poor stony soils will support fennel – better still if on chalk or limestone – though it will grow larger and lusher if mulched each spring with well-rotted manure or compost. Pests and diseases are rare. The worst my plants have suffered was an occasional greenfly on the flower stalks and, once, a bad attack by our goats – which were forgiven when I learnt that fennel increases the milk yield!

For culinary use, the leaves may be picked at any time during the growing season. They do not keep their flavour very well if dried and are best used fresh or frozen. Whole stalks with leaves, for placing under fish, can be gathered from May onwards. They need lengthy drying if they are not to be used fresh. The seeds ripen in late summer and early autumn. They are rather tricky to collect as they drop off the plant as soon as they are fully ripe. The answer is to wait until they have turned from green to brown but are still firmly attached to the stalks, then cut the seedhead off directly into a paper bag and leave it open in a warm dry place. The seeds will finish ripening and, with a shake, will fall to the bottom of the bag.

It would seem that most herbs have, at some time or other, been used to ward off evil powers and witchcraft. In the Middle Ages there were so many recommended that it must have been quite a job to decide exactly what to hang from the rafters or nail to the lintel. But fennel is unique in its reputation for preventing the entry of ghosts into a building. To gain this protection, you must stop up the keyholes with fennel seeds. Of course, you will then be unable to get the key in the lock against more apparent intruders . . .

As with most herbs, we could make far more use of fennel than we do. In the thirteenth century, the household of King Edward I of England got through 4.5 kg (10 lb) of fennel seed a month. It would be very interesting to know how they used such a prodigious amount – either their recipes called for lavish quantities, or they had an enormous problem with ghosts!

VARIEGATED GROUND IVY
Glechoma hederacea 'Variegata'

Many people buy variegated ground ivy along with their bedding plants without realizing what it is. Though evergreen and perfectly hardy, it makes a pretty trailing plant for summertime hanging baskets and window boxes. In the horticultural trade it is generally known as nepeta and if your newly purchased plant bears a label, that will probably be all it says. The reason for this is that it was once classified in the genus *Nepeta*, as are the catmints. Gardeners have stuck with this name but botanists eventually found differences between the catmints and ground ivy, so it was moved to a separate genus of the labiates (Labiatae) and renamed *Glechoma hederacea*. The generic name is from the Greek *glechon*, meaning mint or thyme, referring to its aromatic foliage which, however, is more like blackcurrant than either mint or thyme. Similarly the species name, *hederacea* means ivy-like, but again the resemblance is slight as they have nothing more in common than a generally creeping, ground-covering habit.

Ground ivy grows happily in sun or shade, preferring moisture-retentive soils in hedgerows, woods, thickets and grassy or bare places. The mid-green kidney-shaped leaves are borne in pairs on squarish stems. They tend to redden in the sun and are patterned with a network of veins and scalloped margins – or, as John Gerard describes them, are 'something broad, wrinckled, hairy, nicked in the edges'. The typical two-lipped labiate flowers are violet-blue in colour (occasionally pink) and quite large for the size of the plant. They appear in the axils of erect stems in groups of two to five from spring to summer. Non-flowering creeping stems are sent out some distance from the plant, rooting at intervals when in contact with the soil but otherwise forming long trailing shoots which may reach 1 m (3 ft) long. Ground ivy is a very common plant with a wide distribution throughout western Europe and northern Asia, including Japan. It was taken to North America by the early settlers for use as a medicinal plant and, known there as creeping Charlie, rapidly became established in the wild.

Variegated ground ivy is a plant that needs a niche: delicate and charming in effect but

Variegated ground ivy: an adaptable carpeter or trailer, here seen in damp shade with forget-me-nots, but equally effective in hanging baskets of bedding plants.

42

complementary rather than a dominant feature. I have seen it used in windowboxes at pavement level overhanging a basement boutique in Cheltenham. As you walked down the steps from the pavement to the shop, the petunias and other colourful bedding plants disappeared from view but all down the wall hung chains of variegated scalloped leaves from the ground ivy that had been planted among them. In window boxes and hanging baskets it is usually treated as an annual, but there are many situations where it can fulfil its role as a hardy perennial evergreen: covering old tree stumps and walls in shady corners; trailing over stone sinks planted with choice alpines or ferns; on bare ground under trees; as a carpeter under greenhouse staging; and as a trailing pot plant for unheated rooms.

While the variegated form is both useful and ornamental in the garden, the plain green wild plant is rather too invasive for cultivation. I once had it coming through a fence and making a takeover bid for one corner of my garden. In spite of its brave show of neat foliage and colourful flowers, I finally decided it had to go. Then, while yanking it out by the yard, it made amends for its intrusion by presenting me with a beautifully variegated shoot which I snipped off and potted up. It is quite different from the form sold as 'Variegata', being marbled with cream.

Historically, ground ivy's main claim to fame is as a 'gruit': a herb used in brewing ale. It was widely used in the British Isles until the early 1600s when Henry VIII was on the throne, after which hops became increasingly popular. Herbs were the original 'additives', though, unlike their present-day chemical equivalents, they were often beneficial to health. They clarified the brew, improved the flavour and acted as preservatives. Ground ivy's role in brewing gave rise to several of its common names; alehoof ('hoof' meaning a herb) and tunhoof ('tun' being a beer cask).

The many common names for ground ivy prompted Culpeper to comment that 'there is scarcely any herb growing of that bigness that has got so many'. Some merely describe its creeping habit; Lizzy-run-up-the-hedge and Robin-run-in-the-hedge being obvious examples. Others like Gill-go-over-the-ground, Gill-go-by-the-hedge and gillrun, in spite of their similarity, may nevertheless have a more complicated origin. (Sometimes these long-winded names would be shortened to gill – as in gill tea, a cough syrup based on ground ivy, honey and liquorice.) Originally 'gill' was probably from the French *guiller*, to ferment beer, and *gille* meaning a vat, which explains the unit of liquid measure known as a gill, and why ale houses were sometimes called gill houses. However, gill was also an archaic word for a girl or sweetheart (taken from the name Gillian). These two quite different words inevitably became thoroughly confused, resulting in names such as haymaids and hedgemaids, in which the gill or girl has been changed into a maid. With refreshing simplicity the plant is also known as field balm and catsfoot, the latter referring to the shape of the leaves which are not unlike a cat's footprint.

The medicinal uses of ground ivy are even more numerous than its names. Since Roman times it has been valued for treating eye complaints and failing sight in both people and animals. In traditional Chinese medicine it is known as a herb that generally detoxifies and stimulates, reducing inflammation and relieving fever and pain. Chinese herbalists know it by almost as many different names, including one which translates evocatively as 'the-whole-mountain-is-fragrant'. They use it in much the same way as their European counterparts: for 'flu, stones and infections of the urinary tract, rheumatic and arthritic complaints, and abscesses. In modern European herbal medicine it is regarded as a healing astringent which regulates over-secretion of the mucous membranes and is most commonly prescribed for coughs, bronchitis, catarrh, sinusitis and earache associated with catarrhal conditions.

We owe the most unusual application of this herb's healing powers to those early

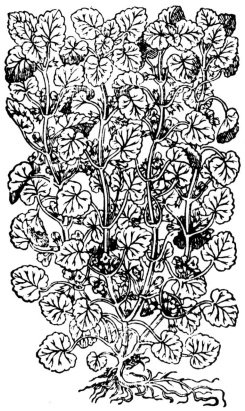

Ground ivy (Glechoma hederacea)

settlers who first introduced creeping Charlie to American soil. In those days paints had a high lead content and lead poisoning was an occupational hazard for painters and decorators. Infusions of ground ivy were taken both as a curative and preventative measure, and those who took regular doses were rarely troubled by 'lead-colic'. Ground ivy was also considered effective in nervous complaints. The fresh juice, sniffed up the nose was said to cure tension headaches instantly. More serious problems, such as 'hypochondria and monomania' were also treated by prescribing ground ivy. This use may have originated in England, as a book published in 1746 and titled *A Collection of above Three Hundred Receipts in Cookery, Physick and Surgery for the use of all Good Wives, Tender Mothers and Careful Nurses* gave the following 'Remedy for Lunacy' by a Dr Wadenfield: 'Take three handfulls of ground ivy, boil it in white wine and mix it

with the best Sallad Oil, boil it up to an Ointment, let the Patient's Head be shaved, then rub and chafe it with the Ointment made warm'. Anyone found carrying out such a treatment these days would undoubtedly be certified on the spot but our ancestors were obviously made of sterner stuff and believed that 'mother knew best'. I can only hope that few mothers came across the fruits of Dr Wadenfield's learning – and that many will go on to discover the more genial uses of this handy little plant.

GOLDEN HOP
Humulus lupulus 'Aureus'

Anyone with a liking for golden-leaved plants soon discovers that although there are plenty of shrubs, conifers, herbaceous perennials and even prostrate creepers and alpines with yellow foliage, there are very few climbers. On this account alone, the golden hop is coveted by plant lovers. There is, however, more to it than that. It is a quick-growing hardy perennial and has bold beautifully shaped leaves reminiscent of those of the grape vine. In addition, female plants produce bunches of fragile papery 'cones' that are not only decorative but very useful, both medicinally and in home brewing.

The genus *Humulus* grows wild over a vast area throughout most northern temperate regions of Europe, Asia and North America, and is cultivated even more widely – from Chile to Australia. There are generally considered to be only two species in the genus; the common hop, *H. lupulus*, and the Japanese hop, *H. japonicus* (the latter being an annual climber with an attractive variegated form). The genus belongs to Moraceae, the same family as the luscious figs and mulberries, hemp (the fibre plant) and the euphoric cannabis – though some botanists consider that *Cannabis* and *Humulus* should form a separate family (Cannabaceae). Hops are also closely related to nettles (*Urtica* spp) and were once included in the family Urticaceae.

The word hop is from the Anglo-Saxon *hoppan*, a verb meaning 'to climb'. *Humulus* may be derived from humus, referring to the hop's liking for rich soil, and *lupulus* from the Latin *lupus*, meaning a wolf. The explanation for the latter is that Pliny the Elder once called the hop a willow wolf (*lupus salictarius*) as in the wild it grows in damp places and creeps up on and strangles willows as a wolf would a sheep.

If you decide to grow a hop, make sure to buy a female plant. Hops are rarely grown from seed, so buying female plants should not be too difficult if you find a nursery that propagates its own and uses only female stock plants. Commercially hops are usually raised from so-called root cuttings which are actually pieces of underground stem. Some nurseries use young shoots as cuttings too. It is also possible to sever suckers, or small divisions with some roots, and pot them up separately to obtain new plants, though this can only be done on a small scale (I managed it when I moved house in midsummer when there was no other way of taking my precious golden hop with me). Pot-grown plants can be planted at any time of the year but traditionally hops are planted during mild spells in the winter or early spring. Though hardy, they prefer genial climates and do not do well in exposed positions where winters are severe. They also like plenty of sun and moisture when in growth, excellent drainage and ample supplies of nutrients. As Thomas Tusser (1524–80) said in his book *June's Husbandrie*: 'Choose soil for the hop of the rottenest mould, well doonged and wrought, as a garden plot should'. In other words, the hop is insatiably hungry and thirsty but likes its feet dry (on a bed of clay it will probably turn up its toes). Artificial fertilizers will do for a time, but for healthy vigorous colourful foliage and large bunches of 'cones', there is no substitute for manure, compost, fishmeal, hoof-and-horn and other such organic treats.

After considering the hop's requirements, it is worth pondering upon your own, as the hop is not only a beautiful climber: it is big! The stout extensive roots may go 4.5 m (15 ft) deep, which might make one think twice about planting it next to the house where it may dry out the soil around the foundations. Though deciduous and dormant in winter, when it puts out new shoots in the spring, it does so with a vengeance and has been known to grow 15 cm (6 in) in 24 hours, finally reaching a length of 6 m (20 ft) or more. Each shoot circles clockwise in half-metre sweeps to find support and tightens up on anything suitable – poles, wires, branches, its own or other plants' stems – with a grasp made firm by bristly hooked hairs. Well-established plants have many shoots or 'bines' as they are known by hop growers, so, all-in-all, the hop is a heavyweight among climbers and needs a sturdy support and plenty of room to spread its golden tresses. It is also worth remembering that every winter there will be a mass of intertwined dead stems and removing these from some supports (such as trees) may be rather difficult.

The leaves of the hop are basically heart-shaped with three to five broad, pointed lobes, serrated margins and a very rough texture due to the hooked hairs which clothe most parts of the plant. Wild plants are dark green in colour, but the golden form is yellowish-lime, colouring best in moist sunny conditions. Plants are wind-pollinated and dioecious, having male and female flowers on separate plants. Males have the same handsome foliage, but are of no use in medicine or brewing. They are not required to fertilize the female flowers, as unfertilized flowers are gathered for drying. (Some commercial growers prefer them fertilized but only because they grow slightly larger.) Male flowers appear in panicles up to 13 cm (5 in) long but are much less decorative than the trusses of female 'cones' or strobiles. These consist of pale green overlapping bracts which look rather like delicate immature fir cones. Tucked away out of sight in the axil of each bract is a tiny flower. If you examine the flowers and bracts, you will see that they appear to be covered in grains. These are actually glands containing soft resins and essential oil: the substances valued by brewers and herbalists – and by perfumers, who add oil of hop to scents of the *chypre* type.

Hops are a relatively recent introduction in brewing. Though widely used elsewhere in Europe by the fourteenth century, they were not common in England until the sixteenth, and even then their introduction met with considerable resistance. Our Viking ancestors drank ale: a brew of malt and bitter aromatic herbs such as ground ivy, yarrow and wood sage. The new-fangled beer based on hops was Dutch or German in origin and regarded with such suspicion that Henry VIII forbade it and the hop was condemned as 'a wicked weed that would spoil the taste of the drink and endanger the people'. As late as 1670, John Evelyn wrote that 'Hops transmuted our wholesome ale into beer, which doubtless much alters its constitution. This one ingredient, by some suspected not unworthily, preserved the drink indeed, but repays the pleasure in tormenting diseases and a shorter life.' It was also suspected of causing melancholy (depression, as we know it).

The use of hops in medicine is more recent still. Physicians as long ago as Avicenna (980–1037) knew of their tonic, diuretic and sedative effects, but it was only in the early nineteenth century that they became popular for treating a wide range of problems. For this purpose the aromatic bitter-tasting female flowers are gathered in late summer and dried rapidly, but gently, to preserve the volatile constituents. They do not keep well and stocks must be replenished annually. There are three main spheres of use: in compresses and lotions for leg ulcers, boils, neuralgic and rheumatic pains (hop is a mild painkiller and antiseptic); internally for sexual problems in men; and for hyperactivity, insomnia, nervous tension, colitis, and headaches and indigestion of nervous origin (usually in conjunction with chamo-

(*above*) Golden hop: the finest of all gold-leaved climbers.
(*opposite*) Golden-variegated orris: a distinguished plant for the front of the border.

mile). Hops are not, however, prescribed for patients with a tendency to depression – the suspicions of the seventeenth century being correct.

The hormonal effects of hops are particularly interesting. They contain oestrogenic substances, so although beer drinking has an image of tough masculinity, the fact is that the hop is a feminizing herb which is used for low-oestrogen problems in women and for depressing an abnormally high sexual urge in men. It is also taken to improve the milk flow in nursing mothers. Lupulin resin, which can be obtained by sifting the dried shaken strobiles, is made into tablets for this purpose.

While hops stimulate and improve digestion, they relax other functions, even to the point of causing drowsiness. Inhaling the heavy odour of the female flowers is quite sufficient – as hop pickers know only too well – and hop pillows are an old cure for insomnia. George III, who ruled Britain from 1760 to 1820, suffered terribly from the disease por-

46

phyria. He was treated as insane by his physicians but at least found relief in the hop pillow he was given to help him sleep. Small pillows filled with a muslin liner of hop flowers and fragrant herbs, such as lemon balm, are also very useful for overnight travel when even those who normally sleep like a log have difficulty in relaxing.

Not only will your golden hop supply you with flowers for brewing and medicinal use, but in the spring a number of new shoots can be cut without detriment to the plant, for eating. Hop shoots are a delicacy like asparagus and may be steamed and served hot with butter, or cold with French dressing.

Few would now argue against the usefulness and value of the hop. Its popularity nowadays is such that there is probably no other herb grown in such quantities worldwide. Of course, even in the stormy days of its introduction there were some who were in favour. The herbalist John Gerard entered the controversy, and in the 1636 edition of his *Herball* wrote: 'The manifold virtues of Hops do manifest argue the wholesomenesse of beere above ale; for the hops rather make it a physicall drinke to keepe the body in health, than an ordinary drinke for the quenching of our thirst'. He also commented that, however beneficial in small amounts, too much in the way of hop-flavoured beer is 'ill for the head': with which no one can disagree!

VARIEGATED ORRIS
Iris pallida 'Variegata Argentea' and 'Variegata Aurea'

There are few flowers as lovely as the iris. It is a satisfying blend of dignity and grace: bold and sculptural yet as delicate and colourful as a butterfly. In sympathy with these qualities, Linnaeus named the genus *Iris* after Juno's messenger who came down from the Olympian heaven on a rainbow. It has been cultivated and revered since earliest times. To the ancient Egyptians it symbolized eloquence, and the temple of Thutmosis III at Karnak, built over 3,000 years ago, bears its image on the walls. The shape of the iris is the origin of the sceptre, a ceremonial staff carried by monarchs as a symbol of power and majesty. Even better known is its role in heraldry as the fleur-de-lis, a stylized iris whose three petals represent faith, wisdom and valour. This symbol is remembered as the emblem of the former French royal family, of the Medici and the city of Florence (long famed for iris cultivation), as well as being the badge of the Scout movement.

The iris flower is indeed a most distinctive shape. Characteristically it has three upturned petal-like lobes (known as 'standards') and three downturned (the 'falls'). In many iris species the centre of each fall is joined to the style (part of the female reproductive organ

47

which, in irises, is often flattened into a colourful crest or 'beard'), forming a tube over the anther (the male organ). Insects are attracted to colours and patterns on the falls, and by nectar in the centre of the flower, which they reach by crawling along the tube – picking up and transferring pollen in the process and thus carrying out pollination.

There are about 250 species of iris worldwide, ranging from diminutive alpines to lush semi-aquatics, and species which can tolerate near-desert conditions. They are found wild throughout the Northern Hemisphere, from the Arctic Circle to the Tropic of Cancer. The genus belongs to the family Iridaceae which includes other horticulturally important genera, such as *Crocus*, *Gladiolus* and *Freesia*. Some of the hardiest, loveliest and longest cultivated irises are the so-called flag or bearded irises which have sword-shaped leaves and thick creeping rhizomes which lie on the surface of the soil. Of these, several species and varieties are of particular interest as the source of the violet-scented powder known as orris which is produced by grinding the dried rhizomes.

Orris has been used medicinally and as a perfume since at least classical times. The rhizomes consist mostly of starch, mucilage, sugar and a complex essential oil. When fresh they are odourless but extremely pungent and acrid. However, chemical changes take place during drying which render them delightfully fragrant and only slightly bitter. The medicinal uses are now almost obsolete but were once highly popular, if rather diversified in their application. Pieces of dried root were given to teething babies and burnt to get rid of musty smells. The powder could be taken externally as snuff or internally for a whole host of complaints. William Turner, the sixteenth-century English herbalist, recommended flag iris for 'gnawings in the belly' and 'for them that have taken a thorowe cold', and Culpeper reckoned it was good for anything from bad breath to aborting the stillborn foetus. Basically it is a mild purgative and

diuretic which also eases bronchial congestion, but on all counts there are other more effective herbal remedies available. In contrast, orris is still in great demand by the pharmaceutical, perfumery and food industries. It is used mainly in toilet powders, scents, cachous and potpourris, and to enhance fruit flavours in soft drinks and candies. Although the powder has its uses, the rhizomes are also distilled to produce an oil known as 'orris butter' which smells strongly of violets. Synthetic violet perfume is one of the most widely used of all artificial scents, but on its own is rather crude. Adding a little oil of orris gives a subtle note and improves the quality considerably. Orris is also one of the best perfume fixatives, extending the life of and intensifying other scents.

The irises grown for orris production have been in cultivation for many hundreds – if not thousands – of years, and as a result they include many different cultivars that may be difficult even for the specialist to put a name to. As with all crops, yields and quality vary from region to region according to conditions and the variety of iris grown. The finest orris is said to come from *I. germanica* 'Florentina' (formerly known as *I. florentina*) which, as one might expect, is grown intensively at San Polo, near the Italian city of Florence. It is native to southern Europe and generally has off-white flowers, sometimes blue-veined or lavender-tinged. The variety which used to be called *I. florentina* var. *albicans* but is now recognized as a species (*I. albicans*) in its own right, has pure white flowers. Though not widely grown in gardens, and of no importance for orris, it is nevertheless one of the most beautiful and graceful of wild irises and has an interesting history. In the Middle East it is a symbol of wealth and is often planted on graves to ensure a bountiful afterlife. Its origins are in Saudi Arabia and the Yemen but it is now widely naturalized in southern Europe, having been taken along by Arab invaders for this purpose. I once found a large group of plants growing beneath a carob tree near the coast in

Crete (which first fell under Arab rule in the ninth century), exactly filling the area cast by the tree's shadow. They were in full flower, their luminous white blooms appearing to hover over the broad glaucous leaves as they fluttered in the sea breeze.

More common in cultivation is the variable *I. pallida* which usually has lavender-blue flowers, though pale blue, lilac and greyish-purple are sometimes seen. Their scent has been likened to vanilla, civet and orange blossom. It is, however, not the flowers, but the leaves of this species which are so effective in the garden, as it has two extremely handsome variegated forms: 'Variegata Argentea' with a stiff fan of glaucous leaves broadly striped with white; and the even more striking 'Variegata Aurea' whose foliage is a blend of blue-green, cream and yellow stripes. Neither is as vigorous as the species, but when well established they are stunning plants for the front of the border, where their clean lines and fresh colours are a relief from the dark and fussy leaves borne by many herbaceous perennials. They reach about 40 cm (16 in) and are at their best in spring when the pristine zebra-striped foliage is as smart as new paint.

It is perfectly possible to grow your own orris, if, that is, you can bear to sacrifice your irises and are patient enough to wait two years for the full aroma to develop in the dried rhizomes. Plants of *I. germanica* might be best for this purpose as they are cheaper to buy and more robust than the horticultural beauties just described. Though they will survive on poor dry soils (*I. germanica* is even grown on roof tops in parts of Europe), all the irises mentioned do best in rich, well-drained, neutral to slightly alkaline soil and, above all, a sunny position. The most important thing is to make sure the rhizomes are on the surface of the soil and angled so that they receive the maximum amount of sun. This will probably increase the amount of essential oil produced and will certainly result in better growth and flowering. Dividing and moving plants should be done in the spring; harvesting in the autumn, preferably after a shower of rain. The rhizomes can be dried whole or cut into slices and threaded on strings to speed up the process. Slicing them also makes grinding easier when they are mature enough to make into powder. If you have the necessary skill, they can even be fashioned into marbles or beads which are convenient for putting among clothes and linen. Some people, I know, dislike the smell of lavender on clean clothes almost as much as that of mothballs; in which case, orris might make a suitable substitute. May I go so far as to suggest they try a mixture of orris and anise (the seeds of the annual umbelliferous spice, *Pimpinella anisum*)? It might seem like a novel idea, but it goes back to the second half of the fifteenth century, being the blend used to scent the royal wardrobe of Edward IV of England.

GOLDEN VARIEGATED JASMINE
Jasminum officinale 'Aureovariegatum'

The perfume of jasmine is one of the loveliest and most distinctive of any flower. It may cost the earth to buy the real thing when it takes half a kilogram (1 lb) of blossoms (about 3,500) to produce a few drops of essential oil (an eighth of a teaspoonful, to be more exact), but for a fraction of the cost you can at least have your own plant. To adapt an old Eastern saying (which usually mentions narcissi or hyacinths): 'If you have two loaves of bread, sell one and buy jasmine to feed the soul'.

There are between 200 and 300 species of jasmine, mostly native to China, India and Iran. They include shrubs and climbers, both deciduous and evergreen, tender and hardy. Their closest relatives are lilac (*Syringa*), forsythia, ash (*Fraxinus*) and privet (*Ligustrum*) – all members of the olive family, Oleaceae. Not every jasmine is fragrant and

some of the most fragrant are, unfortunately, not hardy. Several different species are grown for perfumery. Two of the best are the Arabian jasmine (*J. sambac*) from tropical Asia, and the hardy Spanish jasmine (*J. officinale* 'Affine', also known as 'Grandiflorum') which, in spite of its name, comes from the north-west Himalayas. Of those that are both reasonably hardy and heavily scented, the best for gardens is *J. officinale*. It should survive temperatures as low as $-23°C$ ($-9°F$) and though needing well-drained soil, will thrive in sun or shade. The closely related evergreen *J. polyanthum* is similar in appearance and intensely fragrant, but is not frost-resistant. It is the species generally sold as a houseplant, larger specimens making superb plants for conservatories which it fills with fragrance in spring and early summer.

J. officinale is often referred to as common white jasmine, but a more romantic age knew it as the poet's jessamine. The words *Jasminum* 'jessamine', 'jasmine' and the French *jasmin* are from the eastern names for the plant: the Arabic *yasamin*, Persian *yasmin*, and Chinese *yeh-hsi-ming*. The Garden of Gethsemane was, in other words, a garden of jasmine. In the wild it is found in China, the Himalayas, Afghanistan, northern Iran and even as far west as the Caucasus which it may have reached via the old silk road, an ancient trade route that ran from China and India to Samarkand and thence into Europe. It reached British gardens as early as 1548 and in Tudor times was popular for covering arbours, in whose shelter the perfume would linger.

The species name *officinale* indicates that it

(opposite) Golden-variegated jasmine: yellow-splashed leaves and entrancing scent.
(above) The golden Canadian juniper, whose subtle bronze and yellow tints change through the seasons.

has long been used medicinally. Both the leaves and flowers have sedative properties. It is little used today in western herbal medicine, though it and several other species are still popular in India and aromatherapists value its relaxant qualities. Among the traditional uses, one cannot imagine a more delicious cough remedy than that made by layering jasmine blossoms with sugar and leaving them for a day covered with wet cloths. Whether effective or not, the resulting syrup must have led to an increase in hypochondria as the hale and hearty succumbed to temptation.

J. officinale is a deciduous twining climber that reaches 6–9 m (20–30 ft). It bears dark green pinnate leaves which, in the summer, are studded with terminal clusters of pure white long-tubed starry flowers. The blossoms should be gathered when fully open and dried quickly but gently. They can be added to tea (preferably Hyson, a delicate green China tea), used in potpourris and other fragrant articles and, fresh or dried, may be steeped in oil for massage. Though vigorous and hardy, it will appreciate a sheltered spot in cold northern districts. It is most effective against walls, climbing into trees, or trained up a trellis or arch. No pruning is required other than thinning from the base as necessary after flowering. Shortening the shoots should be avoided as it spoils the shape of the plant, and errant shoots will need tying in – jasmine being not the most organized of plants in its approach to the climbing surface.

There are several varieties of *J. officinale*. 'Affine' has larger flowers which, like those of *J. polyanthum*, have a delicate pink blush. Then there are two variegated forms: 'Argenteovariegatum' with cream dappled leaves, and the brilliant yellow-splashed 'Aureovariegatum' (sometimes called 'Aureum'). Both uprate the jasmine into a foliage plant, even though the highlight is still its flowering. The latter is particularly colourful and could be used to great effect near yellow or white flowered climbing roses, whose origins were also in the East.

GOLDEN CANADIAN AND MINIATURE JUNIPERS
Juniperus communis 'Depressa Aurea' and 'Compressa'

In recent years there has been a tremendous upsurge of interest in conifers, with the result that beds of well-chosen and carefully placed conifers are a common sight in both private gardens and parks. They have an almost abstract quality, reminiscent of Japanese boulders and raked gravel, which complements the lean angular look of modern buildings, just as the leafy and floriferous cottage garden goes so well with thatches and leaded windows. Some conifers are quick-growing and in great demand for hedges and ground cover: others take many years to reach quite modest sizes. In any case, a large part of their appeal is that they are attractive all year round and require remarkably little attention once established.

We are all familiar with the invigorating antiseptic scent of pine, but seldom think of conifers as herbs. In fact, some species are widely used in herbal medicine – and even in cooking – making them eminently worth growing for these properties as well as for their handsome appearance. One of the most important is common juniper, *Juniperus communis.*

The genus *Juniperus* belongs to the cypress family, Cupressaceae. It has 60 or so species, about a dozen of which are common in cultivation. A few others, such as savin (*J. sabina*) are used medicinally. Of them all, the common juniper is the most versatile: a plant of infinitely variable appearance and a multitude of uses. It is found throughout most of Europe, from the Mediterranean to Scandinavia, and in Asia and North America too. Plants usually grow in groups, as the name *communis* suggests, and at high elevations in mountainous regions – in the Caucasus and the Himalayas, for example. As is so often the case with species which have a wide distribution, it can vary greatly in appearance, being anything from bushy and untidy to slim and upright. On average, it reaches about 3 m (10 ft) tall and 1.8 m (6 ft) wide, but in harsh environments may be nowhere near as large. On coastal rocks in western Scotland there are completely prostrate plants, clinging to a spartan existence and bare of needles from salt damage on the seaward side – small, densely compact shrubs, gnarled and twisted over perhaps centuries of minimal growth. In spite of the stresses, rocky windswept barren sites are a favourite habitat, often on thin soils over limestone or chalk. Elsewhere junipers are found on impoverished acid peats.

Juniper foliage is grey-green and takes the form of flat needles with extremely sharp points. They occur in whorls of three, with a greyish stripe on the upper surface. In a number of other species of juniper, this prickly kind of foliage is produced only in juveniles and changes to smooth overlapping scales when the plant reaches maturity.

As with all conifers, junipers are wind-pollinated. Male and female flowers are borne on different plants in the spring: the males releasing pollen from tiny bobble-like catkins onto the receptive female flowers which resemble small pale greenish-grey peas with an indentation at the top. If fertilized, these are destined to become juniper 'berries'. They are, in fact, cones. Each contains two to eight seeds and takes about eighteen months to mature, turning purplish-black with a waxy bloom when ripe.

All parts of juniper are fragrant. The wood is hard, water-resistant and has a fine grain which makes it attractive in marquetry and carvings. One of the nicest things I have seen made from juniper is a little box which was a present from Finland. It is constructed from joined 2 cm-square (1 in sq) cross-sections, each showing the extremely fine and irregular growth rings. Carpenters also utilize its aromatic and insecticidal properties in storage chests for woollens and furs.

The fragrance is strongest in the berry-like cones which are rich in essential oil, resin, bitter substances and an interesting anti-tumour agent called podophyllotoxin. Harvesting them from the hedgehog-like juniper is no easy task. I don't know how it is done commercially, but a combination of stout gloves and beating about the bush seems to be the least fiddly method, as well as the least painful, especially if you first put down a sheet to avoid the tedium of picking them off the ground. They should be gathered in the autumn and may be used, fresh or dried, for a variety of purposes. The resinous fruity flavour is superb in marinades and stuffings for meat, especially game, and in the curing of hams and bacon. Dorothy Hartley, in her classic book *Food in England*, describes a juniper spice pickle for salting hams which are then drained and smoked over a juniper fire. A small amount of crushed juniper berries is a great enlivener of cabbage, either cooked or fermented as sauerkraut. In addition to their appeal as a culinary flavouring, juniper berries are about one third sugar. They have proved to be quite a nutritious subsistence food for several North American Indian tribes who bake the mushed berries into cakes in times of hardship. An infusion of a few crushed berries also makes a very pleasant tea: a fact discovered long ago by the Lapps who drink it regularly.

Medicinally, juniper has a great deal to recommend it. Culpeper, with his customary enthusiasm, prescribed it for almost everything, from the usual bites of venomous beasts which so plagued our ancestors, to the still commonplace coughs, pains in the belly, failing memory and poor eyesight. His optimism was not entirely unfounded, as juniper is highly antiseptic, a good diuretic, an efficient cleanser of accumulated toxins, and an excellent carminative 'for wind in any part of the body'. In present-day herbal medicine it is first and foremost a urinary disinfectant used mainly for cystitis. It also has a reputation for improving rheumatism and arthritis, either externally in a massage oil or through various internal treatments. One of these is known as the Kneipp method after its originator, the Abbé Kneipp. It entails chewing juniper berries in a regular cycle of increase and decrease for a month, beginning with one berry three times a day, and each day increasing the number by one until fifteen berries, three times daily, is reached. Then the whole process is reversed. Taken this way, juniper increases the excretion of acid wastes from the joints, thus increasing mobility and reducing pain. The 'short, sharp shock' approach is favoured because juniper can be toxic if taken over long periods (and in any case is never given in pregnancy or cases of kidney disease).

Given that juniper can survive considerable hardship in the wild, cultivating it should be no problem, however unpromising the conditions (though like any plant it will need attentive watering initially until its roots are well established). Indeed, it is positively recommended for windswept sites and thin poor soils, both calcareous and acid. Needless to say, it is also extremely hardy and will tolerate temperatures of −40°C (−40°F), although some ornamental forms are not quite as tough. The worst problem is likely to be choosing which juniper to grow from the multitude of varieties now available. Herbalists may prefer to grow the true species. Few general nurseries bother to keep it, but specialist herb nurseries should have stocks of labelled male and female plants. (Only one male is needed to pollinate several females.) Wild junipers can also be grown from seed, though they may take over ten years to reach flowering size and will include fairly even numbers of males and females. The seeds remain viable for several years in the berry but may not germinate for a year or more once sown, so you have to be prepared to keep them moist and weed-free for a lengthy period. Cuttings are quicker, giving young plants, with the same sex and growth habit as the parent, in less than a year. They should be taken, preferably with a heel, in early autumn and put into a mixture of peat and sand. An additional advantage of plants raised from cuttings is that they flower within a few years if taken from mature foliage.

Wild junipers are, however, less colourful and shapely than the cultivated varieties, some of which may appeal more or be better suited to certain positions. General nurseries are unlikely to identify male and female plants, but if you make your choice in the spring, you should be able to tell which is which from the flowers. Whatever varieties are chosen, providing there is one male to one or more females, you will get berries. (I have a golden prostrate female which is pollinated by a wild male – botanically speaking.)

Although there have been many exciting

new introductions in recent years, two firm favourites are old-timers. 'Depressa Aurea', the golden prostrate juniper, is a selected form of the Canadian juniper, *J. communis* 'Depressa', and has been known since at least 1887. It forms a bowl-shaped low-growing shrub 30–40 cm (12–16 in) high and about 150 cm (5 ft) across which makes dense ground cover, especially on steep slopes where little else can be grown. The main branches are ascending but the tips are pendent. In spring the new needles are bright yellow, turning gold through the summer and bronzing as winter advances. Like all junipers, it needs an open sunny position, but is otherwise an accommodating plant. Completely different in appearance is 'Compressa'. It was introduced to cultivation before 1855, from the Pyrenees, and has the distinction of being one of the smallest, most compact and slow-growing of all conifers. It rarely reaches more than 80 cm (32 in) and increases by a mere 2–3 cm (1 in) each year, resulting in a meticulously tidy column of minute blue-green needles. This is the perfect juniper for containers, either alone as a doorway sentinel (in which capacity it is reputed to keep witches away), or to give height in a trough of choice alpines. It is also most effective as an accent plant on rock gardens where it is guaranteed never to encroach upon its neighbours.

For me, the name 'juniper' conjures up wild hillsides in all weathers. I well remember many of the junipers I have encountered on hikes: individuals with great character, perching on precipices and pruned by the wind. Just like the plants, the origin of the word 'juniper' is lost in the mists of time, leaving but a string of associations. The English girl's name Jennifer may be derived from it (as in the song 'Jennifer, Juniper'), and possibly Guinevere too. Certainly Leonardo da Vinci made the connection in his portrait of Ginevra de Benci, as the background is a network of juniper twigs. Less romantic is the fact that juniper has given us gin, an alcoholic drink dating back to the seventeenth century. Ironi-

cally, it began as a medicine when Franciscus de la Boe, a professor of medicine at the University of Leiden in Holland, distilled spirits with juniper berries to prepare a potent diuretic. The French name for juniper is *genièvre* which became *genever* in Dutch. Before the end of the eighteenth century, Holland was producing 530,000 hectolitres (14,000,000 gal) of *genever* a year – not, one imagines, for medicinal purposes only. British soldiers in wars on the continent acquired a taste for this 'Hollands Geneva', as they called it, and brought home the drink that was soon to be known just as gin. Its subsequent history is one of urban pleasure and ruin – a far cry from the juniper of wild and rugged places.

GOLDEN BAY
Laurus nobilis 'Aurea'

In Victorian times there were several different forms of bay. One book mentions varieties with willow-shaped, curled and variegated leaves. The former is what is today known as 'Angustifolia' (or 'Salicifolia'), an extra-hardy form with narrow, light-green leaves; the curly-leaved form ('Crispa' or 'Undulata') is rarely seen; and the variegated is either extremely rare or lost to cultivation. A variegated bay tree would indeed be a prize! Of course, the species is an attractive plant in its own right and many people will prefer its classic, rather formal, olive-green foliage to anything else. For container-grown plants which are cut into pyramids, balls and other ornamental shapes, plain green leaves are undoubtedly the best, but for garden shrubs there are situations where a more interesting variety could be used to good effect.

The willow-leaved bay ('Angustifolia') makes a more graceful plant than the species and is well worth trying in cold areas where bays are a doubtful proposition in the open, but the most dramatic variety generally avail-

Golden bay: less hardy but more colourful than the green.

formed. After several years the whole head will be sturdy enough for more general shaping with shears. Pruning and clipping should be done several times in the summer. The well-disciplined bay should also have all suckers removed as soon as they appear, as they are dreadful obstacles to symmetry.

All bays are slow-growing and slightly tender, succumbing – or at least receiving disfiguring damage – in temperatures below −7°C (−19°F). In frost-free areas, unpruned trees will, in time, reach 15 m (49 ft) or more, but in colder regions they rarely exceed 5 m (16 ft). They need well-drained soil and full sun. Plants in containers do best in equal quantities of loam, peat and sand, with a little well-rotted manure or compost. They should never be allowed to dry out and should not be 'over-potted'. Quite large specimens thrive in modest-sized containers, although this can be a problem in strong winds. Regular feeding is important, especially if the plant has been in the same pot for years, in which case a top dressing of manure or compost in the spring will also pay dividends in terms of quality and lustre of the foliage. An eagle eye should be kept on the undersides of the leaves as they are prone to scale insects, particularly when undernourished. These look like limpets and cause sooty mould which makes an awful mess of the plant. They are also difficult to get rid of without the kind of sprays which put you off using your bay leaves long after the scale insects are dead and gone.

The genus *Laurus* belongs to the family Lauraceae which also includes avocado and cinnamon trees. It is a small one, generally considered to consist of just two species: *L. nobilis*, generally known as bay, bay laurel or sweet bay; and the Canary Island bay, known variously as *L. azorica*, *L. canariensis* and *L. maderensis*. It has larger, downy leaves, especially when young. At one time there were forests of bay in the Canary Islands and Madeira, but little now remains. *L. nobilis* is evergreen and native to Mediterranean regions. The leaves of the bay are 5–10 cm (2–4

able today is the golden bay, *Laurus nobilis* 'Aurea'. Its new growths are suffused with yellow and well-grown specimens make colourful and attractive shrubs for sunny sheltered positions (unfortunately it is even less hardy than the species). The particular character of the golden form (and of 'Angustifolia' for that matter) is best appreciated if allowed to grow freely, but if desired it can be trained as a standard and trimmed into geometric shapes in the same way as the species. Standards should be taken in hand at an early age, allowing the main shoot to grow on but nipping back all others to two or three leaves. When it reaches 15 cm (6 in) above the required height, it too should be pinched out to remove the growing point. From then on each lateral should be reduced to four or five leaves as it develops and gradually the basis of a ball shape will be in) long, lanceolate (tapering towards both ends) and clearly veined, with short stalks and slightly wavy margins. They are held stiffly and have a thin, rather brittle, leathery texture and a sweet, cinnamon-like scent. Flowering takes place in the spring: the cream-coloured unisexual flowers appearing in clusters of three or four in the axils, followed by aromatic blue-black berries.

The sweetness of bay is more obvious when dried, but both fresh and dried leaves are used in cooking. They really are indispensable. I always remember my father, whom I doubt could tell sage from thyme, insisting on the importance of adding a bay leaf to almost anything that was cooking. He was right. Stock, marinades, soups, casseroles, pulses, rice, seafood, meat, tripe, pickles, sauces, condiments, olives – the list is endless. Even milk desserts are made more flavoursome by the addition of a bay leaf when the milk is warming. Bay leaves are also added to coffee in the Middle East and packed with rice, liquorice roots, dried figs and dates. (They deter weevils from dried foods as well as giving flavour.) In addition, the essential oil is used in the manufacture of soft and alcoholic drinks and the fragrant wood is used for smoking meat and fish.

At one time extracts from both the leaves and the berries were used in medicine. They benefit the digestion and relieve fevers, but do little that many other herbs do not do as well, if not better. However, the fragrant yellow oil still plays a part in external preparations for rheumatism. As Culpeper said three centuries ago, bay is 'very comfortable in all cold griefs' and for 'cramp, aches, tremblings, and numbness in any part, weariness also, and pains that come by sore travelling'.

The word laurel is from the Latin *laurus*, meaning 'praise' and the species name, *nobilis*, means 'notable' or 'famous'. In classical times winning athletes in the Olympic Games were crowned with bay, as were victors in battle, political leaders and anyone deserving of tribute. We may not go in for crowning successful

Bay (Laurus nobilis), *in fruit*

people today, but the British still retain the title of poet laureate. The origin of this tradition is usually given as the Greek myth in which the virgin Diana was turned into a bay tree to avoid the amorous advances of Apollo. From then on, Apollo extended protection to anyone bearing bay, the symbol of his beloved. This belief still affects us today, in a roundabout sort of way. Apparently the ancient Greeks hung a branch of bay over the door of a sick person to fend off death and evil spirits. This led to the tradition of garlanding newly qualified doctors with bay: a symbol of protection and success known as the *bacca laureus* – laurel berry – which gave us the term baccalaureate (a university degree). Advanced students were discouraged from marrying for fear of distraction from their studies, and in time such baccalaureates became known as bachelors. And from Bachelors of Science and Arts the word took on a more general meaning of any unmarried man.

The avowed protective powers of bay gave rise to some strange superstitions, such as keeping a bay leaf in your mouth all day to avoid misfortune. Another was to put a garland of bay on your head during thunder storms to avoid being struck by lightning. The Emperor Tiberius not only did this but, as an extra precaution, hid under the bed as soon as it started thundering – a less noble approach than relying on the crown of noble bay, but one which obviously proved so effective that it is still a popular tactic today.

PINK LAVENDER
Lavandula angustifolia 'Loddon Pink'

Lavender has an essential place in the cottage garden, alongside roses and pinks, paving slabs and stone walls. Indeed, it should be in every garden, preferably close to the path or in a container near the door where its fragrant foliage and flowers are brushed as you pass. It is an irresistible herb whose uplifting scent tempts casual picking – especially the nipping off of flowerheads – so if you plant it where passersby can reach, you are sure to find it will be lightly pruned all summer long.

The fragrance of lavender is synonymous with cool freshly laundered linen and clean clothes, and it is still, after two thousand years of use, a most popular perfume for toilet water, soap and bath essences. The words lavender, *lavandula* and launder are all from the Latin *lavare*, meaning 'to wash'. Traditionally, laundry was rinsed in lavender-scented water and in Elizabethan times a washerwoman was known as a lavender. The characteristic smell of lavender is due to linalyl acetate, a component of the colourless volatile oil. The oil collects in a sac at the base of each petal and the quantity is dependent upon the weather: warmth and sunshine increasing the amount.

Harvesting is done when the flowers are fully open.

Like so many fragrant herbs, lavender is a labiate – a member of the family Labiatae – with small tubular flowers, five-lobed at the mouth, which are richly supplied with nectar for foraging bees. Although several species are native to southern Europe and Mediterranean lands, numerous varieties and hybrids are grown all over the world so that identification is no easy task. Surprisingly, the finest oils come from cooler regions, often from plants of *L. angustifolia* – possibly because the flowers develop more slowly and the sun is not hot enough to cause much evaporation. The area round Mitcham in Surrey was long famous for quality lavender oil. Large acreages are also grown in other parts of southern England and as far north as Lincolnshire and Norfolk. Oils from southern Europe are mostly derived from *L. latifolia*, or spike lavender, which produces higher yields of a less pleasant, camphoraceous oil.

There is more to the oil than its scent, however. In ancient times it was used externally for skin problems and rheumatic pains, and is still an important ingredient in massage oils (the pure essential oil is always diluted for use). Making your own lavender oil is very simple. All that is needed is a litre (2 pt) of good vegetable oil (olive or safflower for example) and 100 gm (3½ oz) of lavender flowers in a glass jar. Stand in a sunny place for three days; shake occasionally; then strain into a clean bottle for use. As well as relieving aches and pains, it can be applied to burns (including sunburn), scalp irritations and dry eczema, and is even more effective if a little Vitamin E oil is added after straining.

Tests have shown that lavender is a potent antiseptic and kills a number of pathogens, such as diphtheria and typhoid bacilli and *Streptococcus* organisms. It also repels gnats and mosquitoes and has been used with success to get rid of head lice which are now resistant to most proprietary insecticides. For some purposes compound lavender tincture is more

convenient than lavender oil. Both are usually available from pharmacies. The tincture makes a stimulating friction rub for the scalp and may be diluted as a gargle for sore throats.

Herbalists prescribe lavender preparations mainly for depressive and exhausted states which are often associated with headaches, lack of appetite and indigestion. The complex chemistry of lavender has sedative and tonic properties which relieve anxiety and give a feeling of well-being. It is rarely used alone, but blended with several other herbs – with rosemary (*Rosmarinus officinalis*), for example, for depression. A simple infusion of these two herbs is wonderful for low spirits and tension headaches. Both are strongly flavoured so only half a teaspoonful of each is needed. Even then, it takes a little getting used to as it is rather like drinking hot perfume! The calming effect of lavender has always been recognized. The Elizabethan physician John Gerard recommended that the flowers, powdered with cinnamon, nutmeg and cloves and drunk in water 'doth helpe the panting and passion of the heart, prevaileth against giddinesse, turning, or swimming of the braine . . .'. Just inhaling the perfume of lavender oil is said to prevent fainting.

A mature bush of a large-growing lavender such as 'Seal' or 'Grappenhall', which reach 1 m (3 ft) tall or more and as much across, can produce as many as a thousand flower spikes in a season – which should meet all your needs, as well as the whims of passersby. For many gardens, varieties like this are too expansive and compact forms are a better prospect – and in many cases a row of small bushes is easier to accommodate than a single mighty specimen. Most lavenders have, of course, grey-green leaves and lavender-coloured flowers, but a visit to a well-stocked nursery in the summer, at flowering time, will reveal many variations on the theme, including 'Alba' with white,

and *L. viridis* with green flowers which are just the thing for restful silver gardens. My favourite, though, is 'Loddon Pink', a neat bush some 25–30 cm (10–12 in) high, with masses of palest pink spikes above the narrow grey-green leaves. It is quite different in effect from lavender lavenders. Though quite lovely with roses or among cottage garden flowers, such as clove-scented pinks, campanulas and geraniums, it comes into its own next to brown or purple-leaved plants which mauve flowers do little to enhance. One of the loveliest plantings I have seen is 'Loddon Pink' lavender at the foot of bronze fennel (*Foeniculum vulgare* 'Purpureum'): a classic combination for the herb gardener.

Lavender is evergreen and hardy in most temperate regions. The commonest species in cultivation are *L. latifolia* (spike lavender) and *L. angustifolia*: the latter being the name now given to plants formerly listed as *L. officinalis* and *L. spica*. Much less hardy are the woolly *L. lanata*, scallop-leaved *L. dentata* and French lavender, *L. stoechas*, all of which need protection against winter rain and frost. Apart from its doubtful hardiness in areas with severe winters (that is to say, temperatures below $-23°C/-9°F$), *L. angustifolia* and its varieties are easy to grow in sunny well-drained positions and thrive on a spartan diet of light dry stony or chalky soils. Propagation can be done from seed, but it is slow (one to three months) to germinate and offspring will be variable in habit and flower colour. Only cuttings will reproduce a certain variety reliably – which is particularly important if you want to plant a lavender hedge. They should be taken in spring or late summer, inserted in sandy compost and kept in a shaded but not too humid place until established. Mature plants may be layered to produce offsets by pegging down side branches in early spring. When rooted from the point of contact with the soil, they can be severed from their parent plant and carefully removed to their new position.

Although one does see lavender bushes of considerable age in some gardens, the text-

(opposite) A winning combination: pastel 'Loddon Pink' lavender and dark bronze fennel.

books tell you to replace them after about five years as they tend to become woody and sparse. Regular pruning helps keep them youthful: a light trim with shears after flowering and a more thorough cutting in the spring before new growth begins.

Lavender is very much a household herb. In England it used to be sold by street traders who would advertise their wares by cries such as 'Lavender, sweet lavender' and the rhyme 'Here's your sweet lavender, sixteen sprigs a penny, which you will find, my ladies, will smell as sweet as any'. It was an important item for domestic and personal freshness, with housewives making their own toilet water, pot pourris, pomanders and muslin lavender bags. Drawers, cupboards and blanket chests were protected from moths by rubbing the inside wood with bunches of foliage and then the contents were interleaved with muslin bags of flowers. Lavender sachets are still used in this way today, but the custom of giving lavender batons, or faggots, to brides has died out. These were ingeniously made by weaving about a dozen heads so that the flowers were contained within a cage of stalks. Making these delightful fragrant articles was not merely a test of skill or occupation for idle moments; lavender has to be containerized before use as the oils in the flowers will corrode tiny holes in garments if put loose in drawers. If the flowers were stripped for sachets, the stalks were kept in a tin box near the medicine chest for burning like incense sticks when there was illness in the house. The blue smoke freshened the air and killed germs. I am constantly amazed at the patience and ingenuity of the traditional housewife: some would crystallize tiny individual lavender flowers as piquant grains to add zest to boxes of candied fruits which were one of the many homemade treats at Christmas.

From domestic hygiene and sweetmeats, it is a far cry to encountering dangerous wild animals, but apparently lavender has its uses here too. The essential oil is reputed to neutralize viper's venom – which might turn out to be most fortunate as the Romans believed that lavender bushes were home to venomous asps. Another somewhat dubious piece of information is that the scent of lavender renders lions and tigers docile. It would certainly add a new meaning to discretion being the better part of valour if those going on safari were to set forth with a dab of lavender water behind their ears.

GOLDEN CREEPING JENNY
Lysimachia nummularia 'Aurea'

The first time I found creeping Jenny in the wild was beneath an alder tree on soggy ground bordering a stream. The spring flowers were over; the grasses had gone to seed; the dark green of the alders cast a heavy shade. Against this dull backdrop the bright yellow upturned bells and flat pairs of fresh green leaves were an unexpected delight – a spring-like moment in the middle of summer. Sometime later I came across the golden form. It was threading its way through large grey pebbles beside an ornamental pool in full sun and the leaves were almost as yellow as the flowers. There are many myths about people and things being changed into plants at the whim of the gods. Here it was as if the sunshine itself had been turned into vegetation as it struck the stones.

There are few plants more prostrate than creeping Jenny. Its branched stems proceed in an orderly fashion across the surface of the soil, the paired rounded leaves held flat on the ground, with roots sent down at regular intervals to consolidate its progress. Various common names attempt to describe this habit (creeping / running / wandering Jenny / Joan / sailor/tailor) and appearance (herb twopence, tuppenygrass, moneywort and string of sovereigns). The Latin species name, *nummularia*, also means money. However, the generic name (*Lysimachia*) has no such obvious asso-

Lavender (Lavandula angustifolia)   *Creeping Jenny* (Lysimachia nummularia)

ciations. It was inspired by a king of Thracia called Lusimakhos who was supposed to have discovered the plants and whose name means 'ending strife': hence the English name loose-strife which is given to several species of this genus. In the context of their medicinal uses, this has always seemed appropriate.

There are about 200 species of *Lysimachia* and they belong to the primrose family (Primu-laceae). They are, however, more closely related to pimpernels (*Anagallis* spp) than to primroses themselves, as a close look at their flowers will reveal. There is even one species, *L. nemorum*, that is known as the yellow pimpernel. It looks like a mini version of creeping Jenny, but with flowers shaped more like those of a pimpernel. Apart from creeping Jenny, the commonest species in Europe is the similarly yellow-flowered but much larger up-right *L. vulgaris*, the yellow loosestrife, which also enjoys damp sites. Both have escaped from

cultivation and are now naturalized in parts of North America.

Creeping Jenny is not much used in herbal medicine today. It contains tannins and is therefore a mild astringent, but there are any number of equally or more effective herbs. Its main uses are as a poultice for wounds and aching muscles and joints. Taken internally as an infusion, it may help control diarrhoea and minor haemorrhage. In former times it com-manded greater respect. John Gerard who in the sixteenth century gathered it on the banks of the River Thames, 'right against the Queenes palace of Whitehall', considered 'there is not a better wound herb'. He also related the ancient tale that wounded snakes were supposed to heal themselves with it – a belief that gave it the name serpentaria.

Without holding out too much hope for its usefulness as a medicinal herb – for snakes or humans – this is still an indispensable little

61

plant for carpeting moisture-retentive, even wet soils. In shade the foliage will darken to lime-green but in a sunny place will bounce back the sunshine: pennies from heaven!

VARIEGATED AND GOLDEN LEMON BALM
Melissa officinalis 'Aurea' (syn. 'Variegata') and 'All Gold'

At a glance the pointed oval mid-green leaves of the common lemon balm, with their serrated margins, look like those of a rather refined nettle. However, any resemblance between them is purely superficial. This can clearly be seen in the summer when lemon balm elongates to produce leafy whorls of tiny white flowers which are tubular and two-lipped, and altogether typical of the labiate family (Labiatae), to which so many popular herbs, such as sage and thyme, belong. If any doubts remain, crushing a leaf (cautiously) will dispel them – odourless nettles inflicting an unpleasant sting, and balm giving forth a delightful lemon scent.

Fortunately, the variegated and golden forms of balm could never be mistaken for nettles. They bring their own sunshine into the gloomiest corners of any garden, and their resplendent yellow coloration provides a visual reminder of lemons. *M. officinalis* 'Aurea', the variegated lemon balm, has leaves splashed and speckled with yellow. It can be grown in shade or in a more open position, but may scorch in full sun. *M. officinalis* 'All Gold' is, as the name suggests, completely yellow. It is even more sensitive to bright sunshine and is best in a shady place, which it will lighten most effectively. Both prefer slightly damp soils and are much the same size as common lemon balm, that is about 45 cm (18 in) tall and 38 cm (15 in) across. They can be cut back in midsummer around flowering time when the leaves tend to fade, so that there is a second flush of bright new foliage which will last until the leaves fall in autumn. Propagation is easy from cuttings of the young growths, or by dividing the plant when dormant.

Common lemon balm originated in southern Europe but has made its escape from cultivation and is now found wild in many countries. Though it is a hardy and easy-to-grow lemon flavouring and has medicinal uses too, its first claim to fame was as a plant for bees. Its common names include honey plant and beehive pepper. The scientific name *Melissa* is actually the Greek word for 'bee', and in classical times balm was regarded as indispensable to beekeepers. Like so many labiate herbs, it produces copious nectar, but apparently this is not the only thing that attracts bees. Pliny the Elder proclaimed that bees are 'delighted with this herb above all others' and Virgil recommended a mixture of balm and honeywort (several *Cerinthe* species native to Greece) to induce bees to swarm. At the end of the sixteenth century in England, it was still popular in beekeeping circles, and the herbalist John Gerard wrote that 'It is profitably planted where bees are kept. The hives of bees being rubbed with the leaves of balm causeth the bees to keep together and causeth others to come with them. When they are strayed away, they do find their way home by it.'

Lemon balm has a variety of culinary uses. Its complex volatile oil not only smells of lemons, but contains some of the same elements – citral, for example. Fresh or frozen balm leaves, therefore, make a reasonable substitute for lemon rind in stuffings, soups, sauces, milk desserts and any recipe calling for a hint of lemon. The chopped leaves blended into butter are an interesting garnish for fish. They also go well with melon, or as a flavouring for rhubarb or marrow (summer squash) jam or jelly, and make an unusual addition to salads and omelettes.

Lemon balm really comes into its own in drinks. The dried leaves make one of the nicest herb teas. The lemon flavour can be intensified by the addition of a few lemon verbena leaves (from the half-hardy shrub, *Lippia citriodora*) and served with a slice of lemon. It can be taken hot or iced and is a mild sedative. In herbal medicine lemon balm is combined with other herbs in remedies for anxiety and depression, insomnia, tension headaches and stress-related digestive problems. The very word 'balm' suggests its soothing effect – even more so another of its common names: gentle balm. Being a very safe herb, it can be taken regularly as a tea for pleasure or to ease nervous tension. Hyperactive, highly strung or overexcited children benefit from it especially.

Best of all is lemon balm in long cool summer drinks. Sprigs or whole leaves may be floated in blends of fruit juice and white wine, Pimms or punches, or simply in mineral water. It has even been used to make a white wine and recipes can be found in books on homemade country wines. Another alcoholic beverage based on lemon balm is the cordial known as Carmelite water which enjoyed a great vogue in England after its introduction by the Carmelites in the seventeenth century. A modern version can be made by putting several handfuls of flowering tops of balm into a litre (2 pt)

(*opposite*) Golden creeping Jenny: a ray of sunshine in the dullest summer.
(*above*) 'All Gold': the golden form of lemon balm.

of brandy, together with twists of lemon rind, a little dried angelica root, a tablespoon of coriander seed, two cinnamon sticks, a few cloves and a pinch of grated nutmeg. It should be left for a week, then strained and bottled. For medicinal purposes a tot should be taken twice a day, diluted with spring water. This soothing tonic was particularly recommended for headaches and neuralgia. In the original sense of the word cordial, it would undoubtedly bring comfort to the heart.

Lemon balm produces generous amounts of foliage and when you have snipped off bits to add to food and drinks, there should still be an abundance for drying and a second crop for further uses. Bunches of fresh leaves can be hung under the hot tap for a perfumed bath. The dried leaves, over and above the amount needed for tea, provide the basis for lemon-scented herb pillows, sachets and potpourris. And there are the plants themselves to enjoy, their lemon-coloured leaves glowing against darker foliage and filling the air with the scent of lemons as you gather them.

PINEAPPLE AND GINGER MINTS
Mentha suaveolens 'Variegata' and
M. x *gentilis* 'Variegata'

The invigorating taste and smell of mint is a favourite the world over. Indeed, it is probably the most widely used of all flavourings. Botanists recognize about 25 species of wild mint. They form the genus *Mentha* which belongs to the large family Labiatae. Mints are therefore closely related to many other labiate herbs, such as sage, thyme, rosemary, lavender and basil. Cultivated mints are much less easy to define: a medley of hybrids and cultivars, often of uncertain origin, with characteristics of growth, flavour and aroma that may change according to conditions and vary only slightly from plant to plant. Amid this confusion, two cultivated mints stand out clearly: the green and white variegated woolly mint, known as pineapple mint (M. *suaveolens* 'Variegata') and the yellow-variegated ginger mint (M. x *gentilis* 'Variegata').

Pineapple mint is somewhat fancifully named. It has more of an apple scent, but presumably could not be called this because the plain green M. *suaveolens* was already known as apple mint (though ironically it is scarcely apple-scented). Whatever its exact nature, the clean fruity aroma makes pineapple mint particularly nice in salads. In spring its immaculate green and white foliage forms dense soft mounds which plant lovers and flower arrangers find irresistible. It really is one of the prettiest of all mints, with woolly piebald green and white leaves. Occasionally a pure white shoot is produced with no trace of green at all in its stalk or leaves. This is a perfect ground cover plant, smaller all round than the green apple mint and less invasive, and happy in sun or shade, providing the soil is not too dry – though strong sunshine will scorch the white areas on the leaves. As a foliage plant, it provides a fine contrast to plain green and is dramatic amongst purplish-brown plants. I grow it with *Ajuga reptans* 'Atropurpurea': a colourful and impenetrable partnership.

Ginger mint is also rather misleadingly named as it takes some imagination to detect a gingery note in its aroma. Its subtle spicy perfume blends well with melon and other fruits. The leaves are smooth, neatly pointed and evenly marbled with yellow. In some situations it can take over, popping up all over the place as it methodically expands its terri-

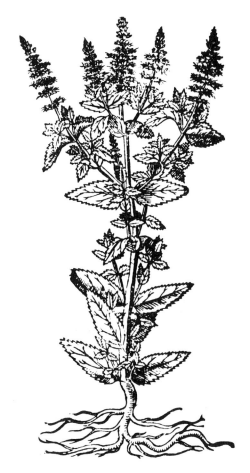

Spearmint (Mentha spicata)

64

tory. As a result, it should be planted where its adventurousness can cause least annoyance – close to larger, more boisterous perennials and low-lying shrubs which will smother its advances. Again, this is a mint for the foliage *aficionado* and flower arranger who always appreciate its gold and lime coloration. Neither pineapple mint nor ginger mint look their best when flowering, so they should be cut back to sprout again.

The genus *Mentha* was named after Minthe, a nymph of Greek mythology who had the misfortune to become the object of Pluto's desires. As a consequence his jealous wife, Persephone, turned her into the herb. Mints are hardy perennials but usually disappear completely in winter, reduced to slender dormant rhizomes. They generally have a creeping rootstock, square stems, opposite leaves, whorled spikes of tiny mauve or pinkish flowers in summer, and a characteristic, but variable minty smell. Many prefer damp, even wet sites. Species of mint are found over most of the world, especially in the northern temperate zones of Eurasia, and in Australia. North America has only one indigenous species, M. *canadensis*, which was used by native peoples long before settlers introduced the many other mints which are now naturalized. In addition to the true mints, there are, in various countries, plants which are known as mints – notably the catmints (*Nepeta* spp) – for a minty scent is not exclusive to the genus *Mentha*.

The smell of mint is quite unmistakable and one that has been enjoyed by human beings for millenia. In peppermint (M. x *piperita*) it is largely due to a fraction of the volatile oil known as menthol. Remains of mint have been found in Egyptian tombs 3,000 years old, and the Japanese have records of menthol production going back over 2,000 years. The extraction of the essential oil is done on a large scale in several countries: England, the United States, Australia, China and Japan are some of the main producers. In England, the area around Mitcham in Surrey

has long been famous for the quality of its peppermint oil. Though peppermint is probably the most important, other mints are also grown for their oils, the best known of which is spearmint (M. *spicata*, formerly known as M. *viridis*). This has quite a different smell, due to the dominance of carvone, rather than methol, in the oil.

Mint contains tannins and bitter substances as well as oils, and the effects of this complex chemistry on the human body are profound. Best known is the decongestant effect, for which menthol is valued in medications for bronchial and nasal congestion. Equally important is its beneficial action on the digestive system, which is why it is included in indigestion remedies – and in after-dinner mints. Basically it improves the bile flow, helping the digestion of fats and relieving spasms of the digestive tract which cause colic and griping pains. It is therefore an excellent household remedy, taken as peppermint tea, for all minor digestive problems.

The most peculiar thing about mint is that it simultaneously warms and cools. It is both a circulatory stimulant, giving a sensation of warmth when swallowed, and a mild anaesthetic, increasing the nerve perception of cold on the skin and mucous membranes. As a result of the latter property, mint is often added to preparations for itching skin conditions to increase their soothing, cooling effects. It is also a traditional remedy for scalp irritations and dandruff. This has recently undergone a revival and several mint shampoos and hair rinses are now on the market. Equally effective is an infusion of peppermint leaves in the final rinsing water.

For most people, mint is synonymous with toothpaste, but what is not generally appreciated is that it not only provides a clean taste, but has a long history of use for whitening the teeth, disinfecting the mouth and freshening the breath. Less familiar is its reputation as an aphrodisiac. The ancient Greeks banned its use by soldiers in the belief that it aroused the passions and diminished courage, and Juliette de Baïracli Levy, in *The Complete Herbal Handbook for Farm and Stable*, recommends it for improving the performance of stallions and bulls. What it does for the female of the species is not recorded, apart from reducing lactation.

For the imaginative cook, few herbs have such potential as mint, for it is equally delicious in sweet or savoury foods and drinks, hot or cold. Peppermint is the world's most popular essential oil, used commercially to flavour confectionery, chocolate, ice cream, chewing gum and liqueurs, as well as medicines and cigarettes. The popularity of mint in the kitchen varies from country to country. It plays little part in French cuisine, whereas it features strongly in Greek, Middle Eastern and Indian food, in which mint is an essential ingredient of various chutneys and salads. Outstanding examples are the Greek mixture of chopped cucumber, mint and yogurt known as *tzatziki*, and the Middle Eastern salad *tabouleh* which is made from bulgur (cracked wheat), parsley and mint. In British cooking, mint is the traditional accompaniment to roast lamb, either in a vinegar sauce or a jelly. Likewise, sprigs of fresh mint are added during the boiling of new potatoes and peas.

Mint-flavoured desserts have a wide appeal, particularly if made with chocolate. A wonderful pale green frosting for a chocolate cake is made by adding *crème de menthe* to icing sugar. Mint sorbets and ice creams are refreshing treats in summer, as is melon, which is as much enhanced by mint as ginger.

Many kinds of drinks owe their appeal to mint. Most famous are *kvass*, a Russian beer made from barley, rye and peppermint, and mint julep, an American concoction of wine, honey, mint and carbonated spring water or ginger ale. Plain simple peppermint tea is one of the most popular of all herb teas. It can be added to apple juice and drunk hot or iced, or to ginger beer. Those who enjoy milk drinks could try a drop of peppermint oil in hot chocolate or a chocolate milk shake.

Cultivating mint is no problem other than that you are likely to have far more than you

(above) As pretty as a flower: the soft green and ivory foliage of pineapple mint.
(opposite) Variegated myrtle: an evergreen, aromatic and floriferous shrub for the conservatory.

need if its progress goes unchecked. Fortunately it is shallow-rooted and quite easy to pull out. Most mints are notoriously invasive, but the reason for this is seldom considered. They appear to be rich feeders, and put out large numbers of runners each year to enable the plant to move onto fresh ground. This strategy ensures that exhausted soil is left behind, minimizing the pests and diseases which affect poorly nourished plants. If mint becomes cramped and starved, as it so often does in the containers generally advised for its restriction, it becomes prone to rust. This is hard to eradicate and often the best solution is to burn affected plants and begin again with new stock on a different site. The disease seldom strikes if plants are well fed in early spring with well-rotted manure or compost and if they are grown alongside other plants, rather than isolated in containers.

If mint should need a helping hand in propagation, it is best done from dormant runners in late winter, or from cuttings of young shoots which root readily in a jar of water or in equal quantities of damp sand and peat. Few cultivated mints come true from seed and it is a seldom-used method of producing stock.

Harvesting mint for kitchen use can be done at any time when there are leaves, checking carefully that the type of mint is suitable for the purpose, as flavours can vary enormously. (Peppermint is best for medicinal use and for drinks and desserts.) Mint dries reasonably well if picked just before flowering on a sunny morning, as this is when the volatile oil content is highest. Bunches should be hung in a warm, airy, shaded place to dry until crisp. Crushing the dried leaves disperses the oils and it is better to store them whole until required. Freezing is an excellent way to preserve mint and the leaves crumble easily while still frozen. Small leaves and tiny sprigs may be frozen in cubes to add to drinks. Preserving mint for mint sauce to accompany lamb is traditionally done by filling jars with finely chopped mint, topping up with cold vinegar and sealing with acid-proof lids. This is then diluted and sweetened for use.

It is estimated that there may be as many as 900 kinds of mint in cultivation worldwide. Most herb nurseries list a dozen or more: some with grey foliage, others dark purplish; in aroma ranging from the heady to the pungent; and in size from the robust 'Bowles Mint' (M. x *villosa* var. *alopecuroides*) at over 1 m (3 ft) tall, to the diminutive prostrate Corsican mint (M. *requienii*) whose leaves measure a millimetre or two and whose flowers are even smaller. There must be a mint for every taste, but for brilliant colour and enticing scents, pineapple and ginger mints are the stars of the multitude.

VARIEGATED MYRTLE
Myrtus communis 'Variegata'

The common myrtle, *Myrtus communis*, is the only European member of the family Myrtaceae. All the rest – some 3,000 species – are denizens of tropical and subtropical regions. Best known is the clove tree (*Syzygium aromaticum* or *Eugenia caryophyllata*), native to the Moluccas, whose dried flower buds have been a valuable article of commerce for centuries, and the many eucalyptuses which are now planted worldwide for their oils and timber.

Myrtus is a genus of about 100 species of tender and half-hardy shrubs and small trees which, characteristically, have aromatic leaves. As a herb, myrtle is less well known than cloves and eucalyptus, yet it has long been valued and cultivated for its fragrance. M. *communis* grows in woods and thickets on hillsides in southern Europe, northern Africa and the Middle East. It is an evergreen small shrub 2.5–3 m (8–10 ft) high, with neatly pointed ovate leaves about 3 cm (1 in) in length, slightly leathery in texture and a glossy dark green in colour. The bark of new shoots is reddish brown, ageing to grey and cracking as it thickens. The wood is prized by woodworkers for turning and inlay work, being hard, fine-grained and a lovely reddish-grey. The delightfully scented flowers are borne singly in the axils on slender red-brown stalks during the summer, their five white (or sometimes pinkish) petals scarcely visible beneath a hemispherical boss of long golden stamens. They are followed by attractive aromatic blue-black berries, 12 mm (½ in) long.

Myrtle has to be given winter protection where long cold spells and heavy frosts occur. It is safest kept above 5°C (41°F), though a touch of frost will only cause superficial damage. In borderline areas, myrtles may survive outdoors if planted in a sunny sheltered place with their backs to a wall. They need good drainage and a fertile, but light soil. Sandy or alkaline soils suit them well. When in growth, they should be given ample water and at no time should they dry out completely. If their chances in the garden are slim, they can be grown in pots as conservatory plants in the winter and placed outside in the summer. They are easy to train as standards and will also thrive as houseplants on a sunny windowsill. Flowering specimens are spectacularly beautiful and scented, and for the rest of the year are attractive evergreens whose fragrant foliage remains neat and tidy. Once a suitable regime has been established, myrtles need little attention other than judicious pruning in the spring to maintain the shape, or to remove frost-damaged shoots on outdoor plants.

All in all, myrtles have much to recommend them and I have never understood why they are not more widely grown. The variegated form is particularly attractive and free-flowering. It has the same habit as the species but its leaves have irregular cream markings, sometimes extending as a border round the margin. When in flower, this variety has a delicacy and charm few other shrubs can match. In cooler climates and in pots they tend to be fairly slow-growing and rarely reach more than 1 m (3 ft), but if space is at a premium there is a dwarf form which could be grown instead. It is smaller all round then the species, with narrower leaves, and likewise comes either plain or variegated. Generally known as 'Tarentina', it is also sometimes listed as 'Nana', 'Microphylla' or 'Jenny Reitenbach'. Myrtles are quite easily propagated from cuttings of non-flowering shoots taken with a heel in summer and placed in sandy compost at 16°C (61°F).

M. *communis* is not just a pretty plant. It is also useful. The aromatic foliage, flowers and fruits have little-known but interesting culinary uses. In southern Europe the leaves are put around roasting meat toward the end of cooking and are traditionally used with lamb, pork and small birds. The wood burns well and makes good charcoal: just the thing for barbecues with a Mediterranean flavour. The fruits have a slightly resinous taste and give an interesting aroma to alcoholic drinks. If dried, they may be ground and used as a spice. In the Middle East they are known as *mursins*.

The healing properties of myrtle are even less known and used, and few herbals mention them. Nevertheless, it is a good antiseptic and astringent. Like all aromatic plants, it contains a volatile oil composed of valuable compounds. One of them, myrtol, is used in medicines to treat gum disease. Another, cineol, is rather like eucalyptol and is effective for bronchial congestion and sinusitis. The compounds are rapidly absorbed when taken internally, giving a violet-like scent to the urine within fifteen minutes of consumption.

Myrtle has been esteemed since biblical times. The prophet Isaiah associated it with goodness, foretelling that 'instead of the brier shall come up the myrtle tree'. The Hebrew name for myrtle is *hadas*, meaning sweetness, from which was derived the name Hadassah

which we now know as Esther. In the English-speaking world, Myrtle is, of course, a girl's name in its own right. The word myrtle is supposedly from the Greek *murtos*, a word for perfume. Both Greeks and Romans regarded myrtle as a symbol of love and honour, making garlands and wreaths from it as a homage to respected members of society. In the Middle East it is carried in wedding bouquets. The foliage is, in fact, excellent for decorative purposes and looks well among cut flowers. In 1981, it was used in the bridal bouquet of Lady Diana Spencer: the sprigs cut from bushes grown from the myrtle in Queen Victoria's bouquet.

The only blot on myrtle's reputation is that later on in classical times it became known as an aphrodisiac which was said to increase inebriation and sensuality if steeped beforehand in the wine. Apart from this, it follows close behind the rose and the lily as a symbol of virginity and chastity. As far as the flowers are concerned, they are much less sensuous than roses and lilies – fragile, ethereal creations which would spoil at a touch. Appropriately, the toilet water made from distilled myrtle is known as *eau d'ange*: angel water.

VARIEGATED OLEANDER
Nerium oleander 'Variegatum'

Oleander is named after the olive because its leaves are similarly slender, dark green and leathery. The resemblance is not very striking, as oleander leaves are longer, more pointed and without silvery undersides, and the plant is definitely a shrub and never achieves the dimensions or appearance of a gnarled old olive tree. Its botanical name, *Nerium oleander*, means 'olive-like plant of moist places', *neros* being a Greek word for damp. Confusingly, it is also sometimes called rosebay, a name shared with willowherb or fireweed (*Epilobium angustifolium*), and is referred to as a rose in the Bible and as rhododendron in Greek literature.

Oleander is an erect shrub reaching about 5 m (16 ft), with a dense mass of upright stems and stiff foliage which tends to point upwards. In summer it bears terminal clusters of large fragrant flowers, usually pink but occasionally white. They measure about 5 cm (2 in) across and have five wedge-shaped petals and a fringe at the opening to the corolla tube. The fruits are borne in pairs and are almost woody, in shape resembling horns some 10 cm (4 in) long. When ripe they split open to release numerous parachute seeds. The beauty of oleander as a flowering shrub has led to its cultivation and naturalization around the world in subtropical regions, but its homelands are watercourses in the Mediterranean region and wadis (seasonal wet places) in North Africa and the Middle East. During winter rains it can often be seen standing in water, protected from the tearing effect of floods by the willow-shaped leaves, which offer little resistance to strong currents.

Oleander belongs to a family known as Apocynaceae, the dogbane family, which has some 1,300 species. They are mostly tropical forest trees, shrubs, and lianas, and include a number of impressively poisonous plants. One of them is *Rauvolfia serpentina*, from which we get the drug reserpine, important in the control of both high blood pressure and schizophrenia. Another is *Catharanthus roseus*, the Madagascan periwinkle, whose alkaloids are used in cancer chemotherapy. Oleander is no exception, as it contains cardiac glycosides which act on the heart in a similar way to the more familiar digitalin, an alkaloid extracted from foxgloves (*Digitalis* spp). One of the substances in its toxic milky juice is pseudo-curarine, which resembles curare, and tribes in central Africa have used oleander for poison darts and arrows. There are several stories about the toxicity of oleander – that simply stirring a hot drink with a twig of oleander is sufficient to poison the drink, and that meat cooked on skewers made from oleander twigs is

likewise deadly. Whatever the truth of these reports, there is no doubt that it is a poisonous plant and sensible precautions should be taken if cultivating it. With good reason the Victorian flower emblemists took it to symbolize 'Beware!'

It goes without saying that oleander is not a herb for home use, but herbalists value it for treating heart conditions. Externally, a lotion made from the leaves is a useful remedy for scabies and lice.

On a more pleasant note, oleander is one of the few members of the dogbane family that is scented. It cannot compare with its relative frangipani (*Plumeria rubra*) which is one of the most fragrant flowers in the world, but in terms of beauty it is in the same league. There are some lovely varieties available now, including the double cerise 'Géant des Batailles', 'Luteum Plenum', a semi-double primrose, and

(opposite) Variegation gives year-round interest to the dull green leaves of oleander.
(above) The dramatic black form of basil.

'Soeur Agnes', a variety with single white flowers which dates back to at least Victorian times. Although these are magnificent when in full flower, they are rather dull for the rest of the year; a disappointment when they take up precious greenhouse or conservatory space. This is where the variegated form comes into its own, either as a specimen plant or grown among other oleanders to brighten an expanse of dull green leaves. Even without the attractive pink flowers, it is worth growing for its fine foliage. The variegation takes the form of irregular cream margins to the leaves, though occasionally a whole leaf may be cream. Like the species, it has pink flowers.

Oleanders need full sun, ample water when producing new leaves and flower buds, and a rich sandy loam (ideally, two parts loam and one part each of sand, well-rotted manure and leafmould). If grown in pots, they should be kept on the dry side during the winter, at a minimum of 7°C (44°F). When grown in cooler climates than their native Mediterranean, a common complaint is that the flowers fail to develop. This is usually because they do not get enough warmth in spring. In fact, it is best to keep them in a greenhouse or conservatory until the first flowers are starting to open, or the flowers may be retarded. After that they may be placed outside in a sheltered spot – a 'sun trap' if possible – until the nights become chilly with the advancing autumn. They should be fed every two weeks, and a high potash feed toward the end of the growing season will help ripen growths for next year's flowering.

Pruning should be done immediately after flowering, by cutting back the flowering shoots by half and the laterals to 10 cm (4 in). Propagation is either by seed sown at 18–21°C (64–70°F), or by half-ripe cuttings, with a heel, taken in summer and put into equal parts peat and sand at 16–18°C (61–64°F). Cuttings will also root in water if kept in a warm place. Oleanders are generally trouble-free, but in adverse conditions may be attacked by oleander scale, mealy bug and red spider.

The oleander was introduced to northern Europe as long ago as 1596, where it has been cultivated ever since as a greenhouse plant. Currently its popularity is increasing as conservatories, sun lounges, and patios continue to gain favour. These areas serve as extensions of both the home and garden where tender subjects, such as olives and oleanders, acacias, citruses and bougainvilleas, can be grown and enjoyed even when the weather is wet and cold. They will provide interest and colour for many months of the year – all year round in the case of the variegated oleander – as well as creating a genial atmosphere, encouraging relaxation and conjuring up memories of their warm and sunny origins.

BLACK BASIL
Ocimum basilicum 'Purpurascens' (syn. 'Dark Opal' and 'Violaceum')

Unlike most popular culinary herbs, basil is not Mediterranean in origin, even though it has been an integral part of southern European cooking for several hundred years. It belongs to the same family as such Mediterranean herbs as sage, thyme, rosemary and oregano – which are all labiates (Labiatae) – but was introduced from India via the Middle East, reaching Europe in the sixteenth century and North America in the century following.

The basil we are most familiar with is sweet basil, *Ocimum basilicum*, which reaches about 50 cm (20 in) and which, in most temperate regions, is grown as a half-hardy annual. It has opposite pairs of smooth bright green ovate leaves and insignificant two-lipped white or pinkish flowers. Less often seen are the more ornamental forms, the most widely available being *O. basilicum* 'Purpurascens', which is also known as 'Violaceum' and 'Dark Opal'. It has the same fragrance, habit and size as the species, but the foliage is a dramatic blackish-purple, complemented by magenta flowers. Not all plants grown from seed will be uniformly purple, some being an attractive half-way form with purple and green marbling. Among other culinary herbs, 'Purpurascens' gives an exciting accent of colour: planted in the flower border it provides a fine contrast to grey foliage and is an unusual subject for subtropical bedding.

The scent of basil is hard to describe: 'a strong healthy scent' as the seventeenth-century herbalist Nicholas Culpeper put it, reminiscent of cloves and coriander seed, slightly camphoraceous, but very sweet. Another variety, *O. basilicum* var. *minimum*, generally known as bush basil, has smaller leaves with a more resinous scent which is not quite as good for culinary use, though certainly acceptable. Bush basil may lose a few marks for flavour, but gains on its more equable disposition, often succeeding where the species is doomed to failure through low summer temperatures and lack of sunlight.

The genus *Ocimum* includes about 100 species, many of which are highly aromatic and useful in a number of different ways. One of the most interesting is *O. sanctum*, the holy or sacred basil, a small shrub of great importance in the Hindu religion. Sacred to Krishna and Vishnu, *tulsi*, as it is known in India, is grown around temples and in pots on pedestals in orthodox homes. A leaf is placed on the breast of a dead believer, and the plant is so revered that during British rule in India Hindus were permitted to take an oath on it in court. Another fascinating basil is the tea bush or fever plant (*O. viride*) of West Africa. Its leaves smell like lemon thyme and, as the name suggests, it is used to make a tea for feverish illnesses. Basil is an important herb in many parts of Africa as well as in Asia, both for medicinal and ritual uses – the Fang tribe chew the leaves to calm the nerves and give inspiration before speaking at a 'palaver'. Several basils have insecticidal properties. *O. gratissimum*, the tree or shrubby basil, is widely grown in India, Africa, Sri Lanka and South America to deter mosquitoes. It has an intense lemon fragrance, hairy leaves and yellow flowers. Other interesting basils include the large *O. kilimandsharicum*, a shrub 3 m (10 ft) tall, which is the most camphoraceous of all and is grown commercially as a source of camphor; *O. menthaefolium* from Egypt and the Sudan, with a strong minty smell; and *O. crispum*, a Japanese species whose purple leaves are, believe it or not, made into a decoction to increase the redness of radishes!

The Latin name *Ocimum* seems to be derived from a Greek word meaning 'to smell', which is appropriate for such an aromatic genus. The meaning of *basilicum* is less obvious, however. One explanation is that it means 'kingly', with the implication that 'the smell thereof is so excellent that it is fit for a king's house', as the herbalist Parkinson wrote. Another is that it has to do with the fabulous mythical serpent-like creature, the basilisk,

Basil (Ocimum basilicum)

whose glance and breath were fatal and who killed all living things in its path, splitting rocks, and poisoning water wherever it drank. This last association is linked with the strange reputation basil has had in the past. Regardless of its glorious aroma, it was always considered an evil and controversial plant. According to the old herbalists who provided astrological interpretations of a herb's qualities, basil is ruled by Mars and influenced by Scorpio, which accounted for the sting in its tail.

This link with the scorpion has led to some extraordinary stories. It might be expected, in the warmer countries where basil is grown, that scorpions might occasionally congregate under pots, but it is quite another thing to claim that pieces of basil left under a pot will turn into scorpions, or that, with a little help from a magic spell, scorpions can be created by crushing basil between two stones (though if this pulp is left in the sun, it will engender worms instead). Oddest of all is the belief that smelling basil – an obviously tempting thing to do – would lead to scorpions breeding in one's brain. A case of this was once sworn to have happened to an acquaintance by a French

physician who was aptly named Hilarius. This grisly tale can only be bettered by the story of Lisabetta (first told by Boccaccio in the *Decameron* and later by John Keats in the poem 'Isabella or the Pot of Basil'), who buried her murdered lover's head in a potful of the herb and watered the plants with her tears. And 'love washed with tears' is just what basil symbolizes in Crete to this day. The only good thing about this unpleasant side to an otherwise delightful herb is that as 'every like draws its like', it can be used as an antidote to the sting of a scorpion and is reputedly effective in relieving insect bites and stings, applied as fresh juice or crushed leaves.

The legendary virulent quality of basil was no doubt behind the arguments it used to provoke among herbalists. Culpeper wrote: 'This is the herb which all authors are together by the ears about, and rail at one another (like lawyers). Galen and Dioscorides hold it not fit to be taken inwardly; and Chrysippus rails at it with downright Billingsgate rhetoric; Pliny the Elder, and the Arabian physicians defend it.' Though he eventually came down in favour, he ended his account on a note of ambiguity: 'To conclude, it expels both birth and afterbirth, and as it helps the deficiency of Venus in the one kind so it spoils all her actions in another. I dare write no more of it.'

Fortunately, modern herbal medicine has come up with more rational explanations of this plant's chemistry and effects on the body. Basil contains a potent essential oil, basil camphor, saponins (soap-like substances) and tannins. Basil oil is very similar in aroma to that of mignonette (*Reseda odorata*) and is used as a substitute in perfumery, as mignonette flowers yield very little. The effects of the oil and other constituents are mainly on the digestive system. Basil is an antispasmodic for stomach cramps and wind, nausea, diarrhoea and vomiting, or constipation of nervous origin. Some headaches and migraines have a dietary origin too and may respond to basil, as may travel sickness. In spite of its former reputation, basil is no more toxic than any other culinary herb (though all contain substances that, in excess, could be harmful) and may be taken as a tea for occasional minor complaints. Neither should we fear for our lives by inhaling its aroma!

Given the popularity of basil in cooking today, it is almost unbelievable that it was once regarded as unfit for consumption. Basil is essential for many dishes and has no substitute, with the result that most herb growers find that demand for the fresh herb usually exceeds supply. The two best known dishes that require basil are *soupe au pistou* from Nice and *pesto* sauce from Genoa (*pistou* and *pesto* both mean basil). The latter is a concentrated paste made from basil leaves pounded together with pine kernels, parmesan and sardo (a hard Sardinian sheep's milk cheese), garlic, salt and olive oil, which is served, in small amounts, on top of pasta. Basil is renowned as the perfect accompaniment to tomatoes in any kind of dish, whether raw, stuffed, in soups or casseroles. It is also excellent with peppers, aubergines, mushrooms and olives, as well as adding an incomparable flavour to wine vinegar and olive oil if a sprig is added to the bottle and left to impart its aroma.

Traditionally basil was preserved by drying or by packing into jars in salted layers which were finally covered with olive oil. Nowadays, for simplicity, ease of use and flavour retention, freezing is hard to beat. Just put whole sprigs into polythene bags and, when frozen, crush with a rolling pin and remove the tough main stalks. Then return to the freezer and take out spoonfuls as needed, resealing each time.

The only problem with developing a taste for this king of herbs is that of getting enough of it in its fresh state. Seeds need brisk warmth for germination and seedlings a genial but buoyant atmosphere to prevent mildew. As one might expect from its tropical origins, basil likes to bask in full sun and enjoys ample warmth, perfect drainage and good feeding. In cool wet dull weather it will damp off, lose its roots, wilt and die with remarkable alacrity.

Growing basil out of doors in regions where chilly damp summers are likely can only be successful with luck and good management. One of the best solutions is to grow it in pots – three to a 30 cm (12 in) diameter pot – which can be whisked inside during an inclement spell. Unlike many other herbs which are better flavoured if grown 'hard', basil is best when young and tender. It can even be grown in seed trays, like giant salad cress, but sown much more thinly and snipped off when 7–15 cm (3–6 in) high.

According to the Greeks and Romans, basil grows better if verbally abused. In my experience as a herb grower in England, where cloudy wet weather is all too frequent, there are few summers when it is possible to grow it without resorting to this extreme – although the worse curses usually fall belatedly upon the dead and the dying and seem to have little success in goading them back into life. But however great the frustrations, there is nothing to compare with the reward of picking your own basil leaves from plants that you have had the pleasure of enjoying first for their richly colourful foliage. A pot of basil – all purple or a mixture of purple and green – will, I assure you, harbour nothing but delight.

GOLDEN AND GOLDEN-TIPPED MARJORAMS
Origanum vulgare 'Aureum' and 'Variegatum'

There has always been a good deal of confusion over exactly what is meant by oregano and marjoram. The fact is that they do not refer to specific plants, but are general terms for several different species with similar flavours. Most belong to the genus *Origanum*, but one source of culinary dried oregano is from a quite different family, the Verbenaceae. Mexican oregano, which is harvested

for sale in the United States, is from either *Lippia graveolens*, a species found in southern Mexico, or *L. palmeri* from northern Mexico – both of which smell and taste like oreganums.

The genus *Origanum* belongs to the family Labiatae and has about 25 species all told, a number of which are widely used for culinary and medicinal purposes. They include sweet or knotted marjoram (*O. majorana*, also known as *Majorana hortensis*), a half-hardy species with small grey-green leaves and knots of tiny white flowers; pot marjoram (*O. onites*), a native of Sicily, which entered cultivation in northern Europe before the end of the six-teenth century; and wild marjoram or oregano (*O. vulgare*), a widespread European species which only develops its full pungency in the south of its range. The latter is perhaps the most confusing of all as there is no comparison in flavour between plants growing, say, on the chalk downs of southern England and those on the limestone hillsides of Greek islands. Though both situations are dry and sunny, there is never enough light or warmth in northern Europe for the plants to produce the

Golden-tipped marjoram. When the colour fades in summer, it should be cut down to produce a second flush of neatly painted leaves.

good quality, abundant essential oils that characterize those in Mediterranean regions. Happily though, all are usable and have a more or less thyme-like fragrance, only warmer and sweeter. Indeed, the main components of the volatile oil (thymol and carvacrol) are the same as in thyme oil. Like thymes, marjorams and oreganos dry well for use in the winter.

If you live anywhere that does not have a Mediterranean climate, you must resign your-self to growing slightly insipid, though still delightfully fragrant, marjoram. Choosing the warmest driest sunniest spot in the garden will obviously encourage plants to produce more oil, but they will grow quite satisfactorily in less favoured situations, and even tolerate partial shade. Sweet marjoram (*O. majorana*) has an excellent flavour and its pale grey-green foliage and white flowers are just right for the front of silver borders. However, it is only perennial in frost-free places. The best general-purpose marjoram is probably O. *vulgare*. Much of what is sold as dried oregano is collected in southern Italy from plants of this species. It is perfectly hardy and easy to grow. As a bonus, its great appeal as a garden plant is that a number of attractive forms are available. There are both compact (O. *vulgare* 'Compactum') and golden compact (O. *vulgare* 'Compactum Aureum') forms, but to my mind the best are the golden and golden-tipped varieties (O. *vulgare* 'Aureum' and 'Variegatum').

Choosing which ornamental form of marjoram to grow presents some problems. Arguably, there is nothing to choose between them in spring when all are neat and bright. As the season advances, however, the compact one loses its shape and the golden compact form scorches badly. Admittedly the golden-tipped form fades as it elongates, but its unusual bicoloured variegation, in which each leaf is symmetrically green at the base and yellow at the apex, is so bewitching that I would rather have it in perfection for three months than not grow it at all. Best of all for colour retention is the golden marjoram with yellow springtime foliage which turns lime-green in the summer. Like most golden forms, it colours best in full sun. Though nowhere near as sensitive as the golden compact form – whose fragile rounded leaves go brown and crisp at the edges so readily – it may scorch in high light intensities, but no worse than many other yellow-leaved plants. I find it a joy throughout the growing season and it can be cut down just before or after flowering for a new flush of colourful leaves that will last until it dies down for winter dormancy.

O. *vulgare* is found wild over much of Europe, Asia and northern Africa. It is also naturalized in North America, especially around the Catskill Mountains in New York State, where it was introduced by the early settlers who valued it as a medicinal plant. It is a hardy perennial with a woody creeping rhizome and tough stems reaching 30–60 cm (1–2 ft) tall. Though not invasive, it will increase steadily over the years and eventually form large clumps. These may be divided in the winter to keep the plant within bounds. For purposes of propagation, small chunks, complete with shoots and roots, can be detached during dormancy or early spring. In the summer the stems branch and produce corymbs of tiny pale pink to mauve flowers with purplish bracts. The two-lipped flowers are rich in nectar and attract large numbers of insects, including honey bees and butterflies. The leaves are small (rarely over 4 cm/1½ in long), oval, soft and slightly downy. For medicinal use, the top 10 cm (4 in) of the plant is gathered while flowering and used dried or fresh. Leaves for culinary use may be picked at any time in the growing season, though for drying they will have the best flavour in early summer just before flowering.

Wild marjoram's favourite situations are sunny well-drained calcareous slopes and dry grassy areas. The word *Origanum* is derived from the Greek *oros*, meaning 'mountain', and *ganos*, 'joy'. Anyone who has encountered it on a mountain hike is bound to agree on the appropriateness of its name. *Vulgare* is the Latin for 'common', and fortunately it is just that – so much so that I could always count on finding some to add to my sandwiches when climbing in Greece. There are about ten different species of *Origanum* in Greece, the commonest being O. *vulgare*. The Greeks have a saying that if marjoram grows on a grave, it's a sign that the deceased is in a state of happiness. Knowing how much pleasure it can bring to the living, this seems a reasonable belief to hold.

The fragrance of marjoram is sweet, with a hint of balsam that, for centuries, made it one of the leading herbs for perfumery and strewing floors. William Coles, who published *The Art of Simpling* in 1656, described how in his time 'it is used in all odoriferous waters, powders, etc.: and is a chief ingredient in most of those powders that barbers use, in whose shops I have seen great store of this herb hanged up.'

Nowadays marjoram and oregano are best

known for their contribution to the Italian recipes which have entered international cuisine: the ever-popular pizzas and pasta-based dishes. Generally it is the pungent dried oregano that is used to enliven almost anything containing tomatoes, mushrooms, aubergines (egg plants), courgettes (zucchini), marrow (summer squash), cheese or beans (including chilli beans). It is also excellent with most meat. In Greece it is a favourite with lamb, and in Germany one of its names is *Wurstkraut* because of its importance as an ingredient in different kinds of sausage. Northern marjorams are sweeter and less peppery and are therefore subtle enough for egg dishes, cottage cheese and such like.

An appetizing flavour is not the only contribution that marjoram makes to our diet. Some of its medicinal uses concern the digestive system. If taken before a meal it stimulates the bile flow, aiding the digestion of fats. It also relieves wind and colic and has been prescribed for morning sickness in pregnancy and for travel sickness. In addition, bronchial complaints and the feverish stages of diseases such as measles, respond well to its antiseptic, stimulant properties. Used externally, a strong infusion is effective for wax in the ears, toothache, sore throats, thrush and hoarseness. The herb can also be heated in oil or cold cream for massaging rheumatic and neuralgic aches and pains. In the 1636 edition of John Gerard's *Herball*, it says that 'organy' or 'wilde marjerome' 'cureth them that have drunk opium, or the juice of black poppy, or hemlocks, especially if it be given with wine and raisins of the sun'. This use goes back a long time as the ancient Greeks are known to have prescribed it for narcotic poisoning.

If there is such a thing as an all-purpose herb, marjoram certainly comes near to it. The present-day herbalist Maurice Mességué confirms that it 'clears the system of toxins' and is an excellent treatment for all problems characterized by sluggishness, congestion and blockages. He also reckons that marjoram is a wonderful relaxant and will ease stresses and strains of all kinds, from the throes of love and feeling at one's wits' end, to over-excitement and insomnia. Indeed, the herb is so high in his estimation that he regards it 'as an unforgiveable omission not to grow marjoram in your garden'. I tend to agree, adding only that the golden and golden-tipped forms of *O. vulgare* should come high on the list of priorities.

DOUBLE PINK PEONY
Paeonia officinalis 'Rosea Plena'

Whenever I see an abandoned garden I am reminded of the two that came into my possession. The first was when I was a student. My upstairs bedsitter looked out on a cherry tree which was the main highway for a family of squirrels. In spring the view from my window was a confection of pink blossoms. Beneath it was the derelict garden. One irresistible blue-skied day I ventured down to explore this miniature urban wilderness. Apart from a clump of peonies, most of the garden's refined inhabitants had been taken over by ground elder, couch grass and dandelions which, liberated from persecution, were now triumphantly tall and lush. I was bewitched at the sight of the dark blood-red flowers in the dappled shade of the cherry tree which showered them and me with pastel petals at each shiver of wind. They were 'Rubrum Plenum', the double form of *Paeonia officinalis*.

My second wild garden was in a very different setting, belonging to a cottage in a small downland village. There was no cherry tree – instead wild roses and flowering privet released from the confines of shrub and hedge – but there again, amidst the ubiquitous ground elder and couch grass, was a clump of peonies. I discovered them as they first came into growth and looked forward to the splendour of their huge ruby red flowers among the weeds.

The double pink peony (bud and open flower) which survived in the derelict garden that came into my possession. I call it 'Rosea Plena' but its identity is uncertain.

Instead, they surprised and delighted me by turning out pink, and have ever since been my favourites.

In the wild, the single flowers of *P. officinalis* are usually crimson and globe-shaped with centres of yellow stamens. They are not particularly common, but can be found in meadows and woods at up to 1,700 m (5,600 ft) in the southern Alps and central Apennines, and ocasionally elsewhere in southern Europe. White- and pink-flowered plants occur too, and all three colours have double forms which are longer-lasting. The commonest, and probably the toughest, is the dark red double 'Rubra Plena', a favourite cottage garden plant since its introduction to northern Europe in 1548. Less often seen today are the double white, 'Alba Plena', whose blush pink flowers age to white, and 'Rosea Plena' with double pink blooms which also fade as they age. Either they were always less common, or they are less robust, but few now survive in gardens and even fewer are planted now that there are so many hybrids to choose from. Scarcer still is the species in its single red form, whose cultivation is now mostly confined to botanic and medicinal herb gardens.

The genus *Paeonia* has 33 species and occurs in Europe, China and north-west America. It was once classified as belonging to the buttercup family, Ranunculaceae, but now stands alone in its own family, Paeoniaceae. Peonies may be herbaceous or shrubby, but all are perennial and rhizomatous. Many are worthy of cultivation and two in particular have been the subject of passionate crazes. In China, the peony once had no equal. *P. lactiflora* (sometimes referred to as *P. albiflora*), the *shaoyao*, has white, scented flowers and is the parent of many fragrant double hybrids. It was cultivated in China as long ago as 900 BC and one collection is recorded as having 60,000 plants. The tree peony or moutan (*P. suffruticosa* or *P. moutan*) was similarly adored, especially in the first century AD when the summer palace of the Emperor Ming Huang had a garden filled with over 10,000 plants in many different varieties.

Peonies are not only beautiful. Behind the neatly cut foliage and goblet-shaped flowers is a wealth of folklore and an interesting chemistry. Several species have been used medicinally, notably *P. officinalis*, *P. mascula* (another red-flowered European species) and the Chinese species just mentioned. In many old herbals, *P. officinalis* is referred to as the female peony and *P. mascula* as the male, though this is not a botanical distinction (all peony flowers are bisexual). Few herbalists today use the European species, but the oriental species are still part of the Chinese herbal pharmacopoeia. In their efforts to integrate traditional and western medicine, the Chinese have tested these herbs and found that *P. lactiflora*, which was traditionally used as a tonic, is antibacterial and inhibits fungal infections; and that *P. suffruticosa*, which was used for fevers and dissolving blood clots caused by wounds, is also antibacterial and effectively lowers blood pressure.

P. officinalis contains an alkaloid and other toxic constituents which, together, have sedative and diuretic effects, also constricting blood vessels and, in women, causing uterine contractions. Peony extracts are also rich in benzoic acid, a substance found in many natural resins, which is used as a food preservative and in the manufacture of dyes, paints and plastics. Medicinally, decoctions of peony roots or seeds were mostly taken for kidney and gall stones, varicose veins, haemorrhoids, expelling afterbirths and especially for complaints involving nervousness and spasms: epilepsy, chorea (St Vitus's dance), nervous twitches and nightmares. In the Middle Ages, illnesses of nervous origin were often regarded as manifestations of lunacy, for which the peony was a sovereign cure. In many cases it was sufficient to cover a lunatic with the plant when he lay down and 'soon he upheaveth himself whole'. Necklaces of the seeds or roots were also considered effective.

The knobbly roots, seeds or petals are used medicinally – the petals being the most poisonous part but the roots and seeds apparently posing the worst problems of collection. For, according to classical authorities, such as Pliny the Elder and Theophrastus, the peony cannot be touched without risking life and limb. By the time Gerard wrote his herbal in 1597, 'such kindes of trifles, and most superstitious and wicked ceremonies' were a thing of the past (or almost). He makes it quite clear that he has no time for tethering a hungry dog to the peony (or to the mandrake plant, which needed the same device) and getting it to do the pulling while you make encouraging noises over a piece of meat. Neither would he go out at dead of night to harvest the seeds, guided by their phosphorescent glow, in order to avoid being seen by woodpeckers and struck blind. Whether or not these superstitions originated with Theophrastus (a Greek philosopher and botanist who lived in the fourth century BC), his mention of the peony is probably the earliest. It was apparently named after Paeon, physician to the Greek gods who was later turned into a peony to escape some dreadful fate or other and then worshipped as the god of healing. From his name also comes the word 'paean', a song of praise.

P. officinalis and its double forms are excellent garden plants. They reach about 70 cm (28 in), with divided leaves of 'a dead green colour', as Culpeper describes them, and in early summer produce many flowers 10–13 cm (4–5 in) across, followed by horn-shaped seed pods which split open to reveal red seeds which turn shiny black when ripe. Peonies prefer rich moist soil on the alkaline side, in sun or partial shade. Though the plants are resilient and hardy, protection from early morning sun will prevent late frosts from damaging the buds. An annual mulch with well rotted manure or compost will pay dividends in terms of the quantity and quality of the flowers. The commonest problem with peonies is that the buds stay hard and small and fail to open. This may be caused by frost damage, dryness at the roots, or starvation. It also tends to happen after transplanting and other root disturbance, or when planting too deep. (Peonies must never be planted more than 5 cm (2 in) below the surface.) The various forms and hybrids do not come true from seed and must be propagated by division when dormant.

Planting a peony is rather like planting a tree. They are plants to last a lifetime, outliving the gardener – and, in many cases, the garden too. Year after year the peony will produce its gracious flowers, however long it may be since the gardener departed and however overgrown the garden.

DOUBLE PINK OPIUM POPPY
Papaver somniferum 'Rosea Plena'

The opium poppy has enthralled mankind for over 5,000 years. Opium is as old as

Double opium poppy (Papaver somniferum) 'Rosea Plena'

medicine itself and there has never been – and may never be – a painkiller to equal it. The uses of this herb were described on clay tablets by the Sumerians, a south-west Asian people whose civilization was at its height in the fourth millenium BC. The ancient Greeks found it indispensable too, and images of poppy capsules are common in Greek art. They dedicated the herb to Nyx, goddess of night; Thanatos, god of death; Hypnos, god of sleep; and his son Morpheus, god of dreams. It is further celebrated for its beauty, with seductive muted shades and a dignified habit which single it out from the gaudier, more untidy members of the poppy clan. The sombre colouring matches its reputation, having a twilight quality, as if faded into the greys of dusk and dawn seen through half-closed eyes. Its scientific name, *Papaver somniferum*, means soporific poppy.

Wild opium poppies are very variable. They originated in the eastern Mediterranean region, but probably reached central Europe as long ago as the Neolithic age. Over thousands of years of cultivation, both as ornamentals and as a crop, many different varieties have arisen which vary mainly in flower and seed colour. Plants are generally 1 m (3 ft) tall and upright, with the main stalk ending in the largest flower (some 10–15 cm (4–6 in) across) and several side branches bearing proportionally smaller blooms. Both stalks and foliage are a dull pale grey-green, overlaid with a waxy bloom. The leaves clasp the stalk and are roughly oblong in shape, with irregular undulations and toothed margins. As with most hardy annuals, flowering takes place in the summer. The flower buds are drooping at first, becoming erect and casting the glaucous protective sepals on the morning of opening to release four fragile crinkled petals which expand like a butterfly emerging from a chrysalis. There is a great variety of petal colour, from white or dusky mauve with a dark purple or white blotch at the base, to a range of pinks and reds. Sometimes the petals are fringed and double flowers are quite common. In the centre of the flower is the familiar capsule – a goblet-shaped seed vessel with lightly ribbed sides and a scalloped cap. When the flower opens, it is small and surrounded by a circle of pollen-laden stamens. As the petals fall – which is within a day or so of unfolding – the capsule begins to swell, reaching the size of an egg in some varieties. When ripe, it turns brown and hard with a ring of perforations beneath the cap, through which the round seeds are shaken like pepper from a pepper pot. The seeds may be white, cream, pinkish, blue-grey, brown or black, according to the variety. There may be anything from 800–32,000 seeds in a single capsule and, as they are small enough to stick to birds' feet, it is no surprise that opium poppies tend to pop up in gardens for miles around after one gardener has planted them.

The opium poppy is simplicity to grow in a sunny position and any well-drained neutral to alkaline soil. For the gardener, the only problem is likely to be the usual one with poppies – that they are difficult to transplant and must be sown (in autumn or spring) where required. Unfortunately, another – and insurmountable – problem may arise for some gardeners; namely, that it is illegal to grow them, even for ornamental purposes in some countries. The easiest way of finding out whether such restrictions apply is to look in seed catalogues. If opium poppies are offered, the implication is that you are free to grow them. However, they are rarely referred to as such. Sometimes the botanical name, *Papaver somniferum*, is not given either, but you can be sure that poppies listed as 'Paeony-flowered' or 'Danebrog' are forms of the opium poppy. The former has large fully double flowers which, as the name suggests, resemble peonies. They are mostly available in mixed colours or in a pale salmon pink known as 'Pink Beauty'. 'Danebrog' is a striking single variety with bright red, fringed petals and large white basal blotches which form a Maltese cross around the capsule. It has been listed by British seed merchants for over a hundred years.

Though 'Danebrog' poppies are showstoppers, and 'Paeony-flowered' forms may be attractive in a blowsy kind of way, to my mind the double fringed 'Rosea Plena' is the loveliest ornamental form. Its shaggy pale-rose flowers harmonize well with the pastel sea-green foliage and have a befittingly forlorn look. In Victorian times a similarly double-fringed variety was listed as 'Mursellii'. I like to grow double opium poppies in a group in the border but prefer to let the single ones sow themselves here and there, weeding out the crowded and badly placed. Both are rewarding garden plants: alive with bees in the heat of the day: eerie in the stillness of the night; and continuing in interest after flowering as the

81

Here in its shaggy double pink form, the opium poppy looks befittingly forlorn.

decorative capsules develop.

Opium poppies are not herbs for amateur use as they contain dangerously toxic and addictive substances. They are grown on a large scale for the pharmaceutical industry, as the medical profession uses upwards of 750 tons of opium annually and it cannot be synthesized. The commercial crop is harvested between nine and fifteen days after petal fall: a labour-intensive business in which the green capsules are lanced with multi-bladed knives several times, at intervals of a few days. A white latex exudes from the cuts and is scraped off when congealed to a brown putty-like consistency. This is crude opium. It contains about 25 alkaloids, the most important of which is morphine. (Codeine is another.) Morphine was first isolated by the German pharmacist Friedrich Sertürner in 1815 and named after the Greek god of sleep, Morpheus. Not all the opium poppy's alkaloids are pain-killers, neither are they all addictive, but of those that are, morphine is incomparable in its effects. In its long history of use, it has undoubtedly soothed more pain than any other drug and, in spite of the many advances in medicine this century, is still the drug of choice for severely painful illnesses and accidents. On the other hand, it has left a trail of casualties, through addiction, that also knows no equal.

Addiction is nothing new. Opium has been eaten, smoked and sniffed for many centuries. Avicenna, the great Arab physician, died of an overdose of opium in 1037 in Persia, where eating opium as a recreational drug may have begun. There are, however, several landmarks in its spread. In the seventeenth century, opium was introduced to China from Java and rapidly gained a hold. Notorious opium dens and serious social problems caused the authorities to ban it, but by then British traders were making such profits from imports into China (most of the Royal Navy's income was dependent on opium) that the edicts were ignored and Britain and China engaged in the ignominious Opium Wars of the 1840s. At the end of the conflict, the defeated Chinese ceded Hong Kong to Britain and the bitterness of their defeat was to culminate in the revolt against imperialism which has dominated twentieth-century China.

As the Elizabethan rhyme 'John Silverpin, fair without and foul within' suggests, the opium poppy's beauty belies an offensive taste and smell. This barrier to consumption was partly solved in the seventeenth century when Paracelsus, the extraordinary Swiss physician and alchemist, first dissolved crude opium in alcohol to make a tincture known as laudanum. This more palatable preparation – affectionately known as 'loddy' by the British public – increased consumption greatly, initially as a household medicine for diarrhoea and coughs. In Victorian England, 20 tons of opium a year were consumed for minor complaints and quasi-medical purposes. Many preparations contained it, including Mother Bailey's Quieting Syrup for fractious babies. As a result, addiction often began with a seemingly innocuous remedy given for a childhood complaint. Though the Industrial Revolution and its attendant urban miseries caused an increase in the use of laudanum to relieve stress (it was,

according to a certain Miss Kent, 'so much used instead of tea by the poorer class of females in Manchester and other manufacturing towns'), people in all walks of life came to depend on it. Among the famous are the poet Samuel Taylor Coleridge, who wrote the poem 'Kubla Khan' under its influence; the reformer William Wilberforce; Jane Austen's mother, who took it to ward off tiredness (in small doses it is a stimulant); Clive of India, who died of an overdose; French film director and writer, Jean Cocteau; poet Charles Baudelaire; and perhaps best known of all, Thomas de Quincey, the English essayist and critic who called himself 'Pope of the true church of opium' and in 1821 published his account of opium's 'abyss of divine enjoyment' in *Confessions of an English Opium Eater*.

The second half of the nineteenth century saw the invention of the hypodermic needle and the advent of heroin – a stronger form of morphine created by the addition of a chemical closely related to acetic acid (vinegar). Ironically, when heroin first came onto the market, it was claimed to be less addictive than morphine, but in spite of the fact that it rapidly breaks down to morphine once in the body, the opposite proved to be the case.

Since then, opium and heroin addiction have continued to increase worldwide. As early as 1909, representatives from thirteen nations met to discuss the problem and initiate measures to curb addiction and illicit trading. More and more countries have subsequently joined the campaign, some banning the growing of opium altogether, others strictly regulating cultivation, harvesting and processing. Up to the 1960s, most opium production, licit and illicit, took place in Asia, mainly in India and Turkey. Nowadays, New Zealand holds the record for the highest yields of morphine per hectare and produces about 20 per cent of the world's codeine. Apparently, the sunnier the climate, the greater amount of alkaloids.

Though the medicinal uses of the opium poppy are paramount, it is also grown for its edible and oil-producing seeds which are free from alkaloids. Indian seeds are very tiny and cream-coloured and are added to curries as a flavouring and thickener. Blue-grey seeds are favoured in Europe and the Middle East, where they are used as a topping or filling for breads, cakes and pastries. They have a delicious nutty flavour when baked and are indispensable in some recipes: sprinkled on Jewish bagels (hard doughnut-shaped bread rolls), for example. The cold-pressed oil from the seed is known as *olivette* in France and is excellent for salad dressings and cooking. Subsequent pressings employ heat and give a drying oil for artists' oil paints, which is superior to linseed oil. The high protein residue is turned into livestock feed.

Economically the opium poppy is by far the most important of the 250 species of the family Papaveraceae. In the world of legend, it is told that the Buddha cut off his eyelids so that sleep would not disrupt his meditation. Where they fell to the ground, up grew opium poppies – greatest of all sleep-inducers – whose formidable chemistry has the power of ministering angel and tormenting devil over human life. For most of us, though, it remains just a homely kitchen spice and lovely garden annual, albeit one with an awesome history.

VARIEGATED SCENTED GERANIUMS
Pelargonium crispum 'Variegatum',
P. x *fragrans* 'Variegatum' and
P. 'Lady Plymouth'

Scented geraniums (or pelargoniums, if you prefer) are living potpourris, their rich and varied scents filling the air as you pass. They are not showy plants like their relatives, the zonal and regal pelargoniums, but rather subtle and homely, mostly with a shrubby habit, incised leaves and demure pastel flowers which, on a windowsill, give the same intimacy as lace curtains.

It makes little difference whether you call them geraniums or pelargoniums. In a way, both are right, as they belong to the genus *Pelargonium* which is one of eleven in the family Geraniaceae. The confusing thing is that there is another genus in the family called *Geranium*. It contains generally hardier species with a quite different distribution in the wild and with certain botanical differences. Originally they were all known as geranium, a name mentioned by the Greek physician Dioscorides in the first century AD and given to describe their beaked fruits: *geranios* being the Greek word for a crane (hence the popular name, cranesbill). As botanical knowledge advanced and the number of known species increased, it became necessary to make subdivisions in the family. One of these was given the name *Pelargonium* from the Greek *pelargos* meaning a stork, which was not very helpful, as few of us can differentiate sufficiently between the bill of a crane and a stork to make any use of the analogy. (And to add to the confusion, another genus in the family, *Erodium*, is usually known as the storksbill!)

From the gardener's point of view, plants in the genus *Pelargonium* fall into four main groups: zonal pelargoniums, commonly known as geraniums, which are some of the most popular plants worldwide for containers and bedding, and often have a semi-circular dark zone on the leaf; ivy-leaved pelargoniums or trailing geraniums which are almost as popular and have five-lobed, shiny brittle leaves; regal pelargoniums which are bigger, leafier plants with larger frilly, often patterned flowers and a more sensitive disposition; and last but not least, the scented geraniums with intensely aromatic leaves and smallish flowers. Of all the groups, the last is the least hybridized. Indeed, most of those common in cultivation are species and, apart from the inevitable selection of superior forms, are identical to their wild ancestors.

Most of the 250 or so species of *Pelargonium* are native to southern Africa, with a scattering in the east of the continent, a handful in Australasia and the odd ones on Madagascar and remote islands like St Helena and Tristan da Cunha. They generally grow in frost-free regions which are subject to periods of extreme dryness, often made more exacting by poor stony soils and blazing sun. Where conditions such as these are found away from their native lands, some have escaped from cultivation and become naturalized: areas around the Mediterranean and in California both now have 'wild' pelargoniums. One of the adaptations which helps them survive such harsh environments is having foliage impregnated with essential oils. The powerful taste and smell of these substances is off-putting to most herbivores – an important consideration for plants growing in drought-stricken areas where any greenery is a tempting mouthful. Another possible adaptation is the way the leaves are lobed and cut into shred-like segments so that they look damaged and hardly worth eating. Hairy, bristly or sticky textures are also repugnant, as well as helping to protect the foliage from scorching and desiccation.

Whatever their effects on herbivores, strong scent and interestingly shaped and textured leaves are exactly what appeals to the plant lover. In these respects, there are few other groups of plants to compare with pelargoniums for variety. They range from the thread-leaved *P. abrotanifolium* whose foliage looks, tastes and smells like that of the pungent southern European herb lad's love (*Artemisia abrotanum*), to the peppermint-scented *P. tomentosum* whose broad lobed leaves are so densely hairy that the plant gathers millions of dew drops in the night and looks as if it has been cut from silvery-green felt. Not all smell nice; some, such as *P. quercifoilium*, the oak-leaf pelargonium, are pungent; others like *P. asperum* are downright unpleasant. In addition to scent, shape and texture, there is also colour – not the flamboyance of the zonals and regals which hits you in the eye, but restful shades and detailed patterns which repay closer acquaintance, as befits herbal plants.

Some of the prettiest scented pelargoniums are the variegated forms of several widely grown species. The largest-leaved is 'Lady Plymouth', a form of the rose geranium, *P. graveolens*. It has small scentless flowers in a delicate mauve, and light green broadly ovate leaves cut into five to seven main lobes which are, in turn, finely lobed and irregularly edged with cream. Their rose scent is overlaid with balsam and nutmeg. The dwarf spreading habit makes this variety an excellent pot plant. *P. graveolens* reached Europe in 1774 and rapidly established itself as a favourite, giving rise to a number of cultivars and hybrids. 'Lady Plymouth' was first mentioned in about 1800 and is still a very popular variety. Several kinds of rose-scented geranium are grown commercially for the perfumery industry. Their essential oil, distilled just before the plant comes into flower, contains geraniol and citronellol, as does the much more expensive attar (oil) of roses.

P. x *fragrans* 'Variegatum' is smaller all round with tiny white flowers and more or less heart-shaped leaves that are regularly lobed and silky soft to the touch. In colour the foliage is grey-green with a subtle yellowish-green around the margins. The scent is pine-like, again with a hint of nutmeg. It seldom reaches more than 45 cm (18 in) and has a densely branched, spreading leafy habit. In general appearance *P.* x *fragrans* resembles *P. odoratissimum* (which smells like Granny Smith apples). It has been described as a species in its own right (*P. fragrans*) but most authorities regard it as a hybrid with *P. odoratissimum* as one parent.

P. crispum 'Variegatum' (also known as 'Variegated Prince Rupert') is most distinctive in appearance and scent. It has erect stems crowded with small, almost tri-lobed leaves which are both crinkled and serrated. The cream margins accentuate the crimped appearance of the foliage which, when grasped, feels quite rough and releases a strong smell of lemons. A well-grown specimen can reach 90 cm (3 ft). Its pale pinkish-mauve flowers are

2 cm (1 in) across – large in comparison with the leaves – with upper petals marked purple. A miniature version, *P. crispum* 'Minor', has been described by Roy Genders as 'one of the most beautiful pot plants in existence'.

Scented geraniums are generally very easy to grow in well-drained, even dryish, sunny positions. In the winter they must be protected from frost and kept on the dry side, but otherwise need little attention. In my experience their worst enemies are overwatering, insufficient light and aphids. To maintain a good shape, cut them back in the spring so that they do not become too leggy, especially if they have been sheltered indoors where light levels are low. Cuttings are best taken in spring or autumn (ideally around the equinoxes when growth is strongest) and placed in sand at about 17°C (63°F), again making sure that after the initial watering they stay on the dry side. (Many pelargoniums resemble succulents and can manage on little water for considerable periods.)

The pleasure of growing scented geraniums is sufficient in itself, but the adventurous might like to try them out as culinary herbs. (They have also been used medicinally – for dysentery and gastric ulcers – but are seldom mentioned in western herbals.) Those smelling of lemons or roses go well with milk desserts (just one leaf is often enough to flavour a dish) and a leaf can also be placed at the bottom of sponge cakes before baking. Spicy and apple scents are good with baked or stewed fruit, and the peppermint ones can be used in the same ways as real peppermint (*Mentha* x *piperita*). Unusual sorbets can be made by flavouring the basic syrup with a few geranium leaves before adding fruit juice.

Even the strongest scents are elusive. Though the memory may last a lifetime, encounters with fragrances are by their nature brief and intense, as our response rapidly diminishes after the initial impact. To get the most from your scented geraniums, position them on steps and near seats and doorways where they will be brushed as you pass. Far

(above) The silky leaves of Pelargonium x fragrans *'Variegatum' are two-toned green and smell like pine and nutmeg.*
(opposite) The fine red form of rat's tail plantain.

from being delicate ornamentals that must be kept out of harm's reach, they are resilient plants that should be allowed to get in the way, each contact releasing a momentary greeting of fragrance that will intrigue, soothe and enliven long after it fades.

RED RAT'S TAIL PLANTAIN
Plantago major 'Rubrifolia'

The rat's rail plantain is everybody's idea of a weed: plain dull green leaves, scraggy spikes of insignificant flowers and the tenacity

to grow in unpromising places like well-trodden paths and regularly mown lawns. Though European in origin, it has spread almost worldwide by tagging on to our colonial ancestors in trouser turn-ups and belongings, falling wherever they trod foreign soil: so much so, that the indigenous peoples came to know it as white man's foot.

There are about 250 species in the family Plantaginaceae, most of which belong to the genus *Plantago*. They are generally plants of temperate regions or mountains in the tropics. The rat's tail plantain is an evergreen perennial with a rosette of broad ovate leaves which have thick chanelled stalks and between five and eleven rib-like main veins. Dense long-stalked spikes of tiny greenish flowers are produced in the summer. and it is these that give it the name of rat's tail. The flowers are wind-pollinated, with conspicuous anthers appearing successively as a fuzzy band up the spike. The size of the plant varies greatly according to conditions, reaching 25–30 cm (10–12 in) in good soil when unimpeded, and barely 10 cm (4 in) with flat rosettes in heavily trampled positions. Apart from the fact that it prefers moisture-retentive soils, it is otherwise not fussy and can tolerate anything from acid to alkaline conditions. All parts are reinforced with tough fibrous strands which enable it to survive the passing of a 10-ton truck unscathed.

Suggesting that one grows a weed which may already have evaded all efforts to eradicate it on the lawn and garden path does, I admit, seem ill-advised. However, most plant lovers will agree that the variety 'Rubrifolia' is a fine foliage plant. Its burgundy leaves are striking near grey-leaved plants and most effective in floral arrangements. In the luxury of cultivation it may grow to 40 cm (16 in) or more, with leaf blades some 20 cm (8 in) long and 15 cm (6 in) across. Further encouragement should not be given though, and it is best to remove the flower spikes before they drop their seed, or your lawn and path will suffer a second wave of plantain invasion from the red form which comes true from seed. (The seedheads do, incidentally, make very good food for cage birds provided, that is, they are uncontaminated.)

Plantains of various species have been used in folk medicine all over the world from earliest times. Those which have been analysed appear to contain similar properties. They were once the mainstay of poultices, lotions and ointments to heal wounds, sores, inflammations, stings and bites. A North American Indian was credited with the discovery that plantain was a cure for rattlesnake bite and given an award by the Assembly of South Carolina. For this reason, plantains are often called snakeweed in the United States. Shakespeare was obviously familiar with plantain's uses and had Romeo tell Benvolio in the first Act of *Romeo and Juliet* that it is excellent for broken shins. We now know that plantain contains substances which are antiseptic, control bleeding and stimulate the healing process, as well as soothing and cooling inflamed tissues. For such purposes the herb was usually applied externally, but it has also proved effective, in conjunction with comfrey (*Symphytum officinale*), for the internal treatment of minor haemorrhages of the digestive tract, as sometimes occur with gastric ulcers and piles.

Although plantain leaves are still a common household remedy for everyday mishaps, herbalists have more specialized uses for them. The leaves are gathered in the summer and have to be dried quickly, without browning, at 40–50°C (104–122°F) to retain potency. They are effective in infusions and tinctures for cystitis and other urinary problems; catarrh and bronchial congestion (the fresh juice is sometimes used for this purpose); and for eye infections such as conjunctivitis.

It is not only the leaves which are useful. There is currently an upsurge of interest in the properties of the seeds which have an outer coating of mucilage (fibre gel) that swells considerably when wet. A number of species are now grown commercially for this valuable commodity, notably *P. ovata* (or ispaghula as it is known in the pharmaceutical industry) and *P. psyllium* (known as psyllium or flea-seed because the dark brown seeds look like fleas). They are processed into a variety of products: gum for fabric finishes; cosmetics, such as face masks, in which they act as skin softeners; bulk laxatives; and in herbal remedies for cleansing the colon of the yeast *Candida albicans* (an infection recently implicated in many different symptoms of ill health). Plantain has always been regarded as a 'spring cleaning' herb, the seeds, in particular, being good for regulating bowel function.

In spite of their many virtues as herbs, there is no getting away from it that on the whole plantains are plain. The only one with any merit as an ornamental is the red rat's tail plantain. It is a little beauty but I have often wondered whether it could be improved upon. Its close relative, the hoary plantain (*P. media*), is less coarse and has fragrant pink-stamened flowers. If it were possible to cross them, we might get a rather more refined red-leaved plant with more colourful scented, spikes, which would be an even greater asset in the garden.

PINK AND DOUBLE WHITE PRIMROSES
Primula x *vulgaris*
'Guinevere' and *P. Vulgaris* 'Alba Plena'

In northern Europe the primrose is the harbinger of spring, symbolic of all that is fresh, sweet and wide-eyed. Along country lanes, banks of streams and ditches, and in budding woodlands, the pale yellow posies beam an assurance that the grip of winter is weakening and a new season of growth is under way. Unlike some of the other symbols – lambs, catkins, and the call of the cuckoo – the primrose thrives just as happily in the confines of garden borders as in the wild. Its English name means 'first rose' (from the Latin *prima rosa*) and the scientific name *Primula* translates as 'first little one'. So well known and loved is the flower that its common name has passed into general usage: everyone knows exactly what shade is meant by primrose yellow, and we are said to be treading 'the primrose path' if we incline to a life of pleasure. In Elizabethan times the word 'primrose' also meant finest. The poet Edmund Spenser wrote, 'She is the pride and primrose of the rest' – a more endearing expression than its present-day equivalent, *crème de la crème*.

One of the loveliest things about primroses is that they do not close up in dull or wet weather. If you look closely at the flowers on several plants, you will see that there are two distinct kinds, but only one kind on each plant. The so-called pin-eyed flowers have the tiny green knob of the stigma visible in the centre; the thrum-eyed have, instead, a circle of five stamens uppermost with the stigma

88

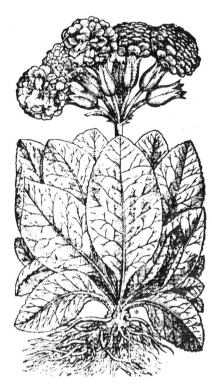

A double form of the polyanthus
(Primula x variabilis)

much lower down (thrum is a weaving term for a fringe or tassel or unwoven ends). This arrangement prevents self-pollination which, in many flowering plants, can take place as a last resort if cross-pollination fails. Primroses are pollinated only by long-tongued bees and moths which can reach to the base of the flower for the nectar. If bad weather prevents pollinators from flying, the primrose blooms in vain and no seed will be produced – hence Shakespeare's lines in *The Winter's Tale*: 'pale primroses, that die unmarried'.

The genus *Primula* has about 500 species, mostly in Europe and Asia, with some in North America and a scattering in regions as far apart as South America, northern Africa and Java. Many grow at high altitudes in mountains or the cool shade of woodland and do not take kindly to cultivation in warmer drier places. Those that do – primroses, polyanthus and auriculas in particular – have

long been among the most popular of all cultivated plants. The primrose family was, in fact, one of the first to undergo intensive selection and cross-breeding. The peak was in the eighteenth and nineteenth centuries when primulas of various kinds were in great demand by gardeners and enthusiasts. At the end of the eighteenth century in northern England, 50 shows for cultivars of the auricula (*P. x pubescens*, a hybrid between *P. auricula* and *P. hirsuta*) were held each year: followers of the cult made special auricula theatres from black velvet and mirrors, and the most perfect – grown to mathematical specifications as regards diameter and width of colour bands – were drawn or painted by the leading artists of the day.

The primrose has a long history as a garden plant. Less formal than the auricula, more suitable for cottage gardens (auriculas had to be kept under glass to protect their mealy bloom from the elements) and less demanding to grow, it produces a profusion of blooms over many weeks, given a moisture-retentive soil, ample humus and partial shade. Even easier is its hybrid, the polyanthus (*P. x variabilis*), a cross between the primrose and the cowslip (*P. veris*), which tolerates full sun and drier soil. They are very similar in appearance: the polyanthus having many flowers on each stalk: the primrose only one. In the sixteenth century, primroses were grown for medicinal and culinary purposes as well as ornamental, and in a far greater variety of forms than is now seen. Double-flowered plants were as common then as they are scarce today. In 1823 Thomas Hogg's *Treatise on the Carnation, Pink, Auricula etc.* listed double primroses in yellow, white, pink, purple, dark red and lilac. Some of the old varieties were curious rather than beautiful, such as 'Jack-in-the-green' which has each flower backed by a frill of tiny leaflets, and 'hose-in-hose' (named after the Elizabethan custom of wearing two pairs of stockings at a time) where one flower produces another flower from its centre. These aberrations, which occur naturally in the wild, reach their most extreme in the 'Franticke' or 'Foolish' primrose, which John Parkinson described in his *Paradisi in sole Paradisus terrestris* (1629) as having 'at the top of the stalk a tuft of small, long, green leaves with some yellow leaves, as it were pieces of flowers broken and standing amongst the green leaves'.

The greatest events in the development of the primrose as a garden plant were in the 1630s when Tradescant's 'Turkie Purple' – the pink or purple-flowered *P. vulgaris* subspecies *sibthorpii* from south-eastern Europe – was introduced; and in 1912 which saw the arrival of the magenta *P. juliae* from the Caucasus. Using these in the breeding, vivid reds, russets, purples and pinks were added to the original pastel yellow. In the mid-seventeenth century, the polyanthus rapidly gained in popularity and within a hundred years there were over a thousand different varieties. Today, most of the Regency and Victorian primulas are extinct, having petered out through a failure to divide plants regularly – a necessary procedure to maintain vigour and propagate the strain – coupled with a loss of interest when bigger, brighter and more robust hybrids came on the scene.

Fortunately, all are not lost and a few are again quite widely available, thanks to specialist nurseries and gardeners with a concern for our vanishing heritage of traditional garden plants. One of the most distinctive is the lovely 'Guinevere' which has polyanthus-type dusky pink flowers with a yellow eye and dark purplish-bronze leaves – the nearest a primrose gets to being a foliage plant. This original Garryarde cultivar is thought to have come from the garden of James Whiteside Dane in Garryarde, Co. Kildare, in the 1920s and to have *P. juliae* in its ancestry. Ireland has the perfect climate for primroses and has produced many adorable cultivars, including the dark 'Tawny Port', striped 'Kinlough Beauty' and the eccentric hose-in-hose 'Lady Lettice' and Jack-in-the green 'Donegal Danny'. Nearly all the original Garryardes have disappeared from cultivation now, leaving 'Guinevere' as the only one easily obtainable.

Double primroses have a special charm and it is sad that they too underwent a period of decline from which they are only just emerging. As with most varieties of primrose, they do not come true from seed (in fact most doubles are sterile) and must be divided regularly. In addition, they are constitutionally weaker than the species. Many of the old named varieties came from Ireland, but the most recent introductions are from the Pacific north west of the United States. This new race of doubles is strong-growing and can be grown from seed, though only about 30 per cent will be double. Meanwhile, cottage garden doubles may still be found at some nurseries, the most delightful of which is the white 'Alba Plena', John Gerard's favourite in the sixteenth century and certainly mine today. Part of the folklore about primroses is that if you eat the flowers you see fairies, but I am more inclined to believe that it happens if you look long enough at a double-white plant in full flower.

Primroses are, in fact, edible and have been used in many ingenious ways: crystallized, pickled, in desserts, wines, vinegars and salads. (Even the smallest amount should not, however, be consumed by anyone with an allergy to primulas – a fairly common form of dermatitis among horticulturists who handle the plants frequently.) Some of the old recipes called for vast quantities of the fragile flowers gathered from the wild and stripped of all green parts; an indication of how prolific plants used to be before modern farming methods took their toll. These days wild primroses are all too few and gardeners may be able and willing to spare a few flowers for crystallizing or strewing on a salad, but are unlikely to be generous or ruthless enough to gather the bucketful needed for a gallon of wine. A modest and delicious recipe is for primrose pottage which can be served as it is or used to fill a baked shortcrust pastry case. The basis is ground rice cooked to a suitable consistency with white wine (ideally a homemade flower wine, even if not primrose), flavoured with a pinch of saffron and two dozen

finely chopped primrose flowers (minus the green bits), sweetened with blossom honey, spiked with flaked almonds and, lastly, decorated with fresh or crystallized primroses.

Primroses, cowslips and their offspring, the polyanthus, have a similar chemistry. Herbalists used to refer to them as 'Herba Paralysis' a widely used remedy for muscular paralysis and rheumatism. The whole plant, gathered when flowering, or the dried roots were used. They have sedative properties and relieve coughs, due to a fragrant volatile oil and saponins (irritant soap-like compounds). Present-day medical herbalists use them little, as more effective remedies are available, but herb suppliers still stock the dried flowers for those who like to drink cowslip or primrose tea to relieve tension, sleeplessness and minor bronchial complaints. Gerard assures us that 'Primrose tea, drunk in the month of May is

(left) If you gaze long enough at double white primroses, you may see fairies!
(below) 'Guinevere': one of the few surviving primroses of a race from Garryarde, Co. Kildare, Eire.

Pasque flower (Pulsatilla vulgaris)

famous for curing the phrensie'. The leaves are also edible and, when new in spring, make a pleasant addition to salads. They were traditionally a 'spring-cleaning' remedy and Gerard described a practitioner in London who was 'accustomed every year in the month of May to dyet his patients after this manner; Take the leaves and flowers of the primrose, boil them in a little fountain water and in some Rose and Bettany waters, adding thereto sugar, pepper, salt, and butter, which being strained he gave them to drink thereof first and last'.

Should any of these edible or medicinal uses of primroses appeal to you, it might be preferable to grow the original pale yellow wild species or the plain yellow polyanthus which is bound to crop up if you grow wild primroses and cowslips too close together. It would be unthinkable to use such beauties as the virginal double white or the pretty pink Guinevere'

for anything but pleasurable observation and the grateful realization that they are the scarce survivors of the primrose's finest hours – and heralds of a new era of popularity.

RUBY PASQUE FLOWER
Pulsatilla vulgaris 'Rubra'

The pasque flower must be one of the loveliest of all temperate wild flowers – a fact that has led to its decline from overcollection in many regions, especially those in the extreme of its range, such as the southern English downs. Favouring well-drained sunny sites in upland areas, the pasque flower starts into growth while snow and wintry weather still linger. The flowers venture out first. Both they and the leaves are suitably equipped with fur coats: a dense outer covering of silky hairs which provides a high degree of insulation from freezing temperatures. It is this soft silvery haze which, when backlit, becomes a halo surrounding all parts of the plant that gives it such appeal.

There are about 30 species of *Pulsatilla* and they belong to the family Ranunculaceae. At one time they were included in the genus *Anemone*, giving *P. vulgaris* its former name of *A. pulsatilla*. *Anemone* is from the Greek *anemos*, meaning 'wind' and *pulsatilla* is an Italian word derived from the Latin *pulsare*, from which we get the word pulsate. The common name, wind flower, is along the same lines, all describing the way that the flowers shake and tremble in the wind. In Culpeper's inimitable style: 'Anemone. Called also wind flower, because they say the flowers never open but when the wind blows. Pliny is my author; if it be not so, blame him.' It is possible that in poor weather when there are few insect pollinators about, this may disperse pollen. Certainly the plumed seeds are shaken free and blown about by the wind.

P. vulgaris is native to northern and central Europe and western Asia. It is found in dry grassy places on chalk or limestone. The plant has a tough woody rootstock and reaches about 30 cm (1 ft) tall, with dark green leaves divided into many narrow fern-like segments. The foliage emerges with or soon after the first flower buds show and is fully expanded by the time the last flowers have faded. At first the scentless flowers are erect, becoming more or less pendent when open. They measure 3–5 cm (1–2 in) in length and the sepals form a bell-shape to begin with, flaring more widely as they age. The colour varies widely, sometimes according to locality. The commonest is lilac, but white, pale pink, opalescent blue, dark purple and burgundy shades are known. All have a large central boss of yellow stamens. The flower stalk continues to lengthen after flowering so that the magnificent heads of feathery seeds are held clear of the foliage and catch the wind.

Although pasque flowers are long-lived and very hardy garden plants, they can be tricky to start with. I tried plant after plant in the open ground and only succeeded when I put one in a large earthenware pot and treated it like an alpine – incorporating plenty of grit in the compost and surrounding it with a generous layer too. They obviously need excellent drainage but don't mind being frozen solid (which mine has been on occasions). Once established, they increase year by year, forming clumps which can produce well over twenty flowers at a time.

Pasque flowers are propagated by seed which fortunately is produced in abundance. It should be sown as soon as ripe in early summer, first cutting off the plumes. On the whole, the various coloured forms do not come true from seed, so it is best to buy pasque flowers when in flower (and who can resist?). *P. vulgaris* 'Rubra' will, however, produce mostly reds, the best of which are the colour of rubies and garnets. This is the richest and darkest of the colour forms; a sophisticated regal crimson and gold that stands out among the other more fragile pastel shades. It could even be said that it has a tendency to dominate the scene, in which case giving it the VIP treatment as a specimen pot-grown plant is the answer. Then it can be displayed where there are no constraints to admiration.

In North America, the species known as pasque flower is *P. patens* (formerly *Anemone patens*). It is found on dry prairies and in open woods from Illinois and Wisconsin westward and northward into the Canadian Rockies. In some places, whole hillsides are silvery purple with it in early spring. It also goes under the names of prairie crocus, prairie smoke, meadow anemone, mayflower and April fool. Like *P. vulgaris*, it has lavender flowers (occasionally darker purple or white) and bipinnate leaves clothed in silky hairs. Its popularity has made it the floral emblem of Manitoba and the state flower of South Dakota.

Most pasque flowers are used medicinally. Like all the buttercup family (Ranunculaceae) they are acrid and potentially poisonous, causing unpleasant and serious symptoms if taken to excess. One of the less endearing names for the pasque flower is laughing parsley, as it was once said that anyone eating it would die laughing – though the hideous grin left on the face of the corpse was undoubtedly more to do with the herb's effect on the nervous system than with amusement. Even handling the plants may cause irritation, especially if the sap rubs into the skin. Nevertheless, when prescribed by homoeopaths and practitioners of herbal medicine, the pasque flower has some remarkable curative properties.

The chemistry of the pasque flower is such that it undergoes a number of changes when cut or crushed and dried. The fresh plant is too toxic for use and professional expertise is needed to process the herb into a safe drug. It is a painkiller, sedative and antispasmodic which is particularly effective for painful conditions of the reproductive system in both men and women. Tension headaches and nervous exhaustion, especially those of menstrual origin, also respond well to preparations containing

pasque flower – as the American name headache plant indicates. It may also be used for hyperactivity and insomnia, for which it is usually combined with passionflower (*Passiflora incarnata*). The chemical constituents have a stimulant effect on mucous membranes and are bactericidal as well, making pasque flower of further use in various bronchial diseases, asthma, skin problems and septicaemia – again, in conjunction with other herbs.

Pasque flowers were originally known as passe flowers – a translation of the French *passefleur* which meant surpassing all other flowers in beauty. It was the herbalist Gerard who, in 1597, renamed it the pasque flower because the plant flowered at Easter and was used for dyeing Easter eggs bright green. Large numbers of flowers must have been gathered for this purpose. Records show that in the household of King Edward I of England, 400 easter eggs were coloured this way. The pasque flower is almost extinct in the wild in England now – possibly because of this ritual sacrifice of so many exquisite lilac blooms for making a green dye. It was said that it only grew where

(opposite) The outstanding ruby red form of the pasque flower steals the show.
(below) Flowering later and lasting longer, double yellow celandines have tightly packed enamelled petals with grass green undersides.

Saxons (or was it Danes?) shed their blood – having a preference for hilltops which became of strategic importance in battles. The truth is that today it grows only where it has, by a miracle, escaped being picked and uprooted. Given its ease of cultivation and our preference these days for using onion skins to colour our Easter eggs, is this not a case for reintroduction to the wild, especially on those historic sites which are now conservation and recreation areas?

COPPER, WHITE AND DOUBLE-FLOWERED CELANDINES
Ranunculus ficaria 'Alba', 'Brazen Hussy', 'Cuprea' and 'Flore Pleno'

Were it not so invasive, pilewort or lesser celandine would be a favourite garden plant. As it is, it must be confined to the wilder parts where it can gloss over muddy ditches and bare damp ground under trees and shrubs without becoming a nuisance – though all is forgiven anyway when its spread of tidy heart-shaped leaves and brilliant yellow enamelled flowers beam at you from the sodden earth of early spring. Victorian florigraphy took it to symbolize 'joys to come' and at a time like that, who thinks about the thousands of bulbils that will find their way to pastures new?

Fortunately it is possible to have one's celandines *and* enjoy them without later regrets if you plant the less invasive white-, copper- and double-flowered forms. The latter has petals exactly the same colour as the species – acid yellow with grass green undersides – but instead of the usual eight to twelve, they are numerous and tightly packed so that the green backs show in the centre. I am not a great fan of double flowers, but find this one quite delightful. The others are single: 'Alba' a gleaming white, and 'Cuprea' and 'Brazen Hussy' both with coppery-orange flowers. All are gems – more subtle than the brassy yellow species and more self-contained, but with the same glistening petals. The foliage is similarly neat and, in the case of 'Brazen Hussy', is an attractive brown which tones perfectly with the apricot flowers.

Pilewort is, as one might guess from its appearance, a member of the buttercup family, Ranunculaceae, which has over 1,800 species divided into some 50 genera, including *Ranunculus*. This genus contains about 300 species, the best known being spearworts, water crowfoots, the many different buttercups and the lesser celandine. *Ranunculus* is the diminutive of the Latin word *rana*, meaning a frog – a name given because many of the species live in wet places. In comparison, the name celandine is rather a misnomer, being from *chelidon*, the Greek for a swallow. Apparently it got this name because of its resemblance (in flower colour only) to the greater celandine (*Chelidonium majus*) – a plant which does indeed begin to flower when the swallows return to Europe from their winter resorts in northern Africa, by which time the lesser celandine is over. To add to the confusion, greater celandine belongs to a quite different family altogether, the Papaveraceae or poppies.

Ranunculus ficaria is found wild all over Europe, western Asia and north Africa in damp, rich, neutral to alkaline soil. It is happy in sun or shade and forms perennial colonies on bare ground along streams and in woods, thickets, hedgerows and ditches. The whole plant reaches 15 cm (6 in) across and about 8 cm (3 in) high, appearing in winter and becoming dormant again in late spring. It survives underground for some eight months, reduced to a bunch of club-shaped tubers. The cordate blades measure 3 cm (1 in) or so and are toothed at the margins, shiny and often handsomely marked with dark blotches. Each plant produces quite a few flowers, 2–3 cm (1 in) in diameter, shortly after the leaves develop. Another of pilewort's names is the five o'clock plant, from its habit of closing its flowers promptly at this time each evening. They open from nine to five, close in the rain, and are quite inconspicuous when only the green undersurfaces of the petals are showing. If the weather is unfavourable, they may not be pollinated and in this case, or when growing in the shade, pilewort reproduces instead by bulbils the size of grains of wheat. These form in the leaf axils and are left behind on the surface of the soil when the plant dies down. The following winter they may be washed away by rain or floods and, in the spring, start growing into new plantlets which are geneti-

cally identical to the parent plant. Records show that in certain conditions bulbils are so numerous on bare soil that people have been under the impression that the sky has rained wheat.

Although most people know *Ranunculus ficaria* as celandine, herbalists refer to it as pilewort on account of its effectiveness in treating piles or haemorrhoids. This unpleasant complaint – in which the veins around the anus become dilated and inflamed – is extremely widespread, affecting half the population at some time or other. It is commonest in pregnant women and people with sedentary occupations or a history of constipation. For many hundreds of years, pilewort has provided an astringent emollient treatment which shrinks and soothes the piles. Present-day herbalists usually prescribe it in the form of an ointment (often blended with extracts of plantain (*Plantago major*) and marigold (*Calendula officinalis*), or as a suppository with witch hazel (*Hamamelis virginiana*)). It may also be taken internally, but only under medical supervision as buttercups and their kin are acrid plants. In the herbalist Gerard's words: 'They require a very exquisite moderation, with a most exact and due manner of tempering, not any of them are to be taken alone by themselves, because they are of a most violent force.'

There is no doubt that pilewort works effectively and contains substances with proven healing properties. The interesting thing is how it came to be used for piles – which has far more to do with myth than chemistry. In the sixteenth century an influential theory, known as the Doctrine of Signatures, was expounded by a charismatic physician who went under the name of Phillipus Aureolus Paracelsus. His real name was, believe it or not, Theophrastus Bombastus von Hohenheim, which more accurately reflected his personality – a forceful mixture of practical scientist, workaholic and verbose dogmatic author and lecturer. Basically the Doctrine of Signatures taught that every medicinal plant resembled the part of the body or affliction it was designed (by God) to cure. Thus a plant with cordate leaves might be good for heart disease; those with yellow roots or flowers would alleviate jaundice and other liver problems. And so it was with pilewort's cluster of tubers, for as one herbalist observed, 'If you dig up the root of it you will perceive the perfect image of the disease commonly called piles.' For all its influence at the time, the doctrine did not result in the discovery of new wonder drugs but rode on the shoulders of established knowledge, finding a religious justification for – and an easy way of remembering – cures which had been discovered by a combination of clinical observation and trial and error over the centuries.

The simple shape of the celandine is that of the archetypal flower. It is also, in shape and colour, like a child's illustration of the sun. Its least known but most beautiful name is the Celtic *grian* which means 'sun'. These images were part of its appeal to the poet William Wordsworth, whose favourite flower it was. He loved its 'glittering countenance' which even on wintry days seems to be 'Telling tales about the sun', and, in turn, its image is engraved on his tombstone.

GILDED ROSEMARY
Rosmarinus officinalis 'Aureus' (syn. 'Variegatus')

For a Mediterranean herb, rosemary flowers early in the year. In unseasonal northern springs, when there is a white Easter, the brittle branches with their porcelain blue flowers may be weighed down with snow. Further south, in its coastal Mediterranean homelands, it flowers throughout the mild winter and stray flowers can be found almost all the year round. In some areas, it grows prolifically. The Elizabethan herbalist, John

Gerard, records that in his day there was so much of it in Languedoc (southern France) that the people rarely burned anything else on their fires. I once found it growing in such quantities on a hillside leading down to the sea in Spain that I can well believe the seventeenth-century diarist, John Evelyn, who wrote that the flowers 'are credibly reported to give their scent above 30 leagues off at sea.' Its Latin name, *Rosmarinus*, means 'dew of the sea'.

Rosemary is an evergreen shrub which can reach over 1.5 m (5 ft), though the main stem usually twists and bends so that the plant seldom remains upright. It has leathery, dark green, needle-like leaves which are highly aromatic, with an invigorating, camphoraceous scent. In the wild it has a wide distribution and is very variable. The most outstanding forms have entered cultivation as named varieties, varying in growth, hardiness and differences in the colours of the foliage and flowers. As far as foliage goes, the most interesting is the gilded rosemary, *R. officinalis* 'Aurea', which is also known as 'Variegata'. It has the usual pale blue flowers, but its needles are banded and mottled with yellow, giving it potential with other golden-variegated plants and making it an intriguing subject for the conservatory, where its detailed variegation may be admired at closer quarters.

Like most Mediterranean herbs, rosemary likes a warm sunny spot on light, dry alkaline soil. In less favoured conditions, the position chosen can make a great deal of difference to its chances of surviving cold winters. Planting it close to a wall often gives sufficient warmth and shelter, but in some areas, in spite of one's efforts, rosemary's hardiness is capricious: well-established shrubs come unscathed through several winters and succumb the next. It can appear to survive a spell of severe weather, only to peter out in the spring. The leaves take on a lacklustre appearance, turn brown at the tips, and you know the plant is doomed. It dies from the feet up, the roots being killed by prolonged cold and wet or very hard frosts, the foliage remaining green until the sap fails to rise in the spring. The only consolation is that you can take cuttings as soon as you suspect the worst, choosing stems that still look a good colour. Put them in equal quantities of sand and peat in a warm place and you should be able to nurture a replacement. One year I managed three plantlets before the parent turned completely brown. Normally, cuttings are best taken in the summer. Plants raised from seed are better still in habit and vigour, though the varieties will not come true. Layering during the growing season is another method of propagation, especially in low-growing forms which can easily be pegged down to the soil.

There is no other plant like rosemary – quite literally, as *R. officinalis* is the only species in the genus *Rosmarinus*. The genus does belong to a very large family, though: the labiates, which include important herbs such as basil, sage, mint and thyme. The second part of its name, *officinalis*, indicates that it was of importance in the herbal pharmacopoeia, and for good reason. It has a wide range of medicinal applications, with records of use going back over 2,000 years. Like many herbs, it is toxic in large amounts. The essential oil, which is distilled from both flowers and leaves, should not be taken internally but, diluted with vegetable oil, is one of the finest oils for massage and embrocations, especially for rheumatism, neuralgia and sciatica. A drop or two of essential oil in the bath will also help relieve tension, tiredness and aching limbs.

Medicinally, rosemary is a mild painkiller and sedative which improves the functioning of the liver and gall bladder. This was known as long ago as the first century AD, when the influential physicians Dioscorides and Galen recommended it for jaundice and 'liverishness'. Herbalists today prescribe it (usually combined with other herbs) for migraine, debility following illness, depressive states and digestive problems associated with anxiety. As a home remedy, it makes a relaxing tea for tension headaches and low spirits. Only half a

teaspoonful per cup of boiling water is needed, as rosemary is a strong-tasting herb. Adding a pinch of lavender leaves or flowers increases its effectiveness. These uses follow a long tradition that rosemary is of value for 'inward griefs', 'cold benumbed joints' and 'drowsiness or dullness of the mind and senses', as listed in Nicholas Culpeper's herbal of 1653.

The virtues of rosemary for more mundane troubles have even been proclaimed from the pulpit. In 1607, a respected clergyman, Roger Hackett, rallied his congregation with the announcement that 'It helpeth the brain, strengtheneth the memorie, and is very medicinable for the head. Let this rosmarinus, this flower of men, ensigne of your wisdom, love and loyaltie, be carried not only in your hands, but in your hearts and heads.' A sermon on rosemary would seem strange today, but in former times it was a familiar herb to churchgoers, symbolizing remembrance and fidelity. At funerals it would be tossed on the coffin as it came to rest, and at weddings was often woven into a bride's bouquet and head-dress, or given – gilded and adorned with ribbons – to the wedding guests. I am always reminded of this last use by the golden variegated rosemary.

It is likely that rosemary was introduced to Britain before the Norman Conquest of 1066, but there is a tradition that Queen Philippa, wife of Edward II, received it from her mother, the Countess of Hainault (south-west Belgium), along with descriptions of its virtues, in about 1350. Philippa is acknowledged as the founder of Queen's College, Oxford, and is commemorated every Christmas by the sprigs of rosemary that decorate the roast boar's head.

Rosemary is a pungent culinary herb with an affinity for robust dishes with red wine and garlic. Most bouquets garnis contain it. Used on its own, it enhances a variety of meats –

The detailed variegation of gilded rosemary is best appreciated in the conservatory, where its delicate porcelain blue flowers also benefit from blooming undamaged by March winds and April showers.

rabbit, hare, venison, duck, pork – and is a favourite with roast lamb (or kid). In Italy it is very popular and sprigs are often included with meat from the butcher. Care is needed in its use, however, as it is not a subtle herb and the 'needles' are tough. Quite often, sufficient flavour is provided by a sprig on top of the dish, removing it (and any detached leaves) after cooking. Powdered rosemary gets round the problem of hard bits of leaf, but inevitably lacks aroma, as the smaller one cuts or grinds an aromatic herb, the more the oils evaporate.

Not least important are the cosmetic uses of rosemary. Shampoos, hair lotions and soaps containing rosemary extracts are well known for maintaining healthy hair and skin. The herb stimulates the peripheral circulation which ensures that the tissues are adequately cleansed of waste products and well supplied with vital nutrients and oxygen. Toilet waters and eau-de-Cologne were originally made for medicinal purposes and rubbed vigorously into the skin or taken as a tonic. The Arabs discovered and perfected the art of distillation and in the thirteenth or fourteenth centuries alcohol was first used as a vehicle for the scents extracted from plants. Hungary water, made from the flowering tops of rosemary macerated in alcohol, dates from this time. It began with Queen Izabella of Hungary who, at the age of 72, crippled with rheumatism and gout, fell in love (so the story goes). One day a hermit mysteriously appeared, divulged the secret recipe for the lotion and was never seen again. After a year of use – drinking it, rubbing her infirm limbs with it, and washing with it – the lady was restored to such health and beauty that the King of Poland proposed to her and she became convinced the recipe had been given by an angel in disguise. Such drastic measures are not always necessary though. Apparently, one can benefit from rosemary without even using it. In Bancke's herbal, dated 1525, we are advised to 'smell of it oft, and it shall keep thee youngly'. What better advice could be given to gardeners who plant this delightful shrub?

VARIEGATED AND BLUE RUES
Ruta graveolens 'Jackman's Blue' and 'Variegata'

'Jackman's Blue' rue is a classic foliage plant: a compact small shrub with such dense foliage that the stems are completely hidden beneath the flawless grey-blue divided leaves. It is smaller, more compact and bluer than the species, and as neat as a conifer, even when producing its waxy yellowish-green flowers. Seldom looking out of place, it is particularly effective near lime-green plants, such as lady's mantle (*Alchemilla mollis*) and golden marjoram (*Origanum vulgare* 'Aureum'). Slightly less blue and more open in habit is the variegated rue. Its new growths are splashed with white or almost wholly white – a feature enjoyed by gardeners and flower arrangers alike. This is one of the few variegated shrubs which comes true from seed. Young plants (from seed sown in warmth in late winter) are very pretty as pot plants and in containers of summer bedding plants. In addition to the visual attraction, the leaves are pungently aromatic and have a long history of medicinal use. Yet for all the popularity of rue as a garden plant, it is rarely appreciated as a herb.

Centuries ago the story was very different. In Greek and Roman times it was a major medicinal herb, respected for its curative and protective properties. It had a powerful reputation for counteracting magic, evil and poison. In those days, poisoning was a favourite method of removing adversaries and few people in positions of authority would eat before a lesser mortal had tasted the food. A chemist-cum-herbalist called Mithridates – one of the leading lights of the influential Alexandrian School of Medicine which was established in Egypt in about 300 BC – specialized in antidotes to poisons and regarded rue as one of the most effective ingredients.

Another claim made for rue was that it preserved good eyesight and relieved eyestrain. Pliny the Elder, the Roman author who wrote a monumental encyclopaedic work on natural history in AD 77, made these recommendations which became traditional among Italian artists and craftspeople. This knowledge obviously spread further afield, as the English poet John Milton (1608–74) refers to it in *Paradise Lost* when the Angel cleansed Adam's sight 'with Euphrasy and Rue' – euphrasy (or eyebright, *Euphrasia officinalis*) being another herb used for eye problems.

Not surprisingly, it was the Romans who introduced this valuable herb to England. It is referred to in the Saxon *Leech Book of Bald* – Bald being the author and 'leech' being another word for doctor, on account of the medical profession's fondness in those days for using leeches to draw out impurities from the long-suffering patient. The respect rue commanded in bygone times is indicated by the fact that it is used in heraldry. It features in the regalia of the Dukedom of Saxony and in the British Order of the Thistle. Generally it is taken to symbolize repentence but, in the case of heraldry, it more likely denotes its reputation for warding off disaster and strengthening whoever uses it. The sixteenth-century English herbalist, John Gerard, reckoned that 'When the Weesell is to fight with the Serpent, shee armeth her selfe by eating Rue'. He even went so far as to say that 'If a man be anointed with the juice of rue, the poison of wolf's bane, mushrooms or todestools, the biting of serpents, stinging of scorpions, spiders, bees, hornets, and wasps will not hurt him' – a claim which it would take considerable courage to disprove.

On a less heroic note, rue is said to kill fleas. For this reason, it was included in the nosegays which were carried by the well-to-do when they went among the unwashed masses. As well as providing distraction from unwholesome smells, the little bunch of aromatic leaves and flowers was thought to keep vermin and pestilence at bay. Assize judges in courts had sprigs of rue placed between them and the defendants to deter the spread of parasites and 'gaol fever'. Rue was also one of the herbs used in the famous 'Four Thieves' Vinegar' (see page 16).

The age-old tradition of relying on rue to fend off the evil and unpleasant was eventually incorporated into ecclesiastical ritual when sprays of the finely cut leaves were employed to sprinkle holy water on the congregation. This use gave it the old name 'herb of grace' which became corrupted to herbygrass. Shakespeare mentions the plant several times in his plays, drawing out all the connotations of its names. Ophelia, in *Act IV*, v – the famous 'mad scene' – of *Hamlet*, says to herself: 'there's rue for you; and here's some for me; we may call it herb of grace o'Sundays. O! you must wear your rue with a difference.' In fact, the word 'rue' as the name of the plant, and the verb 'to rue' (meaning to feel sorrow or regret for events with unpleasant consequences) have nothing at all in common as far as their linguistic origins go. The plant name is derived from a Greek word meaning 'to set free' (i.e. of ills). The verb, on the other hand, is an old Germanic word for regret or pity.

Botanically, *R. graveolens* is one of about 60 species in the genus *Ruta* which, in turn, belongs to a large family of over 600 shrubs and trees – the Rutaceae. Its best known relatives are the citruses and *Choisya*, the Mexican orange blossom bush. At a glance, it would be hard to guess that rue and a lemon tree, for example, are closely related, but one of their similarities is a chemical they have in common. Limonene is a part of the essential oil which gives the characteristic scent to these plants – very strongly in the case of lemon; overlaid with other oils in other citruses; and, to most people's sense of smell, decidedly hidden in rue, which to me smells rather like wet paint.

The strong peculiar odour of rue is matched by its bitter pungent flavour. The very first taste does, indeed, begin on an orange note, but is rapidly swamped by an intensely bitter tang. (I inhale and nibble as I write.) Having sampled rue, you may well conclude that it is quite inedible, but you would be wrong. I once met a lady who swore that no tomato salad was complete without it. I did not enquire about her ancestry, but on the whole it is the Italians who are the greatest enthusiasts – perhaps as a legacy from the days when their illustrious artists used it to strengthen their eyesight. Apparently they, and the Germans too, have been known to include it in salads, vegetable juice cocktails and cream cheese dishes. Even the English have not been completely immune to its fascination – for it is by no means entirely revolting. Sack, the mead drink beloved by Falstaff in Shakespeare's *Henry IV*, included rue in its ingredients. Most notorious of all, though, is the Italian grape spirit, *grappa*. Bottles of this often have a sprig of rue suspended in them. Tom Stobart, the mountaineer and cookery expert, described this 'firewater' as follows:

> The flavour of *grappa*, especially when it has rue in it, is, to many people, rather nasty; at least this ensures that one does not drink too much of it. The guides of Cortina d'Ampezzo often give their clients a thimbleful on the vertical face of some Dolomite needle. It greatly aids the contemplation of eternity, and the rue is appropriate.

Even if rue is added to your list of 'once tried' culinary experiences, its medicinal uses have been well and truly tested and found effective over the centuries. Rue is a toxic herb with a complex chemistry. Tiny amounts in food and drink have a tonic effect; otherwise it should only be used by herbal practitioners. Apart from the essential oil, there are many other compounds, notably Vitamin C and rutin, or Vitamin P (which usually occur together in plants). The latter substance in part accounts for the success of rue in treating eye problems,

as it strengthens capillaries (the finest extensions of the circulatory system which tend to weaken with age). In homoeopathy, rue is also used for the eyes, and for varicose veins.

Gardeners should beware of cutting and handling rue on a sunny day. Another of its compounds, xanthotoxin, makes the skin very sensitive to sunlight and blisters may result after skin contact with the plant. It is unlikely to affect the tough inner surfaces of hands, but wrists, arms and legs are target areas when they brush against the leaves.

Rue is easy to grow in a sunny position on poor dry stony soils, ideally on limestone or chalk, but it will tolerate anything but peat, waterlogging and perpetual shade. To maintain a neat dome, cut back bushes ruthlessly in the spring, though avoid actually cutting into the main stem. For a few weeks, they will look a sad sight, shorn of their lovely blue leaves, but the compact vigorous new growth will be ample reward. A well-tended 'Jackman's Blue'

Variegated rue comes true from seed.

rarely exceeds 60 cm (2 ft) and should have no stems visible at all: just layer after layer of glaucous leaflets. As is the rule with variegated shrubs, variegated rue should have vigorous unvariegated shoots removed.

To propagate rue, use the spring prunings. They may root in a sandy soil outdoors, but in colder regions will need warmth under glass. It is also easy from seed. An early fifteenth-century herbal discloses that 'They sayen the stolen sede is butt the bestte', but if you cannot toughen your nerves sufficiently to test this out – even with a dose of rue – be assured that bought or given seed does very well too!

COLOURED SAGES
Salvia officinalis 'Icterina', 'Purpurascens' and 'Tricolor'

The common sage is pretty enough, with oval grey-green leaves which have the texture of finely puckered velvet. It has given its name to sage green, the most soothing and restful of all green shades. Though the coloured forms are more eye-catching, they share the same subtlety and softness, as well as the same invigorating aroma and valuable culinary and medicinal properties.

Salvia officinalis 'Purpurascens' has greyish-purple leaves, though it is often called red sage. Some plants sold as 'Purpurascens' have a proportion of leaves streaked with green, cyclamen pink, or ivory: a clone which is more correctly described as 'Purpurascens Variegata'. Like common sage, 'Purpurascens' bears vivid purplish-blue flowers in summer, and although some people like to remove them to keep the plant bushy, they are a fine contrast. This is a hardy and vigorous sage, and probably the most versatile in terms of colour. Though undeniably beautiful, it never dominates, and is the perfect complement to grey- and silver-

(above) 'Tricolor': *the least hardy but most beautiful sage.*
(above top) *Red or purple sage at the foot of a climbing rose.*

103

leaved plants, old roses, *Geranium* species, and many plants with pink, purple to blue, or white flowers.

Golden sage is known both as *S. officinalis* 'Aurea' and 'Variegata', as well as 'Icterina'. Again it has crinkly velveteen leaves, but this time the basic grey-green is marbled with yellowish-green. Because of the yellow cast, it can be used in quite different planting schemes where the accent is on gold, lime, yellows and oranges.

S. officinalis 'Tricolor' has such pretty leaves – each one differently patterned in sage green, white and pink – that flowering is only a distraction and is best nipped in the bud. The delicate colouring is, unfortunately, matched by a sensitive disposition, and hard frosts and cold damp weather are anathema to this painted beauty. In areas with hard winters, the best solution is, therefore, to treat it as an annual or to overwinter it under glass in a sunny well-ventilated situation (the leaves tend to moulder in humid shady conditions). Like its relatives, it is easy to root from cuttings of sideshoots in the summer, and these will give sturdy young plants for the following spring. 'Tricolor' is less vigorous altogether than the golden and red sages and is ideal for containers, where it looks delightful with other herbs, or with bedding plants such as *Verbena*, *Lobelia*, white or pale pink geraniums and *Helichrysum petiolatum*.

Sage is one of the commonest herbs in cultivation, and, being an essential component in dried mixed herbs and bouquets garnis, is widely grown for the food industry. Less well known is the respect it commands in herbal medicine, which is indicated by its name. The English word sage may be taken to mean wise, but the roots of the word lie in the Old French *sauge* and the Latin *salvia* and *salvere* (hence the genus name *Salvia*), which mean to be safe or saved – in other words, to be in good health. The plant has even been known as *Salvia salvatrix* – sage the saviour – from which we can deduce that it must once have been credited with life-saving powers. As a consequence, it

has featured in several proverbs and sayings, such as, 'Why should a man die whilst sage grows in his garden?' and 'He that would live for aye must eat sage in May'. They make rather greater claims for the herb than I would dare but, barring actual immortality, most of the other time-honoured applications have been substantiated by modern research into its chemistry. For example, the complex volatile oil – which gives it such an intense aroma – is a potent antiseptic. At one time, sage was boiled and evaporated in sick rooms to kill germs, and made into a medicine to expel internal parasites. Nowadays we are more likely to make use of its disinfectant properties by making a strong infusion of the leaves for a gargle or mouthwash to treat sore throats and dental infections. There is a long tradition, too, that sage leaves are good for cleaning the teeth and gums. Both the American Indians and the Arabs use the leaves for this purpose. A do-it-yourself tooth powder can easily be made by grinding sage leaves and sea salt together with a mortar and pestle. The mixture should be dried out, then reground and stored in an airtight container.

Sage has always been regarded as an excellent hair tonic and colour revitalizer which reduces dandruff and promotes healthy growth. All that is needed is a strong infusion applied as a rinse. Inhaled when steaming hot, an infusion is an effective decongestant too, and is reputed to relieve asthma and other forms of bronchial congestion. Sage is a relaxant as well, alleviating nervous tension, anxiety, depression and headaches associated with such conditions. Traditionally, it was thought to mitigate grief, and the English diarist Samuel Pepys recorded how graves in the Southampton area were sown with sage seeds. Following on from the use of sage to improve the balance of the nervous system is the belief that it benefits higher mental functions. John Gerard, the eminent herbalist of Elizabethan England, wrote that 'Sage is singularly good for the head and the brain, it quickeneth the senses and memory'. Perhaps it is for this reason that the Chinese, renowned for longevity and sagacity, found it incomprehensible that we should want to import their tea when we could grow sage, and at one time would barter several times the weight of their choicest blends for a shipment of this commonplace herb.

Not least in importance are the effects of sage on the digestive system. Its bitter components stimulate the flow of bile and digestive juices, improving both the appetite and the digestion of food – especially of fats. There are also compounds in sage which relieve wind and, even more interestingly, have an inhibitory effect on the growth of organisms which cause infections such as septicaemia, cholera and dysentery. In addition, its tannins combat diarrhoea. Sage tea is therefore a pleasant and practical remedy for minor gastric upsets which do not need medical attention – readily at hand in most kitchens, or growing fresh in the garden.

Sage has an agreeable but strong and bitter flavour which has been described as a cross between lavender and camphor. (Indeed, camphor is one of its components.) In earlier times, it was valued not only as a flavouring, but also as a preservative, especially in sausages and stuffings for meat. A little sage goes a long way, and it is not a herb to add lavishly. In many countries it is used primarily with meat, though exactly which varies. The British like it best with pork, sausages and poultry; Germany and Belgium prefer it with eels; and in Italy liver and veal are flavoured with it. Middle Eastern regions use it for quite another purpose – in their pungent herb salads, though these, in turn, may accompany a rich dish. Vegetarians find that it goes very well with most kinds of dried beans, with fresh broad, or fava beans and with many different cheeses. The English cheese, Sage Derby, has pounded sage leaves added to the curd. To all of these sage imparts a robust, appetizing flavour and aids in their digestion.

The genus *Salvia* has around 700 species worldwide and belongs to the family Labiatae.

Many salvias are highly aromatic. *S. sclarea* (commonly known as clary) is a southern Mediterranean herb important in perfumery and aromatherapy. The European *S. glutinosa* is so rich in essential oils that the leaves feel sticky, and *S. leucophylla*, a native of California, exudes such quantities of terpenes that other plants are unable to germinate or grow near it. In spring, the limestone hillsides of Greece give out the warm camphoraceous scent of *S. triloba* and are alive with countless bees searching the blue flowers. The leaves, which are very similar to those of common sage, but with little leaflets at the base, are picked by the islanders for Greek sage tea which is regularly drunk in many households. Another interesting Greek species is *S. pomifera*, which means 'apple-bearing'. It is attacked by an insect which causes semi-transparent galls to form on the stalks. The little sage 'apples' are gathered and candied as medicinal sweets. These and many other salvias are important bee plants. Of the fifteen or so species in California, two especially (*S. mellifera* and *S. grandiflora*) are noted for their rich and abundant nectar, and the superb honey produced by bees which feed from them.

Common sage originated in the Mediterranean and, though it tolerates partial shade and most soils, is happiest in a warm sunny spot and slightly alkaline conditions. It will thrive in poor stony soil, but if pruned or cropped heavily benefits from a dressing of well-rotted manure or compost in the spring. Pests and diseases are few and far between, and the only problem I have ever encountered is mildew on cuttings and young plants kept in too high humidity.

Sage bushes tend to get woody and sparse with age and are usually past their best after the third year. It is therefore wise to take cuttings each summer and keep a succession of young plants coming along – especially of 'Tricolor' which may succumb in the winter. Pruning helps keep bushes compact and leafy and should be done quite hard in the spring and

wrote: 'Among my herbs, sage holds the place of honour: of good scent it is, and full of virtue for many ills'. The Emperor Charlemagne ordered it to have pride of place in his garden, and the Abbé Kneipp proclaimed that 'No man who owns a garden should forget to plant in it a head of sage'. To these recommendations I can only add that including the colourful 'Purpurascens', 'Icterina' and 'Tricolor' will give plants to delight the eye as well as heal the body.

COLOURED ELDERS
Sambucus nigra 'Albovariegata' (syn. 'Marginata'), 'Aurea', 'Purpurea' and *S. racemosa* 'Plumosa Aurea'

Elder is one of the most magical trees in the world. Its wide distribution throughout Europe, North America, northern Africa and much of Asia, and its uses in healing and folklore in all these regions, have given it a richness of associations that can scarcely be matched. Its roots go deep into history; from its branches spring the rituals of necromancy; behind its leaves lurk all manner of spirits; within its flowers lie the secrets of beauty; and from the wine-red juice of its berries are squeezed the mysteries of longevity.

In all aspects elder is a plant of dramatic contrasts, with a great variety of uses, both noble and humble. It is sacred to the Gypsies and was planted in the dignified courtyards of synagogues in the Israeli town of Safad, where it was probably used in occult practices of the Jewish cabbala. A less illustrious fate befell it in the British Isles where, before the days of indoor sanitation, it used to be planted adjacent to the privy (a lavatory in an outhouse) to deter flies. The flowers offer a similar contradiction – the rather sickly smell of the flowers, though nowhere near as unpleasant as that of the leaves, has a surprisingly delicate bouquet

more lightly after flowering (or before if you do not want flowers).

Even though sage is evergreen and can be gathered all the year round, it is dormant in winter and makes no new growth for several months. It is therefore best to pick enough leaves for winter use when they are at their most vigorous and the essential oil content is at its highest – that is, on a warm dry day before noon, just before flowering. They need very careful drying because of the felty texture and should be spread out individually on trays in a shady well-ventilated place at 23–26°C (73–79°F). Alternatively, they may be frozen. All aromatic herbs should be handled as little as possible, to prevent loss of volatile ingredients, and are best kept in dark airtight containers until required.

Sage has been described as 'the queen of medicinal plants' by the present day herbalist Jean Palaiseul, and many have praised it before him. The ninth-century Walafrid Strabo

when used in desserts, wine and cosmetics. Another contrast is the brittle nature of the young wood, which is full of soft pith, and the old wood which is fine, hard, white and virtually rot-proof. There is a saying that an elder stake or fence will last longer in the ground than an iron bar, and the wood was traditionally used by shoemakers to nail soles to uppers and for fine instruments, turned articles, combs, skewers and the like. On the other hand, the soft new shoots have, since time immemorial, been hollowed into popguns and panpipes, giving elder the other name of pipe tree. The generic name *Sambucus* comes from a Greek word for a musical pipe, from which is derived the present-day Italian *sampagna*, an elder flute. And what more dramatic contrasts could there be than the colours of the dyes it yields – black from the roots and bark, green from the leaves, blues and purples from the berries, whose crimson juice has long been used to improve the colour – and perhaps the

(opposite) Golden elder. Like many gold-leaved plants, it colours best in sun.
(above) Bronze elder has very dark purplish-brown leaves and pink-stamened flowers.

flavour – of wine.

Like many plants which have long been important in the community, elder is steeped in folklore whose origin is hard to determine. What is behind the tradition that one should never prune or harvest elder without first asking and apologizing to the elder tree mother, Hylde-Moer? Why should it never be burnt (the word elder comes from the Anglo-Saxon *aeld* meaning fire, but this was only because the hollow stems were used for blowing fading embers), or used to make cradles, lest the baby should be strangled in revenge by the elder mother? Why is it said that the cross of Christ was made from it, that Judas hanged himself on an elder tree, and that it is a wise

107

practice to doff one's hat or briefly bow in respect as we pass it by? Whatever the answers, there seem to be two sides to this mystifying plant: the dark and sombre of sorrow and death, reflected in the often dank shady places it grows; and the joyous – creamy posies of pollen-laden flowers, festive drinks, music and healing.

As can be seen by dipping into the herbal literature of Europe, North America and the Orient, elder is widely employed in traditional medicine. It has been called 'the medicine chest of the people' and in the past was regarded as a wonder drug which would, among other things, give sight to the blind, stave off epileptic fits and cure malignant skin growths. Herbalists today are more modest in their claims, but it is still a very important medicinal plant. The flowers are valued most, though all parts have their uses. The roots and bark are purgative; the leaves are used in ointments to soothe chilblains, bruises and wounds, and in sprays to kill greenfly and other garden pests; the flowers are distilled for astringent eye and skin lotions and infused for internal uses as a medicine to relieve fevers, colds and 'flu – elderflower, yarrow and peppermint tea being the classic herbal remedy for all respiratory complaints. The juice of the berries, blended with lemon, honey and cinnamon, or preserved as a cordial, is an excellent hot drink for sore throats, coughs, colds, 'flu and catarrh, and in former times was reputed to cleanse the body of toxins, thus relieving degenerative diseases and ensuring longevity. And to complete the illusion of perpetual youth, one can, apparently, die the hair black with it too.

The culinary uses of elder are just as popular today as centuries ago. In many countries the flowerheads are gathered in early summer and stripped of their tiny flowers, whose flavour is akin to muscatel grapes, to make wine and elderflower 'champagne' (a delightful slightly alcoholic fizzy drink). They are also cooked as fritters and used to flavour desserts, jams and jellies (especially goose-berry). The heavy umbels of small black berries are one of the highlights of the hedgerow harvest, whether one turns them into a glorious red wine, pies (with apple), jelly, ketchup or chutney.

Elders belong to the genus *Sambucus*. It is part of the family Caprifoliaceae which also includes the honeysuckles and viburnums. There are about 40 different species of *Sambucus*, many of which are edible and medicinal. European settlers in North America soon discovered that the native American elder, *S. canadensis*, was used by the Indians and made a good substitute for the elder of their homelands, the common or black elder, *S. nigra*.

In the wild, common elder reaches 4–5 m (13–16 ft) and usually has mid-green pinnate leaves with five oval pointed leaflets, cream flowers and black fruits, but a number of variants have been recorded, most of which have been brought into cultivation. The leaves may be deeply cut, golden, purplish-brown, or variegated with cream or yellow. Less variety is apparent in the flowers, though a close look at those of the bronze-leaved form reveals that they have pink stamens when first opened. Forms with white or yellow berries are seen occasionally, as is one with green fruits and white bark. The coloured-leaved varieties are particularly striking shrubs for the backs of borders or shady corners. There are several kinds of variegated elder, the most striking being 'Albovariegata' (syn. 'Marginata'), which has leaflets broadly edged in creamy white and is a wonderful lightener of gloom. The name 'Albovariegata' was in fact first given to a white-speckled form described in 1770, but is now generally used for plants with white margins only. Confusingly, it is also sold as 'Albomarginata' and 'Variegata'. In contrast, the bronze elder ('Purpurea') has very dark purplish-brown leaves and is an effective backdrop for pink or mauve flowers in a sunny position. Most cheerful of all, and one of the hardiest of all golden shrubs, is 'Aurea', the golden elder, whose young yellow leaves age to lime and are practically scorch-proof. It is a fine shrub for planting schemes where gold and green foliage predominates along with mostly yellow, cream and white flowers. As with many golden-leaved plants, it colours better in the sun but retains its glowing yellow tint longer in shade. Though happiest in cool moist positions, all elders tolerate full sun and almost all soils, and are quick-growing. To control the size of shrubs and prevent them becoming sparse and woody, it is best to cut the stems within a few inches of ground level in early spring, before the new leaves start into growth. This gives vigorous new growths with larger, more richly coloured leaves, but, unfortunately, is at the expense of flowers and fruits.

S. *racemosa*, the red elder, is found in Europe (but is not native to the British Isles), western Asia and northern China. It is smaller on average than the black elder, reaching only 2 m (6 ft) or so, and has more slender leaflets, small conical panicles of creamy-yellow flowers in early spring, followed by scarlet berries in the summer. Like the black elder, it is hardy and deciduous. The form usually cultivated is 'Plumosa Aurea' which is, by any standards, an aristocrat among foliage plants. The yellow leaflets have their margins cut into fringes and the new leaves are flushed bronze as they emerge. It forms a beautifully proportioned, graceful, slow-growing shrub and retains its colour well if protected from full sun. Pruning can be less drastic than with the black elder but should be done in alternate years to maintain a good shape and fine foliage.

The red elder is both edible and medicinal but has limited uses in the home. Herbalists have used the roots as a purgative and diuretic, and the pulp of the red fruits makes a nutritious jelly. The seeds inside the berries are, however, poisonous, and should not be included.

There is no doubt that elders have a great deal to recommend them, not least their ease of cultivation and attractive coloured forms. If, in addition, you investigate their folklore and uses, you are sure to be even more enamoured. Remember though, however fond of them you become, never sit too long in the shade of an elder, for it is rumoured that you may be overcome by a deep narcotic slumber . . .

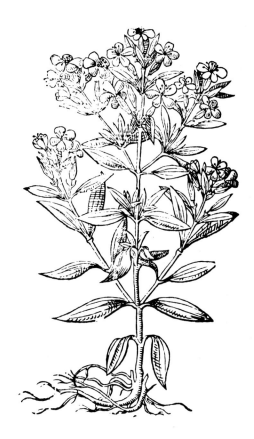

Soapwort (Saponaria officinalis)

DOUBLE-FLOWERED SOAPWORT
Saponaria officinalis 'Rosea Plena'

Soap is such commonplace stuff that we never give it a second thought, but commercial soap production began only in the 1800s and before then every housewife had to produce her own soap for the daily chore of washing. The first soap was made by boiling an unsavoury mixture of goat grease and wood ash, a process known in Roman times. Long before that, however, the plant world was

109

producing much more wholesome soapy substances which can be used both for washing and for medicinal purposes. These substances are known as saponins. They are soluble in water and lower the surface tension, producing a lather. Most plants contain saponins, but some have such high concentrations that they are particularly useful, and not just for washing. Saponins of a certain group yield hormonal substances which are the basis of contraceptive pills and anti-inflammatory cortisone preparations. Others are used to kill fish, as saponins penetrate the delicate gill tissues and break down the blood cells – a

Goodbye-to-summer! – late-flowering double soapwort with a summertime scent and all the untidiness of autumn.

traditional method which leaves the fish safe for consumption, as saponins are poorly absorbed through the digestive system. Even the foaming head on some beers is due to the addition of saponins.

Most of the best known plants which are rich in saponins have common names involving the word 'soap' and sometimes a scientific name involving the Latin word for soap, *sapo*. Often the part of the plant used is indicated in the name too. There is soapbark (*Quillaja saponaria*), a South American tree of the rose family; soaproot (*Chlorogalum pomeridianum*), a bulbous species related to lilies; the tropical American soapberry (*Sapindus saponaria*); soapwoods (the stems of several Central and North American yuccas); and last but not least, soapwort or latherwort (*Saponaria offici-*

nalis), a European species whose rhizomes, leaves and stalks are used.

Saponaria is a genus of the pink and campion family, Caryophyllaceae. The flowers of soapwort are commonly a delicate shell pink, sometimes white or a darker pink, and look very similar to wild campions and pinks. They also have the wonderful scent shared by many members of the family, which attracts butterflies and moths. Flowering takes place fairly late in the summer and goes on into autumn, giving soapwort another of its names, goodbye-to-summer. The five-petalled flowers are borne in clusters towards the top of tall, rather sprawling stems which reach 70 cm (28 in) or more. The odourless leaves are lanceolate in shape and smooth, with deep-set longitudinal veins. They clasp the stalk and where they join it there is a characteristic swelling. This joint fractures easily and is the best place to snap the stalk when gathering soapwort. Soapwort spreads enthusiastically – sometimes excessively – in moist neutral to alkaline soil, by means of runners. Originally it was native to central and southern Europe but has escaped from cultivation in many places and now frequents woodlands, hedgerows and the banks of streams and railways in many parts of Asia and North America as well as northern Europe. Its liking for hedgerows gives it the name hedge pink. Where I live there are blanket mills, and soapwort is common along the river, surviving from the days when it was grown for washing the wool and was known as fuller's herb.

Cottage gardens are other likely places to find corners of soapwort originally planted for practical purposes. Perhaps for this reason it got yet another of its common names, old maid's pink. The sites of Roman baths are also known to harbour these tenacious plants. Double-flowered forms have probably been in cultivation for many centuries and are not uncommon in the wild. Both pale pink and white double forms occur. They are only loosely double and have an untidy look which is far more characterful than the crimped perfection of their well-bred relatives, the garden pinks. Usually I can't resist white forms, but in this case the shell pink 'Rosea Plena' is hard to improve upon. Whichever variety you choose, remember to give it space (in sun or light shade) to spread and flop about. Otherwise it is a trouble-free plant which will flower generously year after year, if not century after century. Should it exceed its welcome, you can always harvest a vast amount (either before or after flowering) and make enough soapwort solution to shampoo the carpets!

Soapwort leaves produce a lather if merely crushed and rubbed together in water. The roots are much tougher and need chopping and boiling for about ten minutes. Soapwort solution has been used to clean almost anything, from tapestries and needlework (apparently some museums still prefer soapwort to modern products) to pewter and wooden utensils and hair. In a dilute form and carefully controlled doses, it is also used medicinally, though, like all saponin-rich compounds, it can be toxic in excess. When taken internally, saponins irritate mucous membranes and trigger reflexes which lead to an increase in glandular secretions and acceleration of waste excretion. This kind of inner cleansing is often effective for skin complaints such as eczema and acne, bronchial congestion and venereal disease. Infusions are used externally too, often by adding to the bath water. Homoeopathic medicine also uses soapwort for skin problems. Another thing that saponins do is to increase the absorption of certain substances (calcium, for example) from food in the digestive system. Most herb teas contain enough to aid digestion in this way, as do common foods such as beans, spinach and oats.

The many common names of soapwort indicate that it has long been a popular plant. Apart from those already mentioned, it is called wild sweet William, sweet Betty and bouncing Bet (or Beth). Whatever its origin, the last name certainly makes it the perfect partner for rock soapwort or tumbling Ted. He, like she, is a saponaria (*S. ocymoides*), but, instead of popping up as large as life in herbaceous borders, is a creeping alpine which pours mats of miniature pinks over every obstacle in its path, having profusion and vigour in common, as well as saponins.

VARIEGATED WATER FIGWORT
Scrophularia auriculata (syn. *S. aquatica*)
'Variegata'

Variegated water figwort is a magnificent foliage plant for wet places. The wild species grows mostly along rivers and canals, reaching an average of 60 cm tall – up to 100 cm (24–40 in) or more in rich mud. The stems are distinctively square in cross section and are winged along each angle: a feature of many aquatic plants which need such reinforcements to withstand water pressure. The leaves alternate in pairs and are oval, often with two small leaflets (auricles) at the base, and lightly toothed at the margin. In summer, sparse panicles of dark red, hooded flowers are produced which attract pollinating wasps. In spite of its size, water figwort is easily overlooked among the profusion of other lush tall waterside plants.

Not so the variegated form. With bold irregular white bands round each leaf and several shades of dark green in the centre, it draws the eye throughout the growing season and makes an outstanding specimen plant. It is particularly effective near bold clumps of green foliage, such as that of skunk cabbages (*Lysichiton* spp) or aquatic reeds and irises, or arising from drifts of sky-blue water forget-me-nots.

The figworts belong to the genus *Scrophularia* and the family Scrophulariaceae, names which were given because some of their members are medicinal plants used to treat scrofula, or the king's evil, a common disease in earlier times which is now referred to as tuberculosis of the lymph glands. Water figwort was one of the ingredients in a renowned remedy for this affliction which its originator, a certain Count Matthei, called 'Anti-Scrofuloso'.

There are about 315 species of *Scrophularia* mostly found in northern temperate regions, but only the variegated water figwort is of any merit in cultivation. It is a hardy perennial which dies down in winter and is easy enough to grow, given fertile moist soil in sun or partial shade. Some growers prefer to remove the flower spikes as they appear, so as to prolong the vigour of the foliage. Propagation is best done in March when clumps may be divided and replanted.

Water figwort is not used much in modern herbal medicine, but in the past was considered a good remedy for tuberculous glands and slow-healing ulcers, sores and wounds. Though closely related and similar in appearance to the common or knotted figwort, *S. nodosa* (an important medicinal herb used for chronic skin diseases, such as eczema and psoriasis), it is not known how far they resemble each other in their chemistry. Both have a strong unpleasant scent when crushed and are poisonous in sufficient quantity. Knotted figwort is known to contain substances that act on the heart in the same way as those in foxgloves (*Digitalis* spp) which are, after all, another branch of the same family. In the wild, common or knotted figwort can be told apart from water figwort by its tuberous 'knotty' rhizome, more pointed leaves without auricles, stems which have no longitudinal wings and, of course, by its habitat which, though often damp, is less likely to be aquatic.

Water figwort is known by a variety of other names, several of which refer to violins: fiddlewood, fiddler and crowdy kit ('kit' being an old Somerset word for a fiddle). The reason for this is that if the winged stalks are rubbed together, they make the somewhat unmusical sound of a bow being scraped on violin strings. Presumably this is more noticeable when the stems are hard and dried in winter.

For years I was under the whimsical illusion that figworts were so called because their little maroon flowers are reminiscent of minute figs. Then I discovered that the Latin word for fig, *ficus*, was the term used for haemorrhoids or piles – hence the name *ficaria* which was given to several other herbs used for this complaint (such as pilewort, *Ranunculus ficaria*) – which is a less endearing, but much more practical explanation.

Figwort (Scrophularia nodosa)

COLOURED HOUSELEEKS
Sempervivum tectorum 'Lancelot' and 'Lavender and Old Lace'

Houseleeks have been associated with human habitation for hundreds, if not thousands of years. The actual word means 'houseplant' – *leac* being Anglo-Saxon for a plant – and even in Roman times it was grown in ornamental pots in front of houses. Its importance in different European cultures is shown in some of the common names it has acquired: Jupiter's eye, Jupiter's beard, Thor's beard, St Patrick's cabbage and Aaron's rod. However fanciful the resemblance to an eye or a beard, the link with Jupiter and Thor is significant. They were gods of sky and thunder respectively, and houseleeks – regardless of their medicinal uses – were first and foremost grown on and around dwellings to protect them from thunderbolts, lightning and fire. (Another of its names is thunder plant.) For this reason it was – and still is – commonly planted on roofs, chimneys and walls in almost every part of Europe.

Some of its other names refer to its habit. Sengreen, ayron, and ayegreen are all versions of evergreen; hen-and-chickens describes a fully grown rosette surrounded by offsets; and live-forever comments on its ability to survive both winter freezing and summer drought unscathed. Its remarkable toughness also in-spired the generic name *Sempervivum; semper* is the Latin word for 'always' and *vivo* means 'I live'. To this is added the species name *tectorum* – 'of roofs'. In contrast to these practical observations, the name welcome-home-husband-however-drunk-you-may-be is delightfully frivolous. How it originated is far from clear. It has been suggested that it refers to the leaning flower stalks – an unlikely explanation that, if nothing else, gives a botanical slant to the expression 'a night on the tiles'.

Houseleeks are found wild in the Alps, Appenines and Pyrenees of southern Europe. They belong to the family Crassulaceae and

are closely related to saxifrages (Saxifragaceae). Crassulas are mostly succulent plants adapted to growing in regions where water is in short supply for long periods. Many species are native to South Africa and undergo drought, heat and high light levels by having compact fleshy leaves protected by devices such as wax, hair-like processes, and substances known as anthocyanins. The latter give a reddish coloration which increases as conditions become more severe. Sempervivums show all these specializations and, in addition, are able to withstand hard frosts.

The genus *Sempervivum* has about 50 species and their enduring popularity in cultivation has led to innumerable hybrids and cultivars. *S. tectorum* crosses readily with *S. arachnoideum* and *S. montanum* and the ancestry of many attractive garden forms is difficult to determine. All sempervivums have either pink or yellow flowers, though white-flowered forms have been recorded. They are perennial succulents with rosettes of 50 or more stalkless fleshy leaves. Some are almost glossy, whereas

(above) Variegated water figwort: a highlight for damp shade.

(opposite, top) 'Lavender and Old Lace': grey-green when lush; pink-tinged in drought.

(opposite, below) 'Lancelot', a burgundy houseleek, studs mats of Acaena microphylla.

others (such as *S. arachnoideum*, the cobweb houseleek) are criss-crossed by long white hairs. *S. tectorum* is the largest species, with rosettes averaging 5–10 cm (2–4 in) across. The leaves are obovate with quite sharply pointed tips and measure some 2–6 cm (1–2½ in) in length. Their margins are reddish and fringed with very short fine hairs. Mature plants flower in the summer, producing panicles of star-shaped unscented flowers about 2 cm (1 in) across on leafy stalks which reach 20 cm (8 in) or more. After flowering, that particular plant dies but its offsets soon fill the gap. They are produced on stolons (runners), but by the time the parent plant is mature, are growing on their own roots. For the plants, this spreading, yet clustered habit is a further

114

protection against the elements, but from the horticulturist's point of view it is an attractive feature.

Given their preference for exposed rocky calcareous sites in the wild, any situation which imitates this will suit houseleeks in cultivation. Sunny aspects on rock gardens and stony slopes are home from home, but there are many other suitable niches, such as tiled or thatched roofs, walls, the edges of paths, between paving slabs, or in containers made from porous material. Establishing houseleeks in precarious positions on rooftops is best done in early spring when there are frequent showers of rain and the rosette is about to produce offsets. Padding the root system with a little moss and anchoring the main root with a piece of wire will also help stabilize the plant quickly and prevent birds from tweeking loose rosettes out of place as they search for insects and nesting material. Once established, houseleeks are virtually trouble and maintenance free. They look immaculately tidy all through the year, with a sculptural simplicity that might almost be acceptable in a Japanese garden. Following the contours of their surroundings, they spread in a restrained way over rocks and the rim of containers as the rosettes methodically increase in number, leaving gardeners nothing to do but admire their handywork.

There are so many attractive sempervivums that it is hard to choose between them. Two of my favourites are 'Lancelot' and 'Lavender and Old Lace'. The former is a deep dark burgundy with a subtle wavelike pattern reminiscent of moiré silk. It looks to me like a strange sea anemone seen through rippled water. 'Lavender and Old Lace' is quite different in colour and texture: a soft grey-green tinged with pinkish-mauve and covered with a haze of fine white stubbly hairs. Both are large and dramatic and look most effective planted next to contrastingly small fresh green cobweb varieties.

Old sinks and stone troughs are excellent for displaying a collection of sempervivums.

From above, a colony of houseleeks looks like a contoured mosaic, and richly coloured patterns can be created by planting different varieties close together. Alternatively, they may be grown with ground-hugging plants, such as the silver moss-like *Raoulia* species, and the more compact acaenas (purplish-brown A. *pulchella* and pale blue-green A. *microphylla* 'Pallidolivacea', for example).

Houseleeks contain a number of substances which cool, soothe and heal damaged tissues. The fleshy leaves used to be slit in two and applied to bites and stings, minor scalds and burns (including sunburn), bruises and inflamed or itching skin. The seventeenth-

Houseleek (Sempervivum tectorum), *in flower.*

116

century herbalist John Parkinson wrote that 'The juice takes away corns from the toes and feet if they be bathed therewith every day, and at night emplastered as it were with the skin of the same houseleek.' Where the affected area was too large for the application of sections of leaves, the foliage of several plants would be infused to make a lotion. They have been part of the household repertoire for treating corns, warts, piles and more serious conditions, such as herpes and shingles, since time immemorial. Although skin problems are the main sphere of action, a variety of other ailments have been treated with this unusual herb. The crushed leaves, rolled into pills with flour and honey, were taken to expel worms. Nicholas Culpeper reckoned 'it easeth also the headache and the distempered heat of the brain in frenzies or through want of sleep, being applied to the temples and forehead.'

Today we may have more convenient remedies for everyday complaints such as sore and irritated skin, but it is still worth trying houseleeks in an emergency or for conditions that fail to respond to other treatments. Several books on herbal cosmetics recommend them highly for their curative and regenerative properties, giving recipes for incorporating them into masks and other preparations to soothe and beautify the skin. According to Victorian flower emblemism, houseleeks represent vivacity and domestic industry. The former may have something to do with their reputation as an anti-wrinkle herb; the latter possibly because they are the herbal equivalent of a sticking plaster, called upon to deal with the minor accidents and discomforts that are part of the daily round in any busy household.

VARIEGATED BITTERSWEET
Solanum dulcamara 'Variegatum'

Compared with their wild counterparts, plants in cultivation are pampered. They are generally better fed and groomed and have more space than in the intense competition of a natural habitat. Not all enjoy the change, but those that take to the new regime of tender loving care respond by forming larger and more impressive specimens. In addition, a well-chosen position accentuates patterns of growth that were difficult to appreciate in the wild, turning some ugly ducklings into swans. A good example of this is bittersweet or woody nightshade (or blue nightshade, mortal, fever twig, wolf grape, tetherdevil or skawcoo, depending on where you live). In many parts of Europe and North America, wild plants of this common perennial climber grow in amongst a rich assortment of other species in hedgerows, along river banks and on shingle beaches, with only the occasional spray of colourful flowers or fruit sufficiently visible to catch the eye. Though attractive in itself, the potential of bittersweet as a climber for the garden is easily overlooked when largely hidden by a dense tangle of vegetation.

Whatever its merits – and it was certainly cultivated in Victorian times – the variegated form brings this species from the obscurity of the hedgerow into the twentieth-century garden. It may never rival classic flowering climbers like honeysuckle and clematis, but it can do much to liven up their lengthy dull periods and thus holds a unique position in being an excellent climber for growing alongside another climber. In spite of appearing sparse and straggly in the wild, cultivated bittersweet will reach surprising dimensions and easily cover a wall, though it may need support if there is no other climber to give it purchase. The fact that it grows quite happily in dry soil, but also enjoys wet (though not acid) conditions, recommends it for positions where few other climbers will thrive. It is also quite hardy (the variegated form less so) and tolerates anything from full sun to semi-shade.

Bittersweet flowers and fruits throughout the summer and autumn, with berries still remaining after the leaves have fallen. It is not flamboyant enough to steal the limelight from a companion climber, but provides plenty of colour and detail during gaps in the star's performance. At Barnsley House in Gloucestershire, there is a superb specimen of variegated bittersweet on the wall of the house, intertwined with clematis. It has a great many stems reaching 3 m (10 ft) or more, and for many months is a cascade of numerous bright purple and yellow shooting-star flowers and berries in every stage, from green to brilliant scarlet. The green and white variegated leaves enhance the display and contrast nicely with the plain green of the clematis. It begins its show before the clematis comes into flower and continues after the feathery clematis seedheads have been blown away by the first winds of winter.

The flowers of bittersweet are similar in shape to those of its close relative, the potato (*Solanum tuberosum*). The flower stalks are purple, as is the calyx and the five petals. When opened, the petals are reflexed and have a green and white pattern at the base which forms a circle round the central cone of bright yellow stamens. The flowers are followed by

poisonous berries, 'more long than round' as Gerard says, and 'growing together in clusters like burnished coral'. They begin green and change through orange to a glowing shiny scarlet. The leaves are variable – mostly small, pointed and oval toward the bottom of the stems, and hastate (spear-shaped) and auriculate (with little basal lobes), or more fully lobed, higher up. Whatever shape the leaves, they tend to face the light and the flower clusters always face the opposite way.

Bittersweet is not a twining or clasping climber. Its technique for going up in the world is less obvious, consisting of vertical growth through the surrounding vegetation with right-angled, or drooping branches sent out to consolidate its position. Though woody at the base, the green stems are quite slender. It is these which are cut for medicinal use. The fresh plant has an unpleasant smell (which disappears on drying) and tastes bitter at first, then sweet, due to the breakdown of its poisonous glycoalkaloids – a characteristic which gave it the medieval Latin name of

amara dulcis and the species name, *dulcamara*, both of which translate as bittersweet.

The status of bittersweet as a medicinal herb is hard to determine, having been praised to the skies and condemned out of hand at various times in its chequered history. As Mrs Grieve said in her herbal of 1931: 'There are few complaints for which it has not at some time been recommended.' Its reputation for curing septic fingers gained it the common names felonwort and felonwood (felon being the medical term for such a complaint). Culpeper rated it highly for internal injuries in 'those that have fallen from high places'. Both herbalists and homoeopaths have used it internally as a tonic and cleanser for rheumatism, chronic skin diseases, such as eczema and psoriasis, and for catarrh, asthma and hay fever. The most recent use is in the form of compresses made from the leaves, which are proving quite successful in the treatment of cellulite ('orange peel' skin on the thighs and upper arms). The closely related *S. lyratum* – which has white flowers and round red berries and goes under the menacing name of sorcerer's eyes – is used in traditional Chinese medicine for cancer of the oesophagus and stomach, and for enlarged thyroid glands. Although bittersweet is certainly poisonous, it is not as toxic as deadly nightshade (*Atropa belladonna*) with which it is often confused – although the latter's non-climbing habit, brownish bell-shaped flowers and large jet black berries are quite distinctive.

The genus *Solanum* is one of the largest in the plant world, with over 1,700 species. It belongs to the nightshades (Solanaceae), a family which includes many medicinal plants, such as deadly nightshade, from which we get atropine (a drug used to dry up secretions before a general anaesthetic), and major food plants, such as potatoes, tomatoes, peppers and aubergines or eggplants – which, in spite of their edible parts, still have poisonous foliage. The names *Solanum* and Solanaceae are thought to be derived from the Latin verb *solor*, meaning to comfort or relieve, which

(opposite) Variegated bittersweet: a brilliant climber.

(above) Variegated Russian comfrey: a bold beauty for shady borders.

refers to the narcotic or soporific effects that many of these poisonous plants have on the body. Similarly, the early medical name for nightshade was *solatrum*. This was later confused with *solem atrum*, meaning black sun, a sinister name which, coincidentally, suits these plants and gave rise to that equally descriptive word, nightshade.

VARIEGATED COMFREYS
Symphytum x uplandicum 'Variegatum'
and *S. grandiflorum* 'Variegatum'

Variegated Russian comfrey (*Symphytum x uplandicum* 'Variegatum') is an eye-catching plant for damp shady places. To most people, the wild comfrey is undistinguished and rather coarse, but the addition of bold

Common comfrey (Symphytum officinale)

cream margins to the large bristly leaves makes the variegated form a stunning foliage plant. As a bonus, the bright fresh leaves of spring have scarcely darkened before the flower stems appear, bearing smaller, but equally brilliant leaves right up to the coil of buds which open successively into lilac-blue bells as summer advances. In good soil it can reach 1 m (3 ft) tall when flowering and as much across. You might fail to notice the wild species beside waterways and in damp hedgerows, but the variegated version is guaranteed to stop you in your tracks.

If your garden is too small to accommodate *S.* x *uplandicum* 'Variegatum', then the variegated dwarf comfrey is a good substitute. It has similar variegation but creamy-white tubular flowers in spring, and reaches only 15 cm (6 in) tall. And, whereas the large comfrey makes an imposing feature, the dwarf species is excellent ground cover. Both should be planted in shade as the cream margins tend to scorch in the sun.

The name comfrey is probably derived from the Latin *con ferva* which means uniting or joining together. This refers to its remarkable healing properties which have been used for centuries to repair broken bones, wounds and obstinate skin problems: hence its popular names of knitbone, consound, bruisewort and boneset. Incredible though it may seem, the leaves and mucilaginous roots contain such an effective healing agent that if they are merely mashed and applied to the damaged area the active ingredient – known as allantoin – will penetrate deeply into the tissues and speed the formation of new cells. The effectiveness of this substance is such that it is now synthesized and used by the pharmaceutical industry in a range of healing creams and ointments. (Herbalists prefer to use natural extracts of the plant, as there is evidence that they are more effective still and have fewer side-effects.)

Comfrey-based preparations can be bought at pharmacies, especially those selling a range of natural health products. They are very good for minor injuries, such as burns, bites, cuts, bruises and sprains, as well as stubborn problems like athlete's foot, varicose veins and haemorrhoids. The ointment is perfectly safe for use on animals who invariably lick their wounds and anything put on them. I once had occasion to test its effectiveness when I received a severe blow to the eye from an ash sapling which felled me, instead of the reverse. I applied the comfrey ointment lavishly and incessantly, and within four days it had healed with only the faintest trace of bruising, in spite of the fact that the doctor had predicted a truly spectacular black eye.

Comfrey can also be taken internally, as a tea or in tablet form. Herbalists prescribe it for serious complaints, such as gastric ulcers and rheumatism. There have, however, been reports in the press that ingesting comfrey can be dangerous and may cause liver damage. They were based on research in which laboratory animals were fed large amounts of an alkaloid found in comfrey. Many herbs contain poten-

120

tially toxic chemicals, as does any medicine, but the evidence of thousands of years of traditional use – with some justification referred to as the longest clinical trial in history – suggests that the whole plant (rather than an isolated ingredient) is quite safe when taken as prescribed by a medical herbalist.

Further evidence for the relative harmlessness of comfrey in moderate amounts is its use as a food. Since earliest times people have gathered the young leaves and chopped them into soups and salads, or cooked them with cabbage, spinach and other spring greens. As a livestock feed, comfrey is renowned for its high protein content (equal to soya beans) and rich supplies of vitamins and minerals, especially of Vitamin B12 (which is extremely rare in land plants, though known to be present in seaweeds and plankton). In some areas, comfrey is grown as a crop which can be cut several times a year, even in temperate zones, giving very high yields. The high nitrogen content, exceeding even that of farmyard manure, also means that comfrey leaves are excellent for making compost and fertilizers. Whether added to the compost heap, buried in trenches, or left to ferment in barrels of water, the resulting plant food will provide all the essential nutrients. It is particularly rich in potash – a crucial mineral for fruit crops, potatoes and legumes – and is better in this respect than many commercial tomato fertilizers.

The usefulness of this herb became the life's work of Henry Doubleday, a Quaker who was so appalled by the Irish potato famine in the nineteenth century that he determined to develop a high-protein crop to feed the starving. His hopes that comfrey would fulfil this role were inspired by a plant sent to him by the gardener to Catherine the Great of Russia. It was larger and more vigorous than the wild British comfrey, *Symphytum officinale*, and would therefore crop more heavily. Unfortunately, it has not proved practicable to turn its protein into a form suitable for large-scale human consumption. His work was not, however, in vain. The Henry Doubleday Research Association, founded by Lawrence D. Hills, continues to investigate comfrey as food, medicine and fertilizer and, in addition, is now one of the world's leading organizations for research into organic farming and gardening.

Botanically, comfrey is a member of the borage family, Boraginaceae. This is a large group of over 1,800 species, found all over the world, but which are particularly numerous around the Mediterranean. They mostly have rough hairy, or bristly stems and leaves, and inflorescences which are coiled inwards like a scorpion's tail. Its best known relatives are the forget-me-nots (*Myosotis* spp), the dye plant alkanet (*Alkanna tinctoria*) and borage (*Borago officinalis*) the cucumber-flavoured herb used in Pimms and other summer drinks. Russian comfrey, S. x *uplandicum*, is a natural hybrid between the huge S. *asperum* from south-west Asia, which reaches almost 2 m (6 ft), and common comfrey (S. *officinale*). As one would expect with an F1 hybrid, it is more vigorous than either parent. It has escaped from cultivation in many places and tolerates drier situations than common comfrey which is usually found close to water. Both Russian and common comfrey are used for culinary and medicinal purposes, fodder and composting, but the dwarf comfrey (S. *grandiflorum*), a native of the Caucasus, is generally grown only as an ornamental.

Comfrey is very hardy but dies down completely in winter. It is easy to grow, given rich, moisture-retentive soil. Underfed plants may suffer from rust which is difficult to eradicate, so new stock should be checked before planting. (Rust shows as powdery orange areas, mostly on the undersurfaces of leaves.) Once planted, comfrey is difficult to move, as its roots often go over 1 m (3 ft) deep and even the smallest piece left in the ground will regrow. It may be eradicated by watering with a solution of sodium chlorate or ammonium sulphamate, both of which are relatively harmless to wildlife. Propagation is best done by dividing the plants when dormant.

A final word of caution: Russian and common comfrey leaves can easily be mistaken for those of foxgloves (*Digitalis* spp) which are highly poisonous, so never plant them near each other in the garden if you intend to use the comfrey for food and medicine. Better still, plant the variegated form of Russian comfrey which is just as usable as the plain green kind, but quite unmistakable.

GOLDEN AND DOUBLE-FLOWERED DWARF FEVERFEWS
Tanacetum parthenium (syn. *Chrysanthemum parthenium*) 'Aureum' and 'Snowball'

Emerson, the nineteenth-century American poet and essayist, described weeds as 'plants whose virtues have not yet been discovered'. The truth of this maxim certainly applies to feverfew which, for much of this century, has been regarded as having little to recommend it, either medicinally or as a garden plant. In modern books on herbs published before about 1980, it receives scarcely a mention. Only the old herbals would give you any idea of the uses that have rocketed this plant into the forefront of herbal medicine in the last few years. Now its virtues have been rediscovered and it is cultivated as never before, both for its long-ignored curative properties and its chrysanthemum-like foliage and pretty daisy flowers – though its ornamental forms still remain poorly known because in horticulture it goes under a confusing variety of names.

The recent rise to fame for feverfew began in the late 1970s in Wales. A Cardiff doctor's wife, Mrs Ann Jenkins, began taking feverfew on the recommendation of a friend in the hope that it might relieve her migraine attacks. She had scant evidence that it would, as her friend had been using it for arthritis, but in spite of the apparent dissimilarity of their complaints,

Golden feverfew, with its lime green chrysanthemum-like leaves and characteristically pungent smell.

she found that after ten months she was, for the first time ever, free from attacks – and that just one leaf a day had succeeded where a variety of proprietary drugs had failed. She passed on the 'cure' to others, with the same degree of success, and soon the news reached associations for migraine sufferers, the London Migraine Clinic – and the media.

Migraine affects some 10 per cent of the population (in Great Britain at least) and causes untold suffering as well as disruption of work and social life. Many sufferers reach their wits' end after drug therapy fails to control attacks, or produces such unpleasant and serious side-effects that medication has to be withdrawn. As with any seemingly incurable disease, when rumours begin that a cure has been found, medical researchers are bound to take notice, though most such 'cures' soon prove to be false hopes. In this case, however, after thorough investigation of its chemistry, double-blind clinical trials, and extensive documentation of successful usage, it was concluded that feverfew was indeed the best treatment yet for this disabling affliction. The results were published in medical journals, and associations for migraine sufferers received thousands of queries on using the herb and products made from it.

Like all medicinal herbs, feverfew has a complex chemistry. From the migraine sufferer's point of view, the most interesting substances it contains are called sesquiterpene lactones. They suppress the formation, or control the effects of amines (such as histamine) and prostaglandins which are formed in the body during inflammatory and allergic responses, and which cause various symptoms, including a narrowing of the blood vessels and pain.

The main benefit of feverfew was, of course, the relief or absence of the crippling headaches and associated disturbances, but researchers noticed other effects. Migraine patients who suffered from other conditions reported marked improvement in some of these too. They included allergies, nervous tension, anxiety and depression, arthritic and rheumatic complaints, hypertension, digestive disorders and Menière's syndrome (a disorder characterized by severe dizziness and ringing in the ears). Exactly why this should be has not been fully established, but it is known, for example, that both migraine and arthritis sufferers have raised levels of prostaglandins, which does at least explain how Mrs Jenkins with migraine and her friend with arthritis were both helped by the sesquiterpene lactones in feverfew.

The sad thing is that almost every complaint which has now been found to respond to feverfew was defined long ago in the herbals which the twentieth century had largely condemned as 'old wives' tales'. John Gerard, whose herbal was published in 1597, described its use for 'melancholie' (depression) and for 'all inflammations and hot swellings', which occur in arthritic and rheumatic conditions. Nicholas Culpeper, in his herbal of 1653, recommended it for 'melancholy and heaviness, or sadness of spirits' and 'wind and cholic', as well as stating that it is 'very effective for all pains in the head'. He also says it works in cases of vertigo 'that is a running or swimming in the head' (Menière's syndrome). In the eighteenth century, the herbalist John Hill claimed that 'in the worst headache this herb exceeds whatever else is known'. And, in one of the last detailed accounts of the plant before herbalism became outmoded by scientific innovation, a book titled *A Welsh Botanology* (published in Welsh in 1813) describes how a woman who was almost driven insane with terrible headaches, was completely cured by infusions of feverfew.

In addition to the range of ailments so far mentioned, feverfew also relieves menstrual problems. One of its former names, *Matricaria*, is from the Latin *matrix* meaning a womb. Again, we should have expected this as Culpeper and other herbalists repeatedly stressed its effectiveness in women's complaints. It was once used to ensure complete expulsion of the afterbirth and 'doth a woman all good she can desire of an herb' by way of strengthening the womb and putting right 'infirmities as a careless midwife hath there caused'. A modern herbalist, Juliette de Baïracli Levy, finds it has 'power over the uterus and ovaries', preventing miscarriages and treating infertility. In her work on veterinary herbalism, she goes on to recommend it for difficult labours and retained afterbirth in domestic animals.

Still more uses include its possible value in drug abuse. Culpeper regarded it as 'an especial remedy against opium when taken too liberally' and a more recent source (*The Herb Book* by John Lust, 1974) indicates its usefulness in the withdrawal symptoms of alcoholism. One practical everyday application is as an antihistamine for the relief of stings and bites. As an on-the-spot remedy, it is more effective than a dock leaf, or can be made into a lotion for the purpose. Strangely enough, in spite of its name, feverfew has rarely been used for fevers.

Needless to say, however remarkable a drug, herbal or synthetic, appears, there will always be some people who find it ineffective and others who have unpleasant side-effects. Feverfew is no exception. The commonest side-effects are mouth ulcers and swelling of the mouth and lips. Fortunately, no more serious side-effects have been reported and on the whole it appears to be an extremely safe herb in spite of its potency. It seems to combine well with other medications and in many instances increases their effectiveness. It is not, however, an instant cure, and anyone thinking of trying it must have proper advice from a qualified medical herbalist or a practitioner at a migraine clinic – and follow instructions, as with any course of medication.

Feverfew is a member of the daisy family, Compositae. Though now in the genus *Tanacetum*, it has previously been included in several other composite genera: *Matricaria*, *Pyrethrum* and *Chrysanthemum*. In seed catalogues it is still usually listed as *Matricaria eximia*, with or without the common name of feverfew to help identification. In summer it reaches about 45 cm (18 in) or more and bears clusters of typical white-rayed daisy flowers with a central yellow disc. The leaves, which remain all winter, are a fresh green and deeply lobed. The wild species does, in fact, look very like a number of other daisy species, but can usually be told apart by its very strong, and rather unpleasant, smell.

The cultivated varieties are much more distinctive in appearance and are well worth a place in any garden, yet can be used medicinally in exactly the same ways. There are a number of different cultivars. Some merely have pure white double flowers and in other respects are the same as the species. They include 'Ball's Double White' and 'White Bonnet', both of which can reach 60 cm (2 ft). These are nice for the border and give tall, long-lasting stems of flowers for cutting. Most

of the other cultivars are smaller, double-flowered, and usually grown as half-hardy annuals. 'Snowball' is one of the best, with ivory white double centres and an outer circle of white ray petals. It reaches 30 cm (1 ft) and is an excellent choice for the front of borders. With similar button flowers and a bushy, floriferous habit, are the really dwarf 'White Gem' and 'Tom Thumb White Stars' which, at about 20 cm (8 in), are suitable for edging, bedding and containers. There are also interesting, but less versatile yellow-flowered dwarf varieties ('Gold Star' and 'Golden Ball', for example). For those with limited growing space, who need fresh leaves for medicinal purposes, dwarf feverfew of any kind is especially useful, providing compact plants which remain attractive all season, even in pots on a sunny windowsill or in windowboxes.

The feverfew with most potential as a foliage plant is *T. parthenium* 'Aureum' which has typical single daisies but brilliant yellow-green foliage. Unlike many golden-leaved plants, it remains bright in partial shade and into the winter. This variety looks very handsome near euphorbias with lime green or red flowerheads, or bronze fennel. It reaches 45 cm (18 in), comes true from seed and sows itself quite freely on open ground, but is not too much trouble in a well-planted border.

Propagating feverfew is straightforward. Seed should be fresh (under a year old), but it is otherwise an easy method, though some double-flowered varieties will produce a proportion of single-flowered offspring. Vegetative propagation has the advantage of ensuring new plants exactly like the parent, though generally fewer offspring are possible than with seed. It can be done by cuttings taken from plants after flowering (even seed-raised plants flower the first year), or by splitting a plant with a sharp knife, which means actually cutting the main stem in half, together with half its root system. The leaves can also be induced to root if the stalks are dipped into hormone rooting powder, though this has a lower success rate than other methods.

Feverfew is a hardy short-lived perennial, seldom surviving more than a few years, though in most gardens it will sow itself sufficiently to ensure a succession of young plants. Its distribution in the wild is very wide, but originally it was probably native to the Balkan region, spreading over the rest of Europe with the advance of the Roman empire, which valued it as a medicinal plant. From the British Isles it then reached North America with the first settlers. As a consequence of its southern origins, it prefers dry sunny sites and readily takes to walls, paths and stony wasteland. In the garden it will, however, tolerate almost any conditions but dense shade and waterlogging. Altogether, it is an immensely useful and adaptable plant whose horticultural varieties should be much better known and more widely grown, and whose medicinal properties could help many people with common and often intractable complaints. A leaf a day . . .

CURLY WOOD SAGE
Teucrium scorodonia 'Crispum'

Wood sage is a plant for those who will look long and carefully. There is nothing whatsoever about it that is showy or even eye-catching. It grows incognito whether in evergreen winter garb, new spring foliage, summer flowers or autumn seedheads, being small, green and unobtrusive. Neither is it rare, being found throughout most of western Europe where dry acid conditions predominate in woodland, scrub, heath, or even on mountain screes and stabilized sand dunes. What does make it attractive is its all-year-round neatness and uniformity. Though a hardy herbacious perennial, it has a shrubby appearance, with a creeping rootstock that sends up a dense mass of shoots clothed in pairs of pointed oval leaves which are etched with a fine network of veins and have the texture of paper-thin suede. Its tiny flowers are a pale green and not unlike those of the mints and marjorams in shape, but lack an upper lip so that the dark pink stamens are clearly exposed.

The curly form of wood sage is exactly the same in habit as the species, reaching somewhere between 30 and 45 cm (12–18 in) in height and remaining compact and tidy regardless of the season. The only difference is in the leaf margins. Instead of being regularly toothed, they are both toothed and frilled, and, in most plants, tinged white or pink – turning a plain leaf into one that is exceptionally pretty and most unusual. In the winter, these ruffles tend to flush purple.

I have to admit that curly wood sage is one of my very favourite plants. It is happy in sun or shade and on any soil, providing it is not too alkaline or wet. Never spreading to excess and needing no pruning or staking, it is perfectly behaved and trouble-free, and equally at home in the front of a border, on a rock garden, as ground cover under trees or shrubs, or among heathers and conifers.

There are several hundred species of *Teucrium* and they belong to the family Labiatae, which includes many of the world's most important culinary herbs. They have a wide distribution but are found mainly in northern temperate zones, the Mediterranean and the subtropical eastern hemisphere. Quite a number are shrubby in appearance and a few, such as the small glossy-leaved wall germander (*T. chamaedrys*) and the blue-flowered *T. fruticans*, are popular in cultivation.

Wood sage is a herbalist's herb though it was once a popular household remedy for a wide range of ailments. The whole herb is gathered in the summer and used fresh in teas and external preparations, or dried for winter use. It is an astringent tonic with antibiotic properties. Internally, it is used for attacks of rheumatism and gout, and for upper respiratory tract infections. Wood sage tea is therefore worth trying at the onset of a feverish cold, perhaps combined with an infusion of yarrow

(*Achillea millefolium*), peppermint (*Mentha x piperita*) and elderflowers (*Sambucus nigra*). As an appetizer, it is said to be as good as gentian and is an excellent cure for flatulent indigestion. For external use, herbalists mix wood sage with chickweed (*Stellaria media*) or comfrey (*Symphytum officinale*) in ointments and poultices for boils, abscesses and skin ulcers. In earlier times it was used to prevent wounds becoming gangrenous and has a reputation for healing superficial tumours and cancers. Wood sage is very bitter in taste and smells rather like hops. As a result, it has in the past been used in brewing, especially in the Channel Islands where it is known as ambroise.

Wood sage resembles common sage (*Salvia officinalis*) when not flowering and is therefore known as wild sage, mountain sage, sage germander and sage-leaved germander. It cannot, however, be used like sage, either in cooking or for medicinal purposes. Another of its names is garlic sage (the word *scorodonia* being from the Greek word for garlic), but as far as I can tell there is nothing garlicky about it. The genus name, *Teucrium*, is also a bit of a mystery. It may commemorate Teucer, King of Troy, who is supposed to have been the first to use these plants medicinally. Then again, Linnaeus is said to have named it after a medical botanist called Dr Teucer.

Its most evocative name is hind heal, from the belief that deer would eat wood sage when they were sick or injured. Whether this is true or not – and it may well be – it seems somehow appropriate that they would search out this plant, whose velvety softness and ability to blend into the surroundings matches their own.

COLOURED THYMES
Thymus 'Silver Posy' and *T. serpyllum* 'Aureus'

Other culinary herbs add piquancy and aroma, but thyme gives a rich savouriness that is unique. The merest pinch transforms even the insipid into something interesting in a trice. It is an essential ingredient in bouquets garnis and at its most subtle yet powerful when blended with wine and garlic (or onions). A whole host of appetizing recipes for pâtés, meat and fish dishes, soups and casseroles depend upon thyme, and many cooks, especially those steeped in French cuisine, regard it as the supreme culinary herb. To their praises are joined those of the medical profession. The French herbalist Maurice Mességué not only shares his country's love of its flavour, but assures us that 'From boils to typhoid fever, from whitlows to tuberculosis, I do not know any infection that cannot be mitigated if treated with this precious herb, thyme' – a bold claim but one that

126

is not without foundation. Thyme is also a gardener's delight, concentrating much fragrance and prettiness into a very small volume of miniature leaves and flowers.

When you start to consider how thyme has been used medicinally over the centuries, it soon becomes obvious that Maurice Mességué's assertion is not far from the mark. The range of applications is truly astonishing, from gout and gastritis to eczema and embalming corpses. The importance of thyme in medicine lies in its essential oil, the main constituent of which is a substance called thymol. This was first isolated in 1725, since when it has become a standard ingredient in many medications, particularly in mouthwashes, and dental and skin preparations. Thymol is a potent antiseptic, about twenty times stronger than phenol but safer to tissues (though it is still toxic in excess). Remarkable though it is, herbalists never extract thymol but prefer to make full use of the plant's chemistry, which contains further fractions in the volatile oil and a variety of other compounds, such as bitter substances, tannins and saponins, which work together in toning and relaxing the body's functions.

The combined effects of these complex ingredients is to reduce spasms (such as the cough reflex and griping pains in the digestive tract), expel mucus from the bronchial tubes, relieve wind, and kill infective organisms (from bacteria to parasites). Elixir of Thyme was listed in the British *Pharmacopoeia* in 1949 and has long been used for coughs. Medical herbalists regard thyme as a major herb in the treatment of whooping cough, bronchitis, dry 'hacking' coughs and nervous coughs. They usually prescribe it in a mixture composed of various herbs, such as coltsfoot (*Tussilago farfara*), wild cherry bark (*Prunus serotina*), white horehound (*Marrubium vulgare*) and the highly effective, but very poisonous *Lobelia inflata*. It can also be given to asthmatics and used with chamomile flowers (*Chamaemelum nobile*) as an inhalant steam bath for both asthma and bronchitis. The only occasion it is

(*opposite*) *Soft and subtle, the leaves of curly wood sage have ruffled margins and the texture of paper-thin suede.*
(*above*) *'Silver Posy' thyme: typical thyme aroma but much prettier in effect.*

not of use for bronchial complaints is when the cough or congestion is 'wet', as thyme increases fluid secretion.

Among the other conditions found to respond to thyme are chronic gastritis, diarrhoea in children, menstrual cramps, acute throat infections, such as laryngitis and tonsillitis, and intestinal parasites (though the dose is large, critical, and potentially dangerous for the last-mentioned problem). It has also proved effective in bed-wetting in older children. In an experiment, 78 per cent of children who were given thyme tea at bedtime, had no further problems. Externally, a strong infusion of thyme is useful for cleaning minor wounds and for soaking warm compresses for mastitis, sciatica, rheumatism and burns.

Thyme is a summer-flowering herb and for medicinal use the flowering tops are gathered and dried quickly, but gently in a shady, airy place. The many different species (some 300 or more) that we refer to generally as thyme, do, of course, differ in aroma and chemistry, but the two commonest – T. vulgaris and T. serpyllum – are similar medicinally. The former is considered more potent but both are used by herbalists.

The genus Thymus is yet another belonging to the Labiatae, the family whose rich conglomeration of essential oils has given us so many aromatic and medicinal plants. Common thyme (T. vulgaris) is a Mediterranean species found wild in Spain and Italy which has been widely cultivated in northern Europe since the sixteenth century, though probably introduced in Roman times. It is a diminutive shrub in habit, with erect, branched, often gnarled stems reaching 15–20 cm (6–8 in) tall, and tiny elliptic leaves 5–10 mm long and a mere 1–2 mm across. The foliage is generally hairy underneath, recurved at the margins and grey-green in colour. Clusters of two-lipped flowers in pale pinkish-mauve are borne at the ends of the shoots and their copious nectar is renowned for attracting honey bees. In fact, thyme honey is one of the finest. It is said to confer some of the beneficial antiseptic and tonic properties of the herb and for this reason is ideal for sweetening herb teas.

In common with many species of thyme, T. vulgaris is variable and this, together with the hybridization that has taken place in cultivation, makes accurate identification difficult in some cases. The flowers may be anything from pink or mauve to white, the leaves more or less leathery and glaucous, and the aroma sometimes decidedly different from plant to plant and from region to region. Of the cultivated varieties, one of the best is 'Silver Posy', with rose pink new stems, white-edged leaves and pale pink flowers. It is reasonably hardy, does not revert, and is not only good for all culinary and medicinal purposes, but is a most decorative plant for rock gardens, containers and the fronts of borders. It is, however, easily confused with 'Silver Queen' which is a form of T. x citriodorous (a cross between T. vulgaris and T. pulegioides). It has similar variegation but is lemon-scented.

Equally good as a garden plant is the golden form of creeping thyme, T. serpyllum. It forms dense low mats of yellowish-green leaves which will spread out into pools from paving cracks, overflow down the sides of containers and carpet warm sunny dry soils. Creeping thyme is, as its name suggests, a prostrate plant which roots as it goes and rarely exceeds 10 cm (4 in) in height. Its leaves tend to be broader than those of common thyme and not recurved at the margins. Though less aromatic and more of a fiddle to use than T. vulgaris and its varieties, creeping thyme offers other possibilities. It is perfect for thyme lawns or seats, in which various creeping thymes make delightfully aromatic and colourful mosaics to walk or sit on during the summer months (if you take your turn with the bees!). T. serpyllum would appear to be even more variable than common thyme, with foliage varying from smooth and golden to grey-green and hairy, and flowers anything from snow-white to orchid-magenta. Some of the prettiest include 'Pink Chintz', with pastel pink flowers and hairy leaves; the even woollier 'Lanuginosus'; bright green, white-flowered 'Albus'; and the contrastingly dark-leaved, carmine-flowered 'Coccineus'. As for foliage, the golden creeping thyme (T. serpyllum 'Aureum') is undoubtedly the most colourful, making a dense yellow-green mat all year round. An area dappled with this and other varieties of creeping thyme would not only be a joy to look at and remarkably easy to maintain once established, but redolent with a scent, described by the author Rudyard Kipling as 'like the perfume of the dawn of Paradise'.

Common thyme is not reliably hardy in more northerly temperate regions and prefers well-drained calcareous soils. Creeping thyme is more adaptable, being found in sub-arctic regions in both acid and alkaline conditions. Both are evergreen and easily propagated by cuttings of non-flowering shoots taken in early summer and put round the edge of a pot containing sandy compost. Plants may also be divided in spring or early autumn. Thyme needs very little in the way of feeding but benefits from a trim after flowering. If plants are growing near deciduous trees and shrubs, care should be taken that falling leaves do not settle and cause rotting as winter advances.

If you watch the constant movement of flowering thyme as it bobs under the weight of foraging bees, it is no surprise that through the ages it has come to symbolize activity and energy. In the days of knights in shining white armour and tales of derring-do, ladies would embroider scarves with the emblem of a bee hovering over a sprig of thyme and give one to their favourite. It is a revitalizing herb whose fragrance makes you want to climb mountains and jump for joy. No wonder it has inspired poets through the ages. Who has not heard Shakespeare's celebrated line from *A Midsummer Night's Dream*: 'I know a bank whereon the wild thyme blows'? Or perhaps Spenser's 'Bees-alluring thyme'; Shelley's 'bees on the bells of thyme'; or T. S. Elliot's 'the wild thyme unseen'? It even induces writers of prose to take flights of fancy – though we may sometimes wish they hadn't. 'How invigorating to ramble across fields begemmed and odoriferous with the crisp and elastic tufts of this bonnie plant!', enthused John Ingram in his *Flora Symbolica*. But whether sublime or ridiculous, the message is clear: thyme is evocative of happy moments in lovely surroundings – perhaps chanced upon in the summer countryside, or more certainly created by planting a variety of thymes in the garden.

YELLOW-VEINED RED CLOVER
Trifolium pratense 'Goldnet'
(syn. 'Reticulatum')

Red clover conjures up pictures of summer countryside with bees buzzing and cows grazing on lush flower-studded meadows – a common, quite pretty wild flower, but in reputation verging on a weed and thus generally dismissed as a garden plant. There is, however, a horticultural variety with exquisite leaves which demands recognition, transforming the humble red clover into a specimen plant worthy of any garden or container. For most of us it will be a case of love at first sight, for 'Goldnet' is a gem with the kind of finely detailed foliage guaranteed to delight the plantsman.

Clover is a member of the large family Leguminosae or legumes, and belongs to the division known as Papilionaceae, whose 10,000 species include not only the ornamental lupins and sweet peas, but valuable fodder crops and protein-rich food plants, such as peas, beans, lentils and peanuts. Red clover, *Trifolium pratense*, has a very wide distribution and is found wild throughout Europe, central and northern Asia, right up to the Arctic Circle and south into the Mediterranean. As the Latin name *Trifolium* suggests, it has leaves divided into three leaflets, each one usually marked with a grey-green V-shape in the centre. In the form 'Goldnet' – also known as 'Reticulatum' – they are adorned instead with a network of clear yellow veins. The stems average 20–40 cm (8–16 in) in length, reaching 60 cm (2 ft) in good conditions, bearing pairs of these filigree trefoils along their length. In the wild, plants are sometimes semi-prostrate, their weak stems largely supported by surrounding foliage. When grown in pots, this means that 'Goldnet' tends to trail and therefore has potential as a plant for window boxes, hanging baskets and other containers. Like the wild clover, 'Goldnet' produces globular to egg-shaped pinkish-purple flowerheads in the growing season.

Though perennial, it is not long-lived (in agriculture it is usually treated as an annual or biennial) and cuttings should be taken every year to guard against its sudden demise.

Farmers and herbalists have always praised red clover to the skies, but for quite different reasons. First and foremost, in economic terms it is a forage crop and soil improver. It appears that the Dutch pioneered the use of clover as an agricultural crop. Following their example, it was introduced to the British Isles from Flanders in the mid-seventeenth century by Sir Richard Weston who is remembered as the initiator of crop rotation, in which red clover played an important part in sustaining soil fertility. With it came the word clover, a derivation from the Dutch *klaver*.

Red clover enriches the land by manufacturing nitrogen in nodules on its roots so that the soil is left more fertile and with its nutrients more readily available to surrounding plants and following crops. Though it likes a deep rich soil with ample phosphorus, calcium and potassium, it gives more than it takes, leaving 23–68 kg (50–150 lb) per acre of nitrogen. In addition, it has a high nutritional value for livestock. Usually it is sown with grass and grazed, cut for hay or silage and finally ploughed under for a subsequent row crop. It does best in cool humid conditions and is grown worldwide, from Siberia to Chile, wherever either the summer or winter climate fulfils these requirements.

To herbalists, red clover is an alterative herb, which is to say that it acts as a tonic to the whole system, improving well-being and vitality. It is the flowerheads that are gathered and dried – very thoroughly on account of their bulk – for medicinal use as a tincture or a herb tea. Present-day herbalists use them as part of the background treatment for cancer, especially of the stomach and throat, for intractable skin diseases, such as psoriasis and eczema, and for bronchial complaints (notably whooping cough). As a home remedy, the flowers make a sweet-tasting tea which acts as a mild relaxant for nervous exhaustion and

(*above*) 'Goldnet', the yellow-veined form of red clover. An example of variegation induced by a virus.

(*opposite*) Nasturtium 'Alaska': heavily marbled leaves and dazzling flowers.

over-excitement. Apart from the chemical constituents of clover, which give mildly sedative effects, clear mucus and cleanse the bloodstream, there are oestrogenic substances, suggesting that it might be a particularly good herb for women during and after the menopause. Clover tea taken once or twice a day is a pleasant drink which will help restore calm, give a clear complexion and generally improve the health. Made stronger, it can be used as a mouthwash for gum infections. For minor wounds when out in the country, the crushed leaves are useful as a rough and ready compress which will quickly stop bleeding. In Culpeper's time (the seventeenth century) clover was used for more serious accidents: adder bites were treated by drinking clover juice, washing the wound with a lotion made from the plant and then applying leaves.

Surprising though it may seem, clover has also been gathered from the wild and cultivated as a vegetable. Several North American

130

Indian tribes are said to have been very fond of it as a food, as well as using it medicinally for skin diseases and wounds. The Pono tribe valued it so highly that they held clover feasts in the spring to celebrate the start of the harvest. The leaflets would certainly make a nutritious addition to a salad in small quantities.

As far as folklore is concerned, clover is on the side of the angels, symbolizing the Holy Trinity through its tripartite leaves, protecting against evil and witchcraft, and bringing good luck – especially if it has four leaflets instead of the usual three. Its greatest claim to fame is as one of the plants identified as possibly being the shamrock of Ireland. St Patrick used the shamrock to demonstrate the concept of the Trinity and it became the country's emblem, worn in the buttonhole every year on St Patrick's Day. What exactly is the shamrock remains a mystery. Surveys have been carried out to discover the answer, but all that has emerged are about a dozen different candidates, including red clover, lesser trefoil (*T. minus*), and white clover (*T. repens*). The debate continues!

With the promise of health and good fortune, and the bonus of added soil fertility, the gardener who grows *Trifolium pratense* 'Goldnet' will soon understand what it means to be 'in clover'. The only possible objection could be that the mauve-pink flowers are not quite the thing with yellow-veined leaves. Herb gardeners have the perfect answer though; picking them, as they appear, for the medicine chest.

VARIEGATED NASTURTIUM
Tropaeolum majus 'Alaska'

How many gardeners, I wonder, began their interest with a packet of nasturtium seeds? The commonplace nasturtium must be one of the easiest plants to grow from seed, with almost 100 per cent germination from its conveniently large seeds and quick robust growth – just the sort of encouragement a budding gardener needs. Given a sunny well-drained site, the only thing you can do wrong is to coddle it on rich soil, which encourages lush leaves but fewer flowers. In the case of the variegated nasturtium – a cultivar known as 'Alaska' – even this results in success, as the cool white-marbled leaves deserve to luxuriate, and plentiful flowers in brilliant shades of yellow, orange and red will still emerge above them to add to the summer-time dazzle.

It comes as no surprise to learn that this gaudy plant comes from tropical America. Like the potato and tomato, it was one of the treasures of the New World which the *conquistadores* acquired in the sixteenth century. In England, John Gerard was probably the first to get hold of seeds of 'this rare and fair plant', receiving them from his friend, John Robin, the King of France's gardener. At first it was called *Nasturtium indicum* and popularly known as Indian cresses, because of the resemblance between its pungent taste and smell and that of watercress (*Nasturtium offici-nale*), though in appearance it is quite different from this well-known member of the cabbage family (Cruciferae). It was also suspected of being a bindweed (*Convolvulus*) on account of its climbing habit and was later, on more scientific grounds, put into Geraniaceae. Botanists finally gave it a family of its own: Tropaeolaceae, a small group with only two genera and under 100 species.

Tropaeolums are mostly succulent climbing plants of mountainous regions in Central and South America, from Mexico to Argentina and Chile. The name *Tropaeolum* is from the Greek *tropaion* meaning trophy, as the flowers look rather like helmets and the leaves are shield-shaped. They have sensitive stalks which kink and twine round supports in much the same way as those of clematis, and long-spurred five-petalled flowers whose upper two petals are smaller than the lower three. In some ways their chemistry resembles that of the Cruciferae, as they contain acrid mustard oil and sulphur compounds. The name 'nasturtium' is apt. It means 'nose-twisting' which is exactly the effect caused by smelling such plants.

The fact that tropaeolums grow at high altitudes in the tropics means that a number are amenable to cultivation in northern temperate regions. Some, such as the scarlet *T. speciosum*, are perfectly hardy and actually need cool summers for successful cultivation. Others are half-hardy or tender and do better with greenhouse protection. No less than 28 species, including the blue-flowered *T. violaefolium* (syn. *T. azureum*), and *T. tuberosum* (which is grown in the Andes as a root crop) were listed in one nineteenth-century gardening encyclopedia. Only a handful of these are available today and right from the beginning the Peruvian *T. majus*, our garden nasturtium, has topped them all in popularity and ease of cultivation.

In temperate zones, nasturtiums are grown as annuals which are sown outdoors or under glass in early spring to provide a display of ground-smothering foliage and colourful flowers until the first frosts of autumn. The fruits have three one-seeded divisions and are reasonably hardy, so that in some gardens nasturtiums sow themselves year after year. Having been familiar with nasturtiums from early childhood, we tend to take them for granted. In fact, their leaves are unusual, being almost round like those of the sacred lotus (*Nelumbo nucifera*) and peltate – that is, with the stalk attached to the centre of the leaf, rather than to its base.

The wild nasturtium has single orange-red flowers and scrambles to a length of 4 m (12 ft) or so. Over the centuries a number of varieties and cultivars have been raised and there is now every shade of cream, bronze, orange, scarlet, crimson, rose and mahogany – some with semi-double or double flowers and compact bushy growth – to choose from. There are also scented forms, descended from the fragrant 'Golden Gleam' which was found in a Californian garden in 1929. Foliage colour is less variable. 'Empress of India' is an old variety that dates back to Victorian times and has darker than average leaves and vivid velvety crimson flowers. Apparently the Victorians had a dwarf compact golden-leaved form too. There is no doubt, though, that 'Alaska' must be the most outstanding in this respect. Though it sends out trailing shoots, it forms a dense mound of variegated round leaves in a dappled medley of cream, white and grey on green; a cheap and cheerful subject for hanging baskets and containers, as well as for summer carpeting.

Whatever the colours of leaves or flowers, all parts of nasturtiums are edible. The pickled unripe seeds make an excellent substitute for capers (the flower buds of *Capparis spinosa* which grows in the Mediterranean), and the flowers are used to make nasturtium vinegar. The leaves are very good finely chopped in potato soup and are a nutritious and piquant addition to salads – as are the flower buds, petals and nectar spurs.

Medicinally, *T. majus* is an antibiotic herb

with a high Vitamin C content. Unlike conventional antibiotics, it does not destroy the intestinal flora. It is best used fresh and has a good track record in treating bronchial and urinary tract infections. Even serious conditions such as emphysema have been known to respond well to the freshly expressed juice taken in milk. It also has a reputation for retarding baldness, possibly through its high sulphur content. For this purpose, a handful or two of the plant is put in a litre (2 pt) of rubbing alcohol for a few weeks, along with some leaves of nettle (*Urtica dioica*), oak (*Quercus* spp) or box (*Buxus sempervirens*). After straining, the lotion should be massaged regularly into the scalp.

Few people realize what a useful plant the nasturtium is. Even fewer know that behind its cheerful innocence lie a few unsolved mysteries. Its less common names, passionflower and flower of love, allude to the tradition that it is a potent aphrodisiac. More intriguing still, if you sit and admire your nasturtiums at dusk on a balmy summer evening, you may see sparks fly from the centres of the flowers. This phenomenon was first observed by the daughter of the Swedish botanist Linné and is thought to have something to do with the high phosphoric acid content. The childhood favourite turns out to be quite a live wire after all.

VARIEGATED GREATER PERIWINKLE
Vinca major 'Variegata'
(syn. 'Elegantissima')

Ground cover plants are chiefly praised for their utilitarian value. When first planted they are condemned to hard labour and, as soon as the task is complete, are seldom given a second look. Parks and gardens everywhere depend on them to render difficult areas presentable. As the owner of a house I was view-ing once said to me, pointing apologetically to a well-established prostrate cotoneaster: 'It covers a multitude'. And such is the lot of ground cover plants. They hide the garden's worst sins – bare shaded ground; thin soil over rubble, disturbed subsoil or steep banks; hedge bottoms; unsightly constructions. To do this they must be evergreen, dense, vigorous and tolerant – and last but not least, reasonably attractive. We may enjoy a garden most for its stars – the specimen plants in their season – but the supporting cast of these loyal retainers is largely responsible for the overall performance.

Periwinkles are definitive ground cover: neat uncomplaining plants that fill dingy corners where lawn and herbaceous delights would pale and wither. They also provide a quick-growing garment of greenery to clothe exposed open areas around newly planted trees and shrubs. For most gardeners, that is all there is to them, but seen through the eyes of a herbalist, there is considerably more.

Although periwinkles are found all over Europe and are in the floras of most regions, they probably originated in southern parts and spread by escaping from cultivation – which in the first place was done largely for their medicinal uses. Like the oleander (*Nerium oleander*), they belong to the dogbane family, Apocynaceae, which consists mostly of tropical rainforest shrubs and trees. Indeed, periwinkle and oleander are its only European representatives. One characteristic of dogbanes is a milky sap which in some species is used for rubber manufacture. From the herbalist's point of view, the most interesting feature of the family is its chemistry – of daunting complexity and enormous potential in medicine. Already we have crucially important psychiatric drugs from the alkaloids of *Rauvolfia*, and cancer chemotherapy is dependent on those of the Madagascar periwinkle (*Catharanthus roseus*). Many more undoubtedly await discovery, if only the destruction of the rainforests can be halted.

The greater periwinkle is similarly endowed with substances which have a pro-

(above) Variegated greater periwinkle: definitive ground cover, blue-eyed in spring.
(opposite) The 'freakish elfin loveliness' of white violets.

finger). The word periwinkle is derived from the Latin *pervinca*, and it could refer to the plant's use as a binding herb, or else to its tendency to conquer its surroundings.

The amateur herbalist can therefore regard periwinkle as a useful plant to have in the garden for first-aid, leaving its internal applications to the professional. If you believe the assurances of Apuleius (who wrote a herbal in the fifteenth century), just having it around will protect you against devil sickness, demoniacal possessions, snakes, wild beasts, poisons, envy and terror, as well as ensuring 'thou shalt be prosperous and ever acceptable'. It was also a vital ingredient in a recipe which was said to guarantee a happy marriage, though it is hard to imagine anything more likely to lead to divorce: 'Perwynke when it is beat into pouder with worms of ye earth wrapped about it and with an herb called houselyke [*Sempervivum tectorum*], it induceth love between man and wife if it be used in their meals.'

Choosing which periwinkle to grow should not present any problems as most are readily available from garden centres and nurseries. There are two species, the greater (*V. major*) and the lesser (*V. minor*). They have some similar uses in herbal medicine, but are not interchangeable. As one might expect, the greater periwinkle is larger all round, with glossy broadly lanceolate leaves, upright stems reaching about 45 cm (18 in) tall and a spread of 100 cm (40 in) or more. *V. minor* has much more slender leaves, is about half the height and has a more trailing prostrate habit. Their flowers are very similar, varying mainly in size. They are twisted in bud and tubular, splaying out into a five-part calyx when open and maintaining the propeller-like twist. Apart from their blue colour, they closely resemble those of oleander. Throughout their long history as garden plants, white and purple forms have been known, as have double ones which are now rarely seen.

Flower colour, though interesting, would not be my criterion for choosing a periwinkle as they are not, on the whole, floriferous

nounced effect on the body when swallowed or applied. It has several alkaloids and is rich in tannins, giving an intensely bitter taste and a powerfully astringent action. In modern herbal medicine, periwinkle leaves are combined wth the root of wake robin (*Trillium erectum*) to treat excessive menstrual loss. Traditionally, it has been used for arresting haemorrhages, discharges and excess fluid loss of various kinds, from nose bleeds (a crushed leaf in the nostril will do the trick) to drying up lactation and controlling diarrhoea in dysentery. Externally, a strong infusion makes a healing lotion for piles and a soothing gargle for sore throats and laryngitis. Folk uses include binding cramped limbs with the stems (hence the name band plant) and applying bruised leaves to wounds (from which it became known as cut plants. In spring the odd flower here and there peeps out from the mass of leaves, causing a quick glance into nether regions of the garden to last a little longer, but the strength of periwinkle lies in its foliage. Variegated and golden forms of the lesser periwinkle are available but for bold smart ground smother there is nothing to beat the variegated greater periwinkle, *V. major* 'Variegata' (or 'Elegantissima' as it is also known). Its shiny leaves have wide irregular cream margins and the stems remain upright to display them well. It performs brilliantly in sun or shade and on damp or dry soils. No wonder periwinkle is also known as joy of the ground!

WHITE VIOLET
Viola odorata 'Alba'

Orris may smell like violets, but violets are the real thing! Theirs is one of the sweetest gentlest fragrances on earth, matched by an endearing appearance which has captured the imagination of poets and romantics in all ages and cultures. The plant hunter Reginald Farrer called it a 'freakish elfin loveliness'; John Keats described it as 'that queen of secrecy'; the nineteenth-century poet Thomas Hood likened it to a nun; and Elizabeth Barrett Browning, who also wrote in early Victorian times, saw violets as 'The kindest eyes that look on you/Without a thought disloyal.' A more practical approach was taken by the seventeenth-century herbalist John Gerard, who observed that 'the mind conceiveth a certain pleasure and recreation by smelling and handling those most odoriferous floures'. The present-day herbalist Maurice Mességué is equally enthralled by these diminutive flowers which 'show up like amethysts' in the hedgerows: 'Ask me for a dainty flower, for a modest flower, for a flower that I

love (except that I love them all) and I will give you a violet'.

Next to the rose, the violet is the most praised and written about flower in the world. It was a favourite with Shakespeare and scarcely a poet before or after him ignored it. The Romans adored it and drank violet-flavoured wine; the Greeks revered it to such an extent that they made it the emblem of Athens; Muslims have a saying that 'the excellence of the violet is as the excellence of Islam above all other religions'; the Bonapartists took it as their symbol because it was the favourite flower of Napoleon, their *Caporal Violette* who, so the story goes, was thrown a bunch by Josephine when they first met and died wearing a locket containing violets taken from her grave.

The violet cult was at its height during the reign of Victoria (1837–1901) and that of her son, Edward VII (1901–10), when everyone from office workers to theatre goers wore small bunches of violets. As a young queen, Victoria visited the perfumery of J. Giraud in Grasse and declared his perfumes 'exquisite'. Of that there can be little doubt, distilled as they were from the fresh flowers grown to perfection in the region of France renowned as the centre of

the perfumery industry. It takes over 220 kg (485 lb) of flowers to produce 50 g (1½ oz) of violet essence by *enfleurage* – a long process in which the tiny blossoms are spread out on sheets of glass coated with grease and replenished daily for a month, by which time the fat has absorbed sufficient floral perfume for alcohol extraction.

Violets have been cultivated for ages. In ancient Greece, as early as 400 BC, they were grown commercially for sale in the Athens market. Horace (65–8 BC) criticized Roman gardeners for spending more time on their beds of violets than on their olive groves, and from the Middle Ages onwards no garden in England was without violets for making posies, perfumes, medicines and sweet dishes. The Victorians had it down to a fine art and gardening manuals give detailed instructions on growing violets for flower production throughout the winter and spring months. Special frames were constructed to protect them from bad weather and they were treated rather like strawberries – old crowns being discarded and replaced by newly rooted offsets every spring. The United States caught the bug too. The largest violet nursery in the world was at Cliftondale, Massachusetts, producing between three and four million flowers a year. Many varieties were grown, most of which are now extremely scarce or extinct. Most popular of all were the Parma violets with their larger, often double and more scented flowers. They were introduced from Italy in about 1820, but their origin and ancestry remain rather a mystery – though quite possibly they came from Asia Minor and are hybrids with *V. odorata* as one parent. 'Marie Louise' (which is still in cultivation) was one of the favourites, with large lilac flowers which were freely produced under the frame system. (Clones in the United States were often described as having red markings.) In the early nineteenth century too, Russian breeders developed some fine hybrids with *V. suavis* (formerly *V. cyanea*). Of the old varieties, doubles such as the blue 'Victoria Regina' and highly scented

white 'Comte Brazza' (also known as 'Swanley White') are difficult to find now, but the robust deep purple 'Czar' is quite widely available.

Occasionally you can come across white sweet violets in the wild. I was once lucky enough to find some growing at the foot of a fallen ash tree. I discovered them when tethering a goat next to an appetizing hedgerow adjoining my garden and fortunately spotted them before the goat did! If anything, they are sweeter than their purple counterparts and grow just as easily. In some areas, such as Hampshire where I was then living, white-flowered plants are commoner than purple. Like the species, 'Alba' has an orange eye but there is also an early-flowering green-centred variety known as 'Christmas' or 'White'.

My favourite may be white, but whichever you grow it is worth going down on your knees to smell them or having enough to pick and enjoy in greater comfort. There is, however, more to violets than their delicate perfume and irresistible prettiness. All parts have medicinal value. The roots have an emetic effect similar to ipecacuanha (*Cephaelis* spp). The leaves and flowers are stimulating expectorants and detoxifiers used mainly in bronchial complaints and, most interestingly, by medical herbalists as part of the background treatment for cancer, particularly of the breast and digestive tract. (Chinese herbalists use another violet, *V. diffusa*, for leukaemia.) The herb may be used fresh or dried, internally or externally, as the condition warrants. It also contains the painkilling anti-inflammatory substance methyl salicylate (similar to aspirin) which is perhaps why Culpeper recommended it for swellings (white violets being especially good) and for various discomforts, such as 'pains in the head, caused through want of sleep' and 'for the piles also, being fried with yolks of eggs and applied thereto'.

Fortunately, more appetizing uses for violets are not hard to find! Both leaves and flowers are edible and can be added in small quantities to salads. The flowers may be crystallized for decorating cakes and encrusting luxurious milk desserts and ice creams; added to white wine vinegar; made into syrup; and put into sugar to scent it. Nothing, however, can compare with the ultimate in violet-flavoured delicacies: the cloying liqueur *parfait amour*!

Violets were once in such demand that you could buy them by the pint in Covent Garden market in London. All this changed at the end of the Victorian era. In 1893, two chemists (F. Tiemann and P. Kruger) developed ionone – synthetic violet – which was to become of such importance that their achievement ranks as a landmark in the perfumery and flavouring industries. But though commercial violet-growing declined, gardeners continued to treasure the large finely scented varieties until the chaos of two world wars finally saw their demise.

Sweet violets grow wild in damp shady hedgerows, grassy banks and woodland in many parts of Europe, Asia and North Africa. They are hardy perennials which produce a crown of foliage and numerous runners that give rise to plantlets. The oval heart-shaped leaves measure 1.5–6 cm (½–2½ in) and are only partly developed when flowering takes place. The flowers are a mere 1.5 cm (½ in), usually velvety purple, but white, pink, and lilac sometimes occur. They have five unequal petals: the top two standing up like ears; the central lower one like a lip extended at the back into a nectar-filled spur; and the two outer lower ones curving protectively on either side. The centre of the flower is patterned with purple and white 'veins' – the honey guides which direct bees to their goal.

The 400 or so species of violet are generally small plants of northern temperate regions or high altitudes in the tropics, and are easy to recognize by their 'little faces'. The genus *Viola* is one of over twenty in the family Violaceae and many of its relatives (especially those in tropical America) are trees and shrubs. Different explanations are given for how *Viola* got its name. The most prosaic is that it comes from the Latin *via*, meaning 'wayside' or 'road';

Sweet violet (Viola odorata)

the most delightful that it is derived from the Greek *Ione*, after the legend that Jupiter changed his darling Io into a white heifer to avoid Juno's jealousy, and violets were created for the lovely animal to feed upon.

However small your garden, there will be a nook or cranny for violets. All they ask is moist soil enriched with peat or leafmould (not manure or they produce leaves at the expense of flowers) and summer shade. Divide and replant them every year, and you will enjoy these fragrant jewels for many years. The only thing to warn you against is inhaling their wondrous scent before giving any sort of vocal performance (should you be called upon to do such a thing). Whether it is true or not, they say that singers should never use violet scents or be given violets, as the perfume makes the vocal chords swell and renders them mute. Apparently this happened to Marie Sass when she was given a bunch of violets before going on stage. Of course, she just might have been speechless with delight!

A NOTE ON THE MEDICINAL USES OF HERBS

The medicinal uses described in *Fine Herbs* should not be taken as a recommendation for their use. Some of the herbs are relatively safe but others are extremely dangerous, and even the safest depend for their effectiveness on toxic compounds which could be poisonous in excess. In addition to this, self-medication is an unwise course of action because we are rarely in a position to make an accurate diagnosis or prescription, which could possibly result in the problem getting worse and lead to a loss of confidence in herbal treatments. If you have a medical condition which you feel might respond to herbal medicine, it would be much better to consult a qualified medical herbalist. Information may be obtained from The School of Herbal Medicine (Phytotherapy), 148 Forest Road, Tunbridge Wells, Kent TN2 5EY and from The Herb Society of America, 2 Independence Court, Concord, MA 01742. Meanwhile, you can of course improve your general health and your knowledge of herbs by using a variety in food preparation and enjoying the wide range of herb teas that are now available.

USING ORNAMENTAL VARIETIES OF HERBS

As far as is known, the decorative forms of herbs do not differ significantly from their plain green counterparts in terms of chemical constituents and uses. Golden marjoram tastes and smells the same as the green species and has exactly the same uses in cooking. On the whole the difference in colour will not show much in cooked dishes but may be quite striking in salads. Personally I like black basil in a tomato salad but it may not be to everyone's taste! As far as herb teas go, the same applies in that the herbs are gathered and used in just the same ways as the common species. I often use purple sage for tea and many herbalists prefer it. Likewise, pink lavender is as fragrant and usable as the purple.

ORNAMENTAL VARIETIES AND THE GARDENER

In terms of cultivation, there are some differences between ornamental varieties and the species which need to be noted.

Choosing a site
Generally speaking, chlorophyll-deficient tissues (that is, variegated and golden leaves) do not tolerate strong sun and can scorch as summer advances. On the other hand, most golden-leaved plants are brightest in a sunny position and tend to become more lime-green than gold in shade. Some plants with these kinds of coloration may therefore need quite careful siting so that they can give their best.

Positions which get the early morning or evening sun and avoid the hours around midday are often a good compromise.

Propagation
In horticultural terms, variations from the norm are known as 'sports' and have always been prized as interesting and often colourful additions to the range of garden plants. The reasons behind spontaneous variation in plants are complex and there is no rule of thumb for detecting the cause or predicting to what extent such variations will be transferred to the next generation. On the whole, varieties

are therefore best propagated vegetatively – that is, by division or cuttings – in which case the new plants should be identical to the material used. Where this is difficult or impossible, in the case of annuals for example, you have to rely on seed and probably only a small proportion of the offspring will retain the variation.

Variegation is particularly interesting. Very few species are normally variegated, though some are known – lungwort (*Pulmonaria saccharata*), for example, always has white-spotted leaves (and will of course breed true from seed). Usually, however, variegation is the result of abnormal changes in the plant's cells. It may come about through genetic mutation, or by changes in the cells or layers of tissues during growth, or by virus infection which damages the chlorophyll but is not severe enough to kill the plant. Variegated rue (*Ruta graveolens* 'Variegata') is a case of genetic mutation and therefore breeds true from seed. Golden-variegated jasmine (*Jasminum officinale* 'Aureovariegatum') is virus-induced and *Pelargonium crispum* 'Variegatum' is a 'chimaera' in which different coloured cells which normally remain in separate layers have become unstable. These are best propagated by cuttings or division. Virus variegation may, of course, be infectious and can be transmitted to normal plants by sap-sucking insects and by cutting tools and grafting. Variegation does occur in the wild but is particularly common among cultivated plants which are subject to vegetative propagation. Nowadays it can also be induced by irradiation and the use of colchicine, an extract of meadow saffron (*Colchicum autumnale*).

Double-flowered and white-flowered forms are equally important in their contribution to horticulture, extending the scope immeasurably for both garden designers and florists. White-flowered forms are rare in species with normally yellow flowers but in those which have flowers in the pink/purple/blue range they may be quite common, even in the wild. This absence of pigment does not breed true from seed, but the proportion of white-flowered seedlings can be increased through selective breeding. As a result, it is now possible to buy seeds of many white-flowered forms, such as white violets (*Viola odorata* 'Alba').

What causes doubling is still rather a mystery and as doubleness tends to be associated with sterility, most double-flowered forms are quite rare in the wild. Among the exceptions are double-flowered opium poppies, *Papaver somniferum* 'Paeoniaeflorum', 'Rosea Plena' and such like, and double chamomile, *Chamaemelum nobile* 'Flore Pleno', whose flowers are fertile. Fortunately for plant breeders, many double-flowered forms do not constantly produce double flowers and those produced later in the season are often semi-double and fertile, giving the chance to use them in breeding and so increase the percentage of double-flowered seedlings in subsequent generations. This is well worth remembering if you like to save your own seed. Double-flowered forms are extremely important in horticulture as the flowers are more spectacular, last longer and are often more fragrant, though this may be offset by their top-heaviness and greater vulnerability to wind and rain damage. In some species, the double form has a slightly different flowering period, which extends the display in the garden. The double celandine (*Ranunculus ficaria* 'Flore Pleno'), for example, flowers later than the species. In common with variegation and unusual colours in leaves, doubleness and colour variation in flowers is most reliably propagated by cuttings and division – unless the plant is an annual, in which case you have to rely on seed.

FINE HERBS BY COLOUR

Purples, browns, reds and pinks

Achillea millefolium 'Cerise Queen' (green leaves, bright pink flowers)

Ajuga reptans 'Atropurpurea' (blackish-purple leaves, blue flowers)

Ajuga reptans 'Rainbow' (bronze/salmon leaves, blue flowers)

Ajuga reptans 'Burgundy Glow' (pink/plum/cream leaves, blue flowers)

Foeniculum vulgare 'Purpureum' (brown leaves, yellow flowers)

Lavandula angustifolia 'Loddon Pink' (grey leaves, pale pink flowers)

Ocimum basilicum 'Purpurascens' (blackish-purple leaves, pink flowers)

Paeonia officinalis 'Rosea Plena' (dark green leaves, pale pink flowers)

Papaver somniferum 'Rosea Plena' (grey-blue leaves, pink flowers)

Plantago major 'Rubrifolia' (maroon leaves, greenish-brown flowers)

Primula x *variabilis* 'Guinevere' (bronze leaves, pink flowers)

Pulsatilla vulgaris 'Rubra' (silver-green leaves, crimson flowers)

Ranunculus ficaria 'Cuprea' (green leaves, apricot flowers)

Ranunculus ficaria 'Brazen Hussy' (bronze leaves, apricot flowers)

Salvia officinalis 'Purpurascens' (greyish-purple leaves, blue flowers)

Salvia officinalis 'Tricolor' (pink, grey-green and white leaves, blue flowers)

Sambucus nigra 'Purpurea' (bronze leaves, pink-stamened white flowers)

Saponaria officinalis 'Rosea Plena' (green leaves, pale pink flowers)

Sempervivum tectorum 'Lancelot' (bronze leaves, pink flowers)

Sempervivum tectorum 'Lavender and Old Lace' (pinkish grey-green leaves, pink flowers)

Silvers, blues and greys

Artemisia 'Powis Castle' (silver leaves, non-flowering)

Artemisia absinthium 'Lambrook Silver' (silver leaves, cream flowers)

Juniperus communis 'Compressa' (grey-green leaves)

Lavandula angustifolia 'Loddon Pink' (grey leaves, pale pink flowers)

Papaver somniferum 'Rosea Plena' (grey-blue leaves, pink flowers)

Ruta graveolens 'Jackman's Blue' (blue-grey leaves, lime flowers)

Ruta graveolens 'Variegata' (grey-green and white leaves, lime flowers)

Greens and white

Acorus calamus 'Variegatus' (green and white striped leaves, green flowers)

Aegopodium podagraria 'Variegata' (green and white leaves, white flowers)

Buxus sempervirens 'Elegantissima (white-margined dark green leaves, insignificant greenish flowers)

Chamaemelum nobile 'Flore Pleno' (green leaves, white flowers)

Colchicum autumnale 'Alboplenum' (green leaves – not present at flowering, white flowers)

Glechoma hederacea 'Variegata' (white-margined green leaves, mauve flowers)

Iris pallida 'Variegata Argentea' (green and white striped leaves, lilac-blue flowers)

Mentha suaveolens 'Variegata' (green and white leaves, mauve flowers)

Myrtus communis 'Variegata' (green and white leaves, white flowers)

Nerium oleander 'Variegata' (cream and white leaves, pink flowers)

Pelargonium 'Lady Plymouth' (white-margined green leaves, pale mauve flowers)

Pelargonium crispum 'Variegatum' (cream and green leaves, pinkish-mauve flowers)

Primula vulgaris 'Alba Plena' (green leaves, white flowers)

Ranunculus ficaria 'Alba' (green leaves, white

flowers)

Ruta graveolens 'Variegata' (grey-green and white leaves, lime flowers)

Sambucus nigra 'Albovariegata' (cream-margined green leaves, cream flowers)

Scrophularia auriculata 'Variegata' (green and white leaves, dark red flowers)

Solanum dulcamara 'Variegatum' (green and white leaves, purple and yellow flowers; bright red berries)

Symphytum x *uplandicum* 'Variegatum' (green and white leaves, lilac-blue flowers)

Symphytum grandiflorum 'Variegatum' (green and white leaves, cream flowers)

Tanacetum parthenium 'Snowball' (green leaves, white flowers)

Thymus 'Silver Posy' (green and white leaves, pink flowers)

Tropaeolum majus 'Alaska' (green and white leaves, red, orange and yellow flowers)

Vinca major 'Variegata' (green and white leaves, blue flowers)

Viola odorata 'Alba' (green leaves, white flowers)

Green, yellow, lime and gold

Achillea millefolium 'Flowers of Sulphur' (green leaves, pale yellow flowers)

Buxus sempervirens 'Latifolia Maculata' (young leaves gold-variegated, insignificant greenish flowers)

Filipendula ulmaria 'Aurea' (plain gold leaves, cream flowers)

Filipendula ulmaria 'Variegata' (green and yellow leaves, cream flowers)

Humulus lupulus 'Aureus' (gold leaves, green flowers)

Iris pallida 'Variegata Aurea' (blue-green, cream and yellow striped leaves, lilac-blue flowers)

Jasminum officinale 'Aureovariegatum' (green and yellow leaves, white flowers)

Juniperus communis 'Depressa Aurea' (yellow/gold/bronze leaves)

Laurus nobilis 'Aurea' (lime to gold leaves, cream flowers)

Lysimachia nummularia 'Aurea' (lime leaves, bright yellow flowers)

Melissa officinalis 'All Gold' (yellow leaves, insignificant white flowers)

Melissa officinalis 'Aurea' (green and yellow leaves, insignificant white flowers)

Mentha x *gentilis* 'Variegata' (green and yellow leaves, lilac flowers)

Origanum vulgare 'Aureum' (lime leaves, mauve flowers)

Origanum vulgare 'Variegatum' (yellow-tipped green leaves, mauve flowers)

Pelargonium x *fragrans* 'Variegatum' (lime and grey-green leaves, white flowers)

Ranunculus ficaria 'Flore Pleno' (green leaves, bright yellow flowers)

Rosmarinus officinalis 'Aureus' (green and yellow leaves, pale blue flowers)

Salvia officinalis 'Icterina' (lime and grey-green leaves, blue flowers)

Sambucus nigra 'Aurea' (lime to gold leaves, cream flowers)

Sambucus racemosa 'Plumosa Aurea' (gold leaves, cream flowers)

Tanacetum parthenium 'Aureum' (lime leaves, white, yellow-centred daisy flowers)

Thymus serpyllum 'Aureum' (lime leaves, pale mauve-pink flowers)

Trifolium pratense 'Goldnet' (yellow-veined green leaves, mauve flowers)

141

FINE HERBS FOR DAMP SHADE

Acorus calamus 'Variegatus'
Aegopodium podagraria 'Variegata'
Ajuga reptans 'Atropurpurea', 'Variegata', 'Rainbow' and 'Burgundy Glow'
Colchicum autumnale 'Alboplenum'
Filipendula ulmaria 'Aurea' and 'Variegata'
Glechoma hederacea 'Variegata'
Jasminum officinale 'Aureovariegatum'
Lysimachia nummularia 'Aurea'
Melissa officinalis 'Aurea' and 'All Gold'
Mentha x *gentilis* 'Variegata'
Mentha suaveolens 'Variegata'
Primula vulgaris 'Alba Plena' and *P.* x *variabilis* 'Guinevere'
Ranunculus ficaria 'Cuprea', 'Brazen Hussy', 'Alba' and 'Flore Pleno'
Sambucus nigra 'Aurea', 'Purpurea' and 'Albo-variegata'
Sambucus racemosa 'Plumosa Aurea'
Scrophularia auriculata 'Variegata'
Solanum dulcamara 'Variegata'
Symphytum grandiflorum 'Variegatum'
Symphytum x *uplandicum* 'Variegatum'
Teucrium scorodonia 'Crispum'
Vinca major 'Variegata'
Viola odorata 'Alba'

Please note that golden-leaved plants colour best in sun, though they may also scorch. In shade they will be more lime-green than gold but will not scorch. A site with dappled sun or partial shade, especially one which is shaded from the midday sun, is the best compromise.

FINE HERBS FOR DRY SUNNY PLACES

Achillea millefolium 'Cerise Queen' and 'Flowers of Sulphur'
Artemisia absinthium 'Lambrook Silver' and 'Powis Castle'
Chamaemelum nobilis 'Flore Pleno'
Foeniculum vulgare 'Purpureum'
Iris pallida 'Variegata Argentea' and 'Variegata Aurea'
Juniperus communis 'Compressa' and 'Depressa Aurea'
Laurus nobilis 'Aurea'
Lavandula angustifolia 'Loddon Pink'
Origanum vulgare 'Aureum' and 'Variegatum'
Papaver somniferum 'Rosea Plena'
Plantago major 'Rubrifolia'
Pulsatilla vulgaris 'Rubra'
Rosmarinus officinalis 'Aureus'
Ruta graveolens 'Jackman's Blue' and 'Variegata'
Salvia officinalis 'Purpurascens', 'Icterina' and 'Tricolor'
Sempervivum tectorum 'Lancelot' and 'Lavender and Old Lace'
Tanacetum parthenium 'Aureum' and 'Snowball'
Thymus 'Silver Posy'
Thymus serpyllum 'Aureum'
Tropaeolum majus 'Alaska'

FINE HERBS FOR CONTAINERS

Ajuga reptans 'Variegata'
Chamaemelum nobile 'Flore Pleno'
Glechoma hederacea 'Variegata'
Juniperus communis 'Compressa'
Laurus nobilis 'Aurea'
Lysimachia nummularia 'Aurea'
Ocimum basilicum 'Purpurascens'
Primula vulgaris 'Alba Plena' and *P.* x *variabilis* 'Guinevere'
Pulsatilla vulgaris 'Rubra'

142

Ruta graveolens 'Variegata'
Salvia officinalis 'Tricolor'
Sempervivum tectorum 'Lancelot' and 'Lavender and Old Lace'
Tanacetum parthenium 'Snowball'

Thymus serpyllum 'Aureum'
Thymus 'Silver Posy'
Trifolium pratense 'Goldnet'
Tropaeolum majus 'Alaska'
Viola odorata 'Alba'

FINE HERBS FOR THE CONSERVATORY

Laurus nobilis 'Aurea'
Myrtus communis 'Variegata'
Nerium oleander 'Variegatum'
Ocimum basilicum 'Purpurascens'
Pelargonium x *fragrans* 'Variegatum'

Pelargonium crispum 'Variegatum'
Pelargonium 'Lady Plymouth'
Rosmarinus officinalis 'Aureus'
Salvia officinalis 'Tricolor'

SUGGESTIONS FOR PLANTING SCHEMES

Circular bed in silver, pink, blue and purple

 1 *Ajuga reptans* 'Burgundy Glow'
 2 *Chamaemelum nobile* 'Flore Pleno'
 3 *Papaver somniferum* 'Rosea Plena'
 4 *Ruta graveolens* 'Jackman's Blue' (or 'Variegata')
 5 *Plantago major* 'Rubrifolia'
 6 *Artemisia* 'Powis Castle'
 7 *Salvia officinalis* 'Purpurascens'
 8 *Iris pallida* 'Variegata Argentea'
 9 *Thymus* 'Silver Posy'
10 *Lavandula angustifolia* 'Loddon Pink'
11 *Achillea millefolium* 'Cerise Queen'
12 *Primula* x *variabilis* 'Guinevere'
13 *Ajuga reptans* 'Atropurpurea'

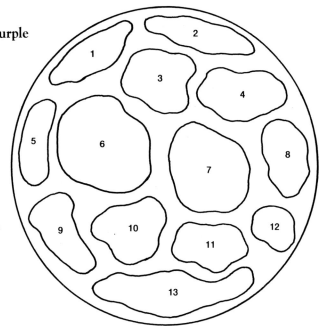

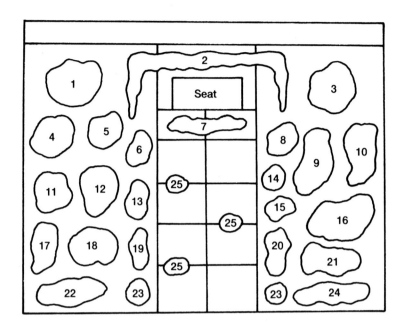

Herb garden with arbour and paved path

1 *Laurus nobilis* 'Aurea' or *Sambucus racemosa* 'Plumosa Aurea'
2 *Humulus lupulus* 'Aureus' (trained onto trellis)
3 *Sambucus nigra* 'Purpurea'
4 *Achillea millefolium* 'Flowers of Sulphur'
5 *Rosmarinus officinalis* 'Aureus'
6 *Viola odorata* 'Alba'
7 *Chamaemelum nobile* 'Flore Pleno'
8 *Lavandula angustifolia* 'Loddon Pink'
9 *Saponaria officinalis* 'Rosea Plena'
10 *Achillea millefolium* 'Cerise Queen'
11 *Filipendula ulmaria* 'Variegata'
12 *Origanum vulgare* 'Variegatum'
13 *Lysimachia nummularia* 'Aurea'
14 *Primula* x *variabilis* 'Guinevere'
15 *Thymus* 'Silver Posy'
16 *Artemisia absinthium* 'Lambrook Silver'
17 *Mentha* x *gentilis* 'Variegata'
18 *Melissa officinalis* 'All Gold'
19 *Iris pallida* 'Variegata Aurea'
20 *Salvia officinalis* 'Purpurascens'
21 *Ruta graveolens* 'Jackman's Blue'
22 *Salvia officinalis* 'Icterina'
23 *Buxus sempervirens* 'Elegantissima'
24 *Mentha suaveolens* 'Variegata'
25 *Thymus serpyllum* 'Aureus'

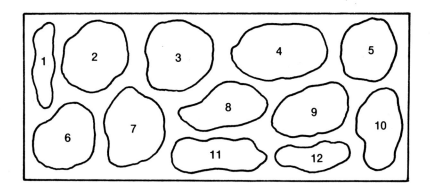

Colourful culinary herb garden

1 *Mentha* x *gentilis* 'Variegata' (ginger mint)
2 *Foeniculum vulgare* 'Purpureum' (fennel)
3 *Laurus nobilis* 'Aurea' (bay)
4 *Melissa officinalis* 'Aurea' (lemon balm)
5 *Rosmarinus officinalis* 'Aureus' (rosemary)
6 *Origanum vulgare* 'Aureum' (marjoram)
7 *Salvia officinalis* 'Purpurascens' (sage)

8 *Thymus* 'Silver Posy' (thyme)
9 *Tropaeolum majus* 'Alaska' (nasturtium)
10 *Parsley or chives* (not described in the book)
11 *Ocimum basilicum* 'Purpurascens' (basil)
12 *Mentha suaveolens* 'Variegata' (pineapple mint)

Container in green, pink and white with all year interest

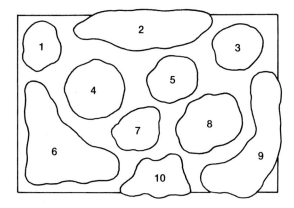

1 *Primula* x *variabilis* 'Guinevere'
2 *Glechoma hederacea* 'Variegata'
3 *Pulsatilla vulgaris* 'Rubra'
4 *Juniperus communis* 'Compressa'
5 *Viola odorata* 'Alba'
6 *Thymus* 'Silver Posy'
7 *Chamaemelum nobile* 'Flore Pleno'
8 *Salvia officinalis* 'Tricolor'
9 *Ajuga reptans* 'Burgundy Glow'
10 *Sempervivum tectorum* 'Lavender and Old Lace'

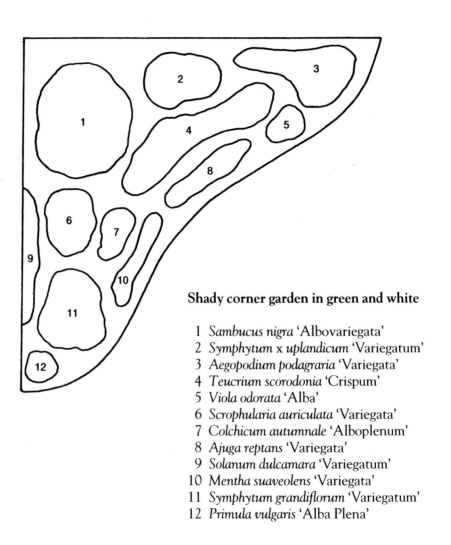

Shady corner garden in green and white

1 *Sambucus nigra* 'Albovariegata'
2 *Symphytum* x *uplandicum* 'Variegatum'
3 *Aegopodium podagraria* 'Variegata'
4 *Teucrium scorodonia* 'Crispum'
5 *Viola odorata* 'Alba'
6 *Scrophularia auriculata* 'Variegata'
7 *Colchicum autumnale* 'Alboplenum'
8 *Ajuga reptans* 'Variegata'
9 *Solanum dulcamara* 'Variegatum'
10 *Mentha suaveolens* 'Variegata'
11 *Symphytum grandiflorum* 'Variegatum'
12 *Primula vulgaris* 'Alba Plena'

FACTS AND FIGURES

Plant name	average height	soil	situation	character and hardiness	foliage	flowers	fruits	uses
Achillea millefolium 'Cerise Queen' and 'Flowers of Sulphur' (yarrow)	40–60 cm	well-drained, neutral to alkaline	sunny	hardy; perennial; herbaceous	dark green, feathery; dies down in winter	summer; flat heads of bright pink ('Cerise Queen') and pale yellow ('Flowers of Sulphur')		aromatic; medicinal
Acorus calamus 'Variegatus' (sweet flag)	1 m	most if con stantly moist or wet, will stand in water	sun – shade	hardy; perennial; rhizomatous	green and white striped; sword-shaped	green spadix; summer	green	aromatic, tangerine-like scent; medicinal
Aegopodium podagraria 'Variegata'	10–20 cm (leaves) 60–80 cm (when flower-ing)	any (but acid)	sun – shade	hardy perennial; rhizomatous	green and white; divided; deciduous groundcover	white, in umbels; summer		edible leaves: medicinal
Ajuga reptans (bugle)		most preferably moist	partial shade – shade	hardy; perennial creeper	evergreen rosettes with runners; ground cover	spring; blue		medicinal
'Atropurpurea' 'Burgundy Glow'	10 cm 10 cm				dark bronze pink/bronze/ cream			
'Rainbow'	10 cm				brown/pink/ cream/yellow			
'Variegata'	5 cm		scorches in sun		pale green/grey-green/white			
Artemisia absinthium (wormwood)		well-drained; even poor, dry and stony	sun	hardy; perennial; sub-shrub	silver, finely cut, semi-evergreen			aromatic; medicinal
'Lambrook Silver' 'Powis Castle'	40–50 cm 50–60 cm				tiny yellow sprays; summer non-flowering			

147

Plant name	average height	soil	situation	character and hardiness	foliage	flowers	fruits	uses
Buxus sempervirens (box)		neutral-alkaline	sun – partial shade	hardy except in severe winters; perennial shrub	evergreen, small oval	insignificant yellowish-green in spring	greenish egg-shaped	poisonous; medicinal
'Elegantissima' 'Latifolia Maculata'	2 m 1.8 m				cream-margined irregularly marked yellow, especially on new growths			
Chamaemelum nobile 'Flore Pleno' (chamomile)	10 cm	well-drained, neutral to alkaline	sunny	hardy; perennial; creeper	dark green, feathery, evergreen rosettes and runners; ground cover	double cream daisies; summer		aromatic; medicinal
Colchicum autumnale 'Alboplenum' (meadow saffron)	15 cm (flowers) 20–25 cm (leaves)	damp, neutral to alkaline; even heavy	sun – shade	hardy; perennial; bulbous	broad ovate – lanceolate, glossy, appearing spring and dying down in summer	double white; autumn	large capsules maturing spring to summer	poison-ous; medicinal
Filipendula ulmaria (meadowsweet)		damp or wet, neutral to alkaline	sun – shade scorches in sun	hardy; perennial; herbaceous		cream, in fluffy heads; summer		aromatic; culinary; medicinal
'Aurea' 'Variegata'	45 cm 60 cm				gold dark green, slashed yellow			
Foeniculum vulgare 'Purpureum' (fennel)	1.5 m	well-drained, neutral to alkaline	sunny	hardy; perennial; herbaceous	brown, feathery dying down in winter	tiny yellow; in flat heads; summer	ribbed, grey-brown	culinary; aromatic; medicinal
Glechoma hederacea 'Variegata' (ground ivy)	10 cm	most	sun – shade	hardy; perennial creeper	kidney-shaped, scalloped; white-margined; evergreen on long runners; ground cover; trailer	lilac-blue; spring-summer		aromatic; medicinal

148

Name	Height	Soil	Aspect	Habit	Leaves	Flowers	Fruit	Uses
Humulus lupulus 'Aureus' (hop)	5 m+	damp, neutral to alkaline, rich	sun	hardy; perennial climber	large, lobed, gold; deciduous	insignificant; summer	pale-green, cone-like (on female plants)	aromatic seed-heads; medicinal; edible young shoots
Iris pallida (orris)	30–40 cm	well-drained, neutral to alkaline	sunny	hardy except in cold areas; perennial, rhizomatous	sword-shaped, dying down in winter	lavender, scented; summer		aromatic rootstock (when dried); medicinal
'Variegata Argentea'					blue-green and white stripes			
'Variegata Aurea'					blue-green, cream and yellow stripes			
Jasminum officinale 'Aureovariegatum' (jasmine)	5 m+	well-drained, most	sun – partial shade	hardy; perennial climber	small divided leaves, bright yellow and green	scented, white; summer		perfumery; medicinal
Juniperus communis (juniper)		well-drained, acid to alkaline	sun	hardy coniferous shrub	evergreen sharp needles	insignificant; male and female on separate plants in spring	blue-black 'berries' (cones)	culinary; medicinal
'Compressa'	80 cm			compact pencil-shaped	grey-green needles			
'Depressa Aurea'	30–40 cm × 150 cm			bowl-shaped; ground cover	gold/bronze needles			
Laurus nobilis 'Aurea' (bay)	3 m+	well-drained, neutral to alkaline	sun	not hardy in exposed sites and cold areas; shrub	evergreen; gold	cream; spring		culinary
Lavandula angustifolia 'Loddon Pink' (lavender)	40–60 cm	well-drained, neutral to alkaline	sun	hardy sub-shrub	evergreen; narrow, grey-green	pale pink; summer; fragrant		perfumery; aromatic; medicinal

Plant name	average height	soil	situation	character and hardiness	foliage	flowers	fruits	uses
Lysimachia nummularia 'Aurea' (creeping Jenny)	3–5 cm	most, if damp	sun – partial shade	hardy creeper	evergreen; bright gold in sun; lime in shade; ground cover	bright yellow		medicinal
Melissa officinalis (lemon balm)	60 cm	most	sun – shade	hardy; perennial; herbaceous	nettle-shaped leaves; dies down in winter	tiny, white; summer		lemon-scent; culinary; medicinal
'All Gold'			scorches in sun		bright gold			
'Aurea'					yellow and green			
Mentha x gentilis 'Variegata' (ginger mint)	30–40 cm	most, if damp	sun – shade	hardy; perennial; herbaceous	yellow and green; dies down in winter; ground cover	lilac; summer		aromatic; culinary
Mentha suaveolens 'Variegata' (pineapple mint)	45 cm	most, if damp	sun – shade (but scorches in full sun)	hardy; perennial; herbaceous	woolly, white and green; dies down in winter, ground cover	lilac; summer		aromatic; culinary
Myrtus communis 'Variegata' (myrtle)	1–2 m	well-drained, neutral to alkaline	sun – partial shade	tender; perennial shrub	evergreen; glossy green and white	white, many-stamened; summer	blue-black	aromatic; culinary; medicinal
Nerium oleander 'Variegatum' (oleander)	2–5 m	neutral to alkaline; rich; damp in summer; on the dry side in winter	sun	tender perennial shrub, needs warmth in spring for flowering	evergreen; long narrow cream and green	pink; summer	large horned pods with parachute seeds	poisonous; medicinal
Ocimum basilicum 'Purpurascens' (basil)	30 cm	well-drained; neutral to alkaline	sun	tender annual	oval; purplish-black	dark pink; summer		aromatic; culinary; medicinal

Name	Height	Soil	Aspect	Type	Foliage	Flower	Seeds	Uses
Origanum vulgare (marjoram) 'Aureum' 'Variegatum'	20–30 cm	well-drained; neutral to alkaline	sun – partial shade slight tendency to scorch in full sun	hardy; perennial; herbaceous	dies down in winter; small, oval, golden; small oval, pointed; green with bright gold tips in spring	pinkish-mauve, summer		aromatic; culinary; medicinal
Paeonia officinalis 'Rosea Plena' (peony)	50–60 cm	well-drained, neutral to alkaline; rich; evenly moist	sun – partial shade, avoiding early morning sun	hardy; perennial; herbaceous	divided; dark green; dies down in winter	pale pink, double; summer		medicinal
Papaver somniferum 'Rosea Plena' (opium poppy)	1 m	well-drained; neutral to alkaline	sun	hardy; annual	waxy, grey-green	pale pink; double; summer	large 'pepper-pot' seedheads and tiny blue-grey seeds	poisonous; medicinal (seeds non-poisonous and culinary)
Pelargonium crispum 'Variegatum' (scented geranium)	90 cm	well-drained to dry; neutral – alkaline	sun	tender; perennial; sub-shrub	small, crinkled, green and white; evergreen	pinkish-mauve; summer		lemon-scent, aromatic; culinary
Pelargonium x *fragrans* 'Variegatum' (scented geranium)	45 cm	well-drained to dry; neutral to alkaline	sun	tender; perennial; sub-shrub	lobed, velvety; grey-green and yellowish-green; evergreen	small, white; summer		aromatic
Pelargonium 'Lady Plymouth' (scented geranium)	90 cm	well-drained to dry; neutral to alkaline	sun	tender; perennial; sub-shrub	large, divided; green and cream, evergreen	pinkish-mauve; summer		rose-scent; aromatic

Plant name	average height	soil	situation	character and hardiness	foliage	flowers	fruits	uses
Plantago major 'Rubrifolia' (red rat's tail plantain)	25–35 cm	any!	sun – partial shade	hardy; perennial; herbaceous	ovate, ribbed, maroon; in rosettes; evergreen	tiny, greenish; in thin spikes; summer	brown seeds	medicinal
Primula vulgaris (primrose) 'Alba Plena'	15 cm	most, if evenly damp	partial shade	hardy; perennial (but may be short-lived); herbaceous	evergreen green	double white; spring		culinary; medicinal
Primula x variabilis 'Guinevere'	15 cm	most, if evenly damp	partial shade	hardy perennial; herbaceous	purplish-bronze	dusky pink; spring		culinary, medicinal
Pulsatilla vulgaris 'Rubra' (pasque flower)	25 cm	well-drained, neutral to alkaline	sun	hardy; perennial; herbaceous	finely divided; green with silvery hairs; dies down in winter	crimson; spring	silky plumed seedheads	poisonous; medicinal
Ranunculus ficaria (celandine) 'Alba' 'Brazen Hussy' 'Cuprea' 'Flore Plena'	8–10 cm	neutral to alkaline; damp	sun – shade	hardy; perennial; tuberous	small, heart-shaped; dies down in summer green bronze green green	early spring white pale orange pale orange double; bright yellow with green petal undersides	bulbils often produced	medicinal
Rosmarinus officinalis 'Aureus' (rosemary)	1–1.5 m	well-drained, neutral to alkaline	sun	not hardy in cold areas; perennial shrub	evergreen; green and yellow	pale blue; spring		aromatic; culinary; medicinal
Ruta graveolens (rue) 'Jackman's Blue' 'Variegata'	45 cm	well-drained, neutral to alkaline	sun	hardy shrub	evergreen, divided blue-grey grey-green and white	yellowish-green; summer		aromatic; culinary; medicinal

Name	Height	Soil	Light	Type	Foliage	Flowers	Berry	Uses
Salvia officinalis (sage)		well-drained, neutral to alkaline	sun	perennial; sub-shrub	evergreen, velvety	purplish-blue; summer	-	aromatic; culinary; medicinal
'Icterina'	60 cm			hardy	grey-green and yellowish-green			
'Purpurascens'	60 cm			hardy	greyish-purple			
'Tricolor'	40 cm			not hardy in cold areas	sage-green, pink and white			
Sambucus nigra (common elder)	3 m (if pruned)	most; damp	sun – shade	hardy; perennial shrub	deciduous; divided	cream; early summer; fragrant	black	culinary (flowers and fruit); medicinal (all parts)
'Albovariegata'					cream and green			
'Aurea'			colours best in sun		golden			
'Purpurea'					dark bronze	pink stamens		
Sambucus racemosa 'Plumosa Aurea' (red elder)	2–3 m (if pruned)	most, damp	partial shade	hardy; perennial shrub	deciduous; gold; divided with finely cut margins	cream	red	medicinal
Saponaria officinalis 'Rosea Plena' (soapwort)	75 cm	neutral to alkaline; damp	partial shade – sun	hardy; perennial; herbaceous	green; dies down in winter	pale pink; loosely double; fragrant		medicinal; detergent
Scrophularia auriculata 'Variegata' (water figwort)	60 cm+	acid to alkaline; damp to wet (and in water)	sun to heavy shade	hardy; perennial; herbaceous	green and white; dies down in winter	small, dark red-brown; summer		medicinal
Sempervivum tectorum (houseleek)	3–5 cm (without flowers)	well-drained to dry; neutral to alkaline	sun	hardy; perennial; succulent	evergreen; fleshy; in rosettes with runners	pink, on tall stalks		medicinal; cosmetic
'Lancelot'					dark maroon with ripple pattern; smooth			
'Lavender and Old Lace'					grey-green tinged pink; slightly hairy			

Plant name	average height	soil	situation	character and hardiness	foliage	flowers	fruits	uses
Solanum dulcamara 'Variegatum' (bittersweet)	3 m+	neutral to alkaline; dry to wet	sun – partial shade	not hardy in cold areas; perennial climber	deciduous; green and white	purple and yellow	bright red (green to orange unripe)	poisonous; medicinal
Symphytum grandiflorum 'Variegatum' (dwarf comfrey)	15 cm	neutral to alkaline; damp	shade	hardy; perennial; herbaceous	green and cream	cream bells; spring		medicinal
Symphytum x uplandicum 'Variegatum' (Russian comfrey)	1 m	neutral to alkaline; damp	sun – partial shade	hardy; perennial; herbaceous	large, green and cream; dies down in winter	lilac-blue bells; summer		culinary; medicinal
Tanacetum parthenium (feverfew)		well-drained; neutral to alkaline	sun – partial shade	hardy; short-lived perennial (often treated as annual)	evergreen	summer		medicinal; aromatic
'Aureum'	45 cm				bright yellow-green			
'Snowball'	30 cm				green	white, yellow-centred daisies double white pompons with white outer rays		
Teucrium scorodonia 'Crispum' (wood sage)	30–45 cm		sun – shade	hardy; perennial; herbaceous	green with frilled cut margins; dies down in winter	pale green, tiny; summer		medicinal
Thymus serpyllum 'Aureum' (creeping thyme)	5–10 cm	neutral to alkaline; even dry	sun	hardy; perennial; creeper	evergreen; tiny; yellow-green; ground cover	pinkish-mauve; summer		aromatic; culinary; medicinal
Thymus 'Silver Posy' (thyme)	15–20 cm	neutral to alkaline, even dry	sun	hardy; perennial; sub-shrub	evergreen; tiny; green and white	pink; summer		aromatic; culinary; medicinal

Trifolium pratense 'Goldnet' (red clover)	20–40 cm	neutral to alkaline; moist to dry	sun	hardy; short-lived perennial; herbaceous	three-lobed; green with yellow veins; semi-evergreen	pinkish-mauve; summer		medicinal
Tropaeolum majus 'Alaska' (nasturtium)	20–30 cm	well-drained; almost dry	sun	hardy; annual	circular; peltate; marbled green and white	various; red, orange, yellow	large round, three-sectioned seeds	culinary; medicinal
Vinca major 'Variegata' (periwinkle)	45 cm	well-drained; most	shade	hardy; perennial; creeping; sub-shrub	oval green and white	blue; spring to summer		medicinal
Viola odorata 'Alba' (violet)	10–15 cm	acid – alkaline; damp	partial – heavy shade	hardy; perennial; herbaceous	heart-shaped, green; with runners	white; late winter-spring; scented		perfumery; culinary; medicinal

LIST OF STOCKISTS

List of stockists in the UK
(no single supplier stocks all of them!)

Avon Bulbs, Bradford-on-Avon, Wilts BA15 2AT. Tel: 02216–3723 (bulbous plants)

Beth Chatto Gardens, Elmstead Market, Colchester C07 7DB. Tel: 0206–222007 (unusual herbaceous plants)

Bressingham Gardens, Diss, Norfolk 1P22 2AB. Tel: 037–988–464 (shrubs, conifers, climbers and herbaceous plants)

Foxgrove Plants, Foxgrove Farm, Enborne, Newbury, Berks RG14 6RE. Tel: 0635–40554 (alpines, primulas and unusual hardy plants)

Hoecroft Plants, Sheringham Road, West Beckham, Holt, Norfolk NR25 6PQ. Mail order only (variegated and coloured-leaved plants)

Hollington Nurseries, Woolton Hill, Newbury, Berks RG15 9XT. Tel: 0635–253908 (culinary, medicinal, aromatic and conservatory plants)

Norfolk Lavender, Caley Hill, Heacham, King's Lynn, Norfolk PE31 7JE. Tel: 0485–70384 (lavenders)

Penwood Nurseries, The Drove, Penwood, Highclere, Hants. Tel: 0635–254366 (trees, shrubs and herbaceous plants)

Rodney Fuller, Coachman's Cottage, Higher Bratton Seymour, Wincanton, Somerset BA9 9BY. Mail order only (violas)

Thompson and Morgan, London Road, Ipswich IP2 0BA. Tel: 0437–688821 (seeds)

List of stockists in the USA

Caprilands Herb Farm, 534 Silver Street, Coventry, Connecticut 06238. Tel: 203-742-7244.

Catnip Acres Farm, 67 Christian Street, Coventry, Connecticut 06483. Tel: 203-888-5649 (over 300 different herbs and 80 kinds of scented leaf geraniums)

Cricket Hill Herb Farm, Glen Street, Rowley, Massachusetts 01969. Tel: 617-948-2818 (over 300 varieties of herbs)

Far North Gardens, 16785 Harrison, Livonia, Michigan 48154 (offers thousands of rare seeds)

Hilltop Herb Farm, PO Box 1734, Cleveland, Texas 77327. Tel: 713-592-5859 (rare and unusual plants)

International Growers Exchange Inc, Box 397, Farmington, Michigan 48024. Mail order only (rare and unusual herbs)

Logee's Greenhouses, 55 North Street, Danielson, Connecticut 06239 (specializes in scented geraniums and rare herbs)

Mellinger's Inc, 3210 West South Range Road, North Lima, Ohio 44452. Tel: 216-549-9861

Merry Gardens Herbs, Camden, Maine 04843. Tel: 207-236-9064 (rare and unusual herbs)

Nichols Garden Nursery, 1190 North Pacific Highway, Albany, Oregon 97321. Tel: 503-928-9280. Mail order only

Redwood City Seed Company, Box 361, Redwood City, California 94064. Tel: 415-325-7333

Rosemary House Inc, 120 South Market Street, Mechanicsburg, Pennsylvania 17055. Tel: 717-697-5111 (large selection)

Rutland of Kentucky, PO Box 182, Washington, Kentucky, 41096. Tel: 606-759-7815

Sandy Mush Herb Nursery, Rte. 2, Surrett Cove Road, Leicester, North Carolina 28748

Shady Hill Gardens, 821 Walnut Street, Batavia, Illinois 60510 (the largest commercial collection of geraniums in the USA)

Stillridge Herb Farm, 10370 Rte. 99 Woodstock, Maryland 21163. Tel: 301-465-8348

Sunnypoint Gardens, Hwy 42, #6939, Egg Harbor, Wisconsin 54209. Tel: 414-868-3646 (200 varieties of herbs and scented geraniums)

Sunrise Enterprises, PO Box 10058, Elmwood, Connecticut 06110 (rare and unusual herbs from the Orient)

Taylor's Garden Inc, 1535 Lone Oak Road, Vista, California 92083. Tel: 619-727-3485

Vita Green Farms, 217 Escondido Avenue, Vista, California 92083. Tel: 619-724-2163

Well-Sweep Herb Farm, 317 Mt. Bethel Road, Port Murray, New Jersey 07865. Tel: 201-852-5390

List of stockists in Australia

NEW SOUTH WALES

The Fragrant Garden, Portsmouth Road, Erina 2250

Medicinal Herb Nursery, Bergmui South 2547

VICTORIA

Apothecary Herbs, 228 Union Road, Surrey Hills, 3127

The Botanic Ark, Cnr. Sutton & Copeland Roads, Warragui 3820

Herb Patch, Priors Road, The Patch 3792

SOUTH AUSTRALIA

Meadow Herbs, Simms Road, Mt Barker 5251

QUEENSLAND

Rushbrooks Herb Farm, Long Road, Eagle Heights 4271

TASMANIA

Middle Earth Herbs, Middle Street, Granton 7013

Select Bibliography

Bianchini, F, F Corbetta and M Pistoia *The Kindly Fruits.* Cassell (translated from the Italian) 1977 – a beautifully illustrated guide to herbal plants and their uses.

Brickell, C and F Sharman *The Vanishing Garden.* John Murray, 1986 – a guide to garden plants which are now rare, endangered or extinct.

Grieve, M *A modern Herbal.* Jonathan Cape, 1931 (reprinted as a paperback in 1976 by Peregrine Books) – still the best general guide to the uses of herbal plants.

Griggs, B *Green Pharmacy.* Jill Norman and P Hobhouse, 1981 – the definitive history of herbal medicine – essential reading for the serious student of herbalism.

Johnson, S *Feverfew.* Sheldon Press, 1984 – an account, written by a doctor, of the use of feverfew in treating migraine and arthritis.

Lust, J *The Herb Book.* Bantam Books, 1974 – a low-priced comprehensive guide to the uses of herbal plants.

Philip, C *The Plant Finder.* Headmain Ltd, 1987 – the Hardy Plant Society's plant directory – an invaluable list for those trying to find unusual plants (if you know what you're looking for) and a useful compilation of names and synonyms in current usage.

Stuart, M (ed) *The Encyclopaedia of Herbs and Herbalism.* Orbis Publishing, 1979 – a well-illustrated guide to herbal plants and their uses.

INDEX

(Figures in bold denote illustrations)

ACKNOWLEDGEMENTS

The preparation of this book has made demands in various ways on many people and I would like to thank them all for their contribution.

I am most grateful to Judith and Simon Hopkinson who allowed me to photograph plants, both in their private garden and in those of Hollington Nurseries, on numerous occasions. Thanks also go to Beth Chatto, Nigel Taylor, Esther Merton and Louise Vockins who allowed me to photograph their plants, and to Ray Jeffs and Mr Linegar of the Iris Society, Brian Davies and Clare Calvert who kindly answered queries.

In the course of research, visits were made to the gardens and libraries of the Royal Botanic Gardens, Kew and to the Royal Horticultural Society's library: I am indebted to the directors and staff – and particularly the librarians – who maintain and make available these marvellous collections.

Special thanks are due to Adrian Whiteley, assistant botanist at the Royal Horticultural Society's Garden at Wisley, whose advice on problems of nomenclature has been invaluable. Many of the plants described in this book have been in cultivation for hundreds, if not thousands of years, and during the course of time innumerable varieties and hybrids have arisen. I have endeavoured to provide the 'correct' (i.e. currently accepted) name for each herb described but I beg readers to bear in mind three things regarding the naming of garden plants: that in some cases the origin is uncertain and this may give rise to several different names which can only be sorted out through empirical research; that plants which are probably or decidedly different may be sold bearing the same name (and vice versa); and that even the experts sometimes disagree! (Having said this, I do of course accept responsibility for any actual errors that may remain.)

Lastly, I am most grateful for the enthusiasm and guidance given by my editors, Connie Austen-Smith, Jane Elliot and Lesley Young; and, above all, for the tolerance, consideration and affection shown by my children, who have not only coped wonderfully with the gestation and birth of another book at the same time as moving house, but are unfailingly good-natured about my passion for plants.